INDIANS, CATTLE, SHIPS, AND OIL
The Story of W. M. D. Lee

INDIANS

CATTLE

SHIPS

AND OIL

THE STORY OF
W.M.D. LEE

By DONALD F. SCHOFIELD

University of Texas Press ◆ Austin

First edition, 1985

Requests for permission to reproduce material
from this work should be sent to:
Permissions
University of Texas Press
Box 7819
Austin, Texas 78713

**Publication of this work has been made possible in part
by a grant from the Andrew W. Mellon Foundation.**

LIBRARY OF CONGRESS CATALOGING IN PUBLICATION DATA
Schofield, Donald F. (Donald Frank), 1944–
    Indians, cattle, ships, and oil.
    Bibliography: p.
    Includes index.
    1. Lee, William McDole. 2. Pioneers—Texas—
Biography. 3. Businessmen—Texas—Biography. 4. Indians
of North America—Texas—History. 5. Fur trade—Texas—
History—19th century. 6. Ranch life—Texas—Texas—
Panhandle—History—19th century. 7. Velasco (Tex.)—
Harbor—History—19th century. 8. Cattle trade—Texas—
Texas Panhandle—History—19th century. 9. Texas
Panhandle (Tex.)—History. 10. Texas—Industries—
History—19th century. I. Title.
F391.L43S36   1985   976.4'06   84-28421
ISBN 0-292-79028-7

*Photo of William McDole Lee courtesy of the late
Mrs. Ruth Sutton-Doland, Columbus, Wisconsin.*

For my parents, Delbert F. and Lois M. Schofield

Contents

Illustrations

Photo section begins after page 70.

Acknowledgments

I could not have completed this biography without the assistance of William C. Griggs, Byron Price, Claire Kuehn, and T. Lindsay Baker of the Panhandle-Plains Historical Society, who gave me permission to search the society's extensive collection of Western history documents. The society further encouraged the completion of the biography by publishing in part the introduction and first three chapters under the title, "W. M. D. Lee, Indian Trader," in the *Panhandle-Plains Historical Review* in 1981.

I am also indebted to the aid of Stuart L. Butler, assistant archivist, Military Division, Navy and Old Army Branch, National Archives; Martha Blaine and Mary Lee Ervin, archivists, Oklahoma Historical Society; David J. Murrah, archivist, Southwest Collection, Texas Tech University; Jack W. Traylor, archivist, Kansas State Historical Society; and Jack D. Haley, curator, Western History Collection, University of Oklahoma. I also express my appreciation to the clerks and staffs of several county governments in Texas, Kansas, Louisiana, and New Mexico who opened their local archives to my research.

I express particular gratitude to Frederick W. Rathjen of the History Department, West Texas State University, who planted the seed of the idea and later directed the writing of the first section of this study. I also credit Duane C. Guy and Garry Nall with many suggestions adopted in the first three chapters. Moreover, without the courtesies shown me by the staff at Cornette Library, West Texas State University, I could not have succeeded. Of these individuals I am considerably indebted to Pat Donovan, Norma Reger, Sylvia Shields, Frances Slagle, and Annette Nall.

I particularly single out five individuals who aided in every step of the project's development. Clyde M. Hudson and LaVonne listened patiently over the years to my excitements and disappointments while resolving Lee's story. Likewise, Faye Hendrickson, librarian and archivist at Cornette Library, was a willing listener; but, more important, by professional diligence she resolved many difficult passages of Lee's activities. Furthermore, I would have known little of the man's youth or of his family roots had it not been for Ruth Sutton-Doland, and nothing would have been known of his later years had it not been for J. G. Phillips, Jr.

The reader should note a recent and significant acquisition by the Western Business History Research Center, Colorado Historical Society, at Denver, Colorado—the papers of Albert E. Reynolds, donated by members of his family. When the collection is opened to the public it will undoubtedly expand the recorded history of business enterprise as practiced on the Great Plains during the 1870s and 1880s. My use of this material is through a one-year correspondence with Louisa Arps, a confidant of Reynolds's daughter, in regard to the Lee and Reynolds partnership. I now look forward to the diligent efforts of the society in assembling the collection and for the discovery of new details in the Lee and Reynolds experience.

I am grateful to all who gave their support, and I hope the writing in some way justifies the interest.

DONALD F. SCHOFIELD

Amarillo, Texas
October 1983

Introduction

Although Portage, Wisconsin, in 1856, still bore the scar of a pioneer's axe, it was a community populated by nearly four thousand residents. The attraction was its location—strategically placed between the Fox and Wisconsin rivers on the fertile Wisconsin frontier. Here the different tribes of the Northwest Territory once camped on the passage between waterways—thus the town's name. The whites, when they discovered the region, also laid claim to the lands by raising an imposing Fort Winnebago on a nearby prominence (see Map 1). No longer needing protection, the local inhabitants were now proud to boast of the community as one of the fastest developing townships in the state. Yet these same resident farmers and merchants felt their kinship to the thousands of men and women who continued to embark on the journey west. Men such as Perry Lee, proprietor of a boardinghouse and saloon located at one end of the main thoroughfare, especially welcomed the migrant traveler.[1]

Lee and his wife Esther were themselves recent immigrants to Wisconsin, having settled at Portage in 1850. Their roots were elsewhere, however—in the arable Susquehanna Valley of Pennsylvania—where both were born and married. Tiring of a farmer's lot, Perry, in 1844, at the age of twenty-eight, pulled stakes for the uncertain fate of a life on the frontier. It was a family that traveled west, for a son, William McDole, had been born on 25 August 1841.[2]

For fourteen months the three lived in Milwaukee until a more suitable homestead could be found near Hampden, in Columbia County, where they lived until uprooted again and resettled at Portage. In 1850, Perry opened the Wisconsin House, his first travelers' inn, followed in 1852 by the Lee House. Four daughters and another son were additions to the family by 1856.[3]

During that same year Portage also entered its transition from the once self-reliant frontier settlement to a dependent, organized township. In 1856 alone, nearly one hundred buildings were constructed, including three new schoolhouses and five churches, each necessary accommodations to the ever-increasing population. Repairs on a canal and system of locks linking Portage to the Wisconsin and Fox rivers were also planned.[4] Although many recalled the colorful details of Indians and log cabins, for all practical matters that frontier had been pushed miles beyond the present town boundaries. Instead, the young now matured in a relatively tranquil environment in which every child had the opportunity of a high-school education.[5] Yet for one lanky, blue-eyed, fifteen-year-old youngster, "Mac" Lee, not everything was commonplace.[6]

His father, Perry, was an exceptionally strong-willed individual noted for his active role in community affairs. After only two years in the county, in 1852 he was elected sheriff and served in that position until 1856. In that critical year, Lee fell victim to an emerging Republican Party that had as an objective control of the sheriff's office. Still, by the spring of 1857, Perry again stood at the forefront of Portage City politics when he took office as a town councilman.[7]

Perhaps the man's appeal was his free-spirited, independent ways. Certainly the children were awed by their father. A particular wonder must have been the many different and colorful individuals who nightly lodged at the family inn. Perry himself added to the excitement by renting an adjacent lot to Orton and Older's Circus and Theatrical Company. In December 1857, while a fire burned out of control through an adjacent saloon, two lions "kept in the back end of the building" even had to be coaxed outside before they could be caged. The only shadow to darken this image was speculation by certain parties that each of three fires at the Lee House during a two-year period was "the work of an incendiary." As townsfolk were reminded soon after the third blaze in 1859, "There was an insurance of $3000 on the building . . . [and] the policy . . . expired at noon of the same day on which the building was burned."[8]

Whether he feared detection of a fraud or merely yearned for adventure, Perry left both family and community during mid-1860 to prospect at a newly discovered goldfield in the northern New Mexico mountains. For all his troubles, the man died alone that November in a miner's camp at Abiquiu (see Map 1).[9]

News of her husband's death probably reached Esther and the six children while temporarily residing at the farm of Elija Lee (Perry's brother) near Hampden in Wisconsin. Mac Lee, then nineteen, would have been expected to assume the role of head of the family. But like

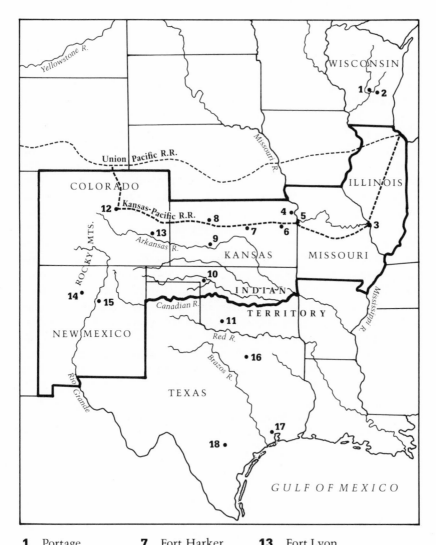

1	Portage	**7**	Fort Harker	**13**	Fort Lyon
2	Columbus	**8**	Fort Hays	**14**	Abiquiu
3	St. Louis	**9**	Fort Dodge	**15**	Santa Fe
4	Leavenworth	**10**	Camp Supply	**16**	Fort Worth
5	Kansas City	**11**	Fort Sill	**17**	Houston
6	Lawrence	**12**	Denver	**18**	San Antonio

——— Department of the Missouri

Map 1. The Frontier, ca. 1869

his father the young man had a restless side to his nature, and the last recorded contact with Portage was an unclaimed letter found at the local post office in May 1862.[10] By now a twenty-year-old Lee had experienced the first exhilarating independence of adulthood; yet the bonds tied in youth would never fully unravel.

Only brief episodes of Lee's experiences after he left Portage are known. A first job was as a Wells Fargo driver on a route connecting several remote Kansas settlements. It was perhaps more than coincidence that J. B. Fargo, an owner of the service, was also an ex–Portage City resident.[11] The experience was short-lived, however, as the Civil War intervened, and the young Lee volunteered for duty and served as a quartermaster in Sherman's army, marching with the general as the North burned its way across Georgia to the Atlantic coast. When the war ended, Lee remained as a civilian attached to the Department of the Missouri (see Map 1), probably supervising wagon transportation along supply trails that linked outposts within the command.[12]

During these same years, Esther and her younger children suffered a decade of hardship, with the Columbia County sheriff selling family property for back taxes. The tragedy of Lee's fifteen-year-old brother Jesse, who died in May 1869 after being kicked unconscious by a horse, must have added to the family's burdens.[13] But the welfare of his mother and four sisters was now only secondary to Lee, for he had recently made a critical decision affecting his own life. Ahead lay an opportunity for adventure, with the immediate concern being the uncertain obligations of a frontier trade.

CHAPTER ONE

Buffalo Robes

About 1:30 P.M. on Tuesday, 30 November 1869, an anxious twenty-eight-year-old William McDole Lee walked the main street of Lawrence, Kansas, past two-storied shops into a red brick building at the corner of Massachusetts and Fourth streets. Inside, Enoch Hoag, central superintendent for the Bureau of Indian Affairs, prepared to address the young man's questions in regard to trade among the southern Cheyenne and Arapaho tribes. Nearly three months had passed since Lee had submitted an application to trade with the Indians; yet, without explanation, Hoag had delayed a necessary endorsement.[1] Understandably, Lee now approached the meeting cautiously.

He had reached this day quite by chance. That fall he and Albert Eugene Reynolds, a man already in business as post trader at Fort Lyon, Colorado, had formed an informal, handshake partnership to open a similar operation at Camp Supply, Indian Territory. Reynolds, born 13 February 1840 to Henry and Caroline Reynolds of New York, had apprenticed as a shopkeeper with his father at a family store in Niagara County until 1865, when he moved and established his own businesses, first at Leavenworth, Kansas, and then at Richmond, Missouri. Both towns were located on the busy eastern termini of the American plains and, therefore, ideally suited to the particulars of a frontier trade. But as the boundary dividing settled lands from unclaimed territory had moved nearer to the Rocky Mountains, Reynolds likewise was forced to adapt, and by October 1867 he had relocated at Fort Lyon, Colorado. Another outlet was established at the new military post of Camp Supply, Indian Territory, during the late summer of 1869, when Lee came into the enterprise through the partnership Lee and Reynolds. In fact, it was not until 15 November, two weeks before Lee's meeting with Hoag, that the army finally approved either man's right to do business at Camp Supply. Their firm was only one of more than three outfits doing business at the post.[2]

Yet a sutler's trade was merely a part of what both intended. They also hoped to take their business into the camps of Indians located near Supply. As bands of southern Cheyenne and Arapaho were head-quartered at the western limits of Indian Territory, Lee had placed his application into the hands of Brinton Darlington, the local agent, who promised a license—subject to the appropriate review. There-fore, having forwarded all necessary papers to Hoag, not much atten-tion was given the issue because it was hoped that acceptance would only be a matter of time. A recent telegram from Reynolds suggested otherwise. At the time Lee was involved at Hays City, Kansas, with an inventory of the company's first shipment of merchandise, and the message forced him to put aside the ledgers in order to book pas-sage on the next train headed east. It was this deadline that now brought Lee to the superintendent's doorstep.[3]

Like all under his authority, Enoch Hoag was a Quaker recently appointed by President Ulysses Grant to the central superintendency in an effort to eliminate corruption within the maligned Indian Bu-reau.[4] At the meeting of 20 November, Lee confronted Hoag with the matter of his application. But Hoag, anticipating the young man's con-cern, matter-of-factly stated that two firms were already in business with the tribes; therefore, he saw no advantage in having yet another outfit operating on the reservation. Lee's petition was refused.

The arguments used to answer Hoag's decision were not recorded. However, at the conclusion of their meeting, Lee emerged from the superintendent's office with a note in hand addressed to the local Cheyenne and Arapaho agent endorsing a qualified right to trade.[5] His next concern was delivery of that message to a man headquar-tered approximately three hundred miles southwest of Lawrence.

Camp Supply was located in the far northwest corner of Indian Territory where Beaver and Wolf creeks joined to form the North Fork of the Canadian River (see Map 2). The post came into being in November 1868, when Major General Philip Sheridan approved the site as his headquarters for a planned winter campaign against the southern Cheyenne nation. Elements of the Seventh Cavalry, under the command of Brevet Major General George Armstrong Custer, opened the attack during a surprise raid on Black Kettle's band in which over 150 men, women, and children were killed. When Lee ar-rived at Camp Supply on 10 December 1869, he would have entered the compound of an active frontier garrison. Brevet Colonel A. D. Nelson was in command of three companies of Third Infantry and four companies of Tenth Cavalry, all stockaded in typical fashion with cut logs palisading a headquarters and parade ground. Two cor-

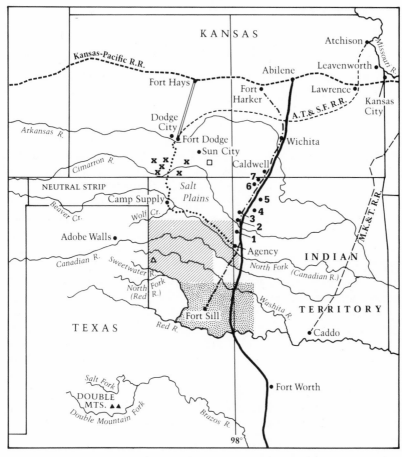

Trails

—— Chisholm Trail

········· Fort Dodge/Camp Supply
/Cheyenne & Arapaho Agency

·—·—· Fort Sill/Fort Harker Road

===== Fort Hays/Fort Dodge Trail

▨ Cheyenne & Arapaho
Reservation

▨ Kiowa & Comanche
Reservation

△ Battle of Washita

"Whiskey" Ranches

1 Kingfisher Ranch

2 Lee and Reynolds's Ranch

3 Baker's Ranch

4 Buffalo Springs Ranch

5 Skelton Springs Ranch

6 Pond Creek Ranch

7 Pole Cat Ranch

☐ Medicine Lodge Creek

✗ Unnamed Kansas ranches

Map 2. Indian Territory, ca. 1874

ners of the compound had been left open while tents and other log buildings stood not far from the center. Wild game, particularly herds of buffalo and antelope, abounded on the surrounding plains.[6]

Brinton Darlington, the man Lee now confronted, was as improbable a government agent as might be found. Yet this tall, slender, sixty-five-year-old Quaker was responsible for the peaceful transition of the southern Cheyenne and Arapaho to reservation life. Darlington faced no easy task, for after Custer's Battle of the Washita the Cheyenne had scattered throughout Indian Territory and were only now accepting the government's uneasy terms of peace. The situation was made all the more delicate as Grant's generals were pressing for the return of the Indian Bureau to military control while politicians with designs on the Territory were determined to continue a policy of "extermination."[7] As exasperating as these issues must have been, a more immediate problem was that neither the Cheyenne nor the Arapaho would accept the arid north-central prairie reserved them by the 1867 Medicine Lodge Treaty.

Seeking to resolve the impasse, several chiefs, with Darlington as escort, rode southeast into the Territory during early September of 1869, where about 150 miles out of Supply they discovered an oasis of jack oaks and cottonwoods located on a bluff near the North Fork of the Canadian River. After closer inspection, the chiefs promised to lead their individual bands to the site, which, if done, would seal the peace.[8] Thus, the demands of one young man with as personal a matter as Indian trade was naturally low on Darlington's list of priorities.

But Lee again pressed his application and, as before, was disappointed. Darlington insisted that he knew of only one Kansas firm, W. A. Rankin and Company, authorized to do business with either tribe. In fact, by coincidence Rankin was visiting in September 1869 and rode with the chiefs in search of a new agency. Along the way the trader had suggested to Darlington's son-in-law that they go into partnership and share profits, which Darlington, when informed of the matter, forbad. Nevertheless, Rankin remained Hoag's favorite, so Darlington could only offer Lee a temporary permit by which he might trade. Yet when the Indians broke camp and moved to their new headquarters, the privilege would automatically expire. It was an offer Lee had to accept.[9]

Meanwhile, Albert Reynolds had returned from Washington, first stopping at Lawrence, when he also confronted Hoag. But the superintendent again refused the request to examine Lee's file. Reynolds did not argue the point, but before leaving he made it clear that the slight would not be forgotten.[10]

Soon after, while Lee continued to request Darlington's "special permits," Hoag began to experience the pressures brought on by Reynolds's complaints. As a consequence, the superintendent wisely returned Lee's application, which was immediately submitted to the Indian Bureau in Washington for action. The man for whom Hoag had shown preference—W. A. Rankin—fared no better. On occasion he had even been found trading ammunition with Indians other than the Cheyenne and Arapaho, a certain breach of license. Therefore, by early February both Colonel Nelson and agent Darlington had sufficient cause to demand Rankin's expulsion from the Territory, and the Department of the Missouri diligently published the order denying Rankin further entry into Indian country. The next month, on 14 March, E. S. Parker, commissioner of Indian Affairs, finally endorsed Lee's application to trade with both the Cheyenne and the Arapaho.[11] Thus the partners might look forward to a near monopoly in the lucrative exchange with Indians. Yet neither was completely satisfied; another license had caught both's attention, and its acquisition would be even more keenly contested.

By directive of an 1870 law, the secretary of war was empowered to appoint one government trader at each military post in the country. The three sutlers doing business at Camp Supply had each applied for the position, as had four others, including Reynolds. Indeed, both Reynolds and Lee had individually submitted applications, probably believing that should one fail then the other might succeed. But it was Reynolds who took the most interest in the appointment, even to the point of attempting personal contacts with the secretary of war, William Belknap. All efforts were rebuffed, however, and it was not until 20 October that Belknap ended the suspense by awarding the Camp Supply tradership to Edwin C. Latimer of Nebraska.[12]

The appointment momentarily took Reynolds by surprise, and he at once retraced a journey to Washington. Only this time one of the secretary's clerks informed the sutler that a former brigadier general, J. M. Hedrick, had considerable influence with Belknap. Reynolds therefore set out to visit Hedrick at the general's Iowa home. The two spent more than one week together during early November 1870 in the small Mississippi River town of Ottumwa. The result was that Hedrick agreed to telegraph the secretary with a request that Reynolds be affirmed in Latimer's stead. Reynolds's "retainer" of $1,000 and the promise of $5,500 to be paid annually from the partnership accounts certainly influenced Hedrick's decision. The expected order was finally issued on 17 November, and four days later Reynolds acknowledged the appointment. Only now, with competition effectively silenced, did the partners feel confident enough of their positions to begin in earnest the servicing of the 3,000 to 3,800 Indians living on the reservation and the 300 to 600 military assigned to duty at Camp Supply.[13]

As early as September 1870, Brinton Darlington had observed that the once independent Cheyenne and Arapaho would be ". . . dependent upon the Government for their subsistence, with the exception of what meat they [obtained] from the wild buffalo." As to other, less critical needs, Darlington found ". . . [the Indians'] minds often fixed upon obtaining some trifling article, or some small favor which the agent had no authority to grant or means to procure."[14] It was an ideal situation for any trader ambitious enough to overlook the hardships of the frontier, as Indians were willing to exchange "services" for their prized buffalo robes.

Like most tribes, the Cheyenne and Arapaho rode to the hunt twice a year—once in early summer and again from late fall through early winter. It was during the latter season that the valued thick-fur robes were collected; after being traded they were sent to either an East Coast or European marketplace. Short-fur summer hides were traded infrequently and then only as a source of leather. This distinction was important, as the Indians dealt almost exclusively in robes while whites pursued the herds in order to acquire hides.

Lee understood the distinction and readily accepted the challenge. He also recognized that he must weigh the demands of yet another interest, the military, whose concern was neither goods nor robes but rather information pertaining to Indian activity. Certainly authorities at Camp Supply felt this need, for on such details local policy would be established. Indeed, on a frontier like the southern plains during the early 1870s—where whites eyed the territory south of the Kansas border and west of the ninety-eighth meridian for settlement—it was critical that the government contain if not subjugate a major obstacle to migration. Thus, daily knowledge of a tribe's whereabouts was required.[15] And what better source of information than white traders who had both the confidence and trust of individual bands.

Consequently, one of Lee's first concerns was winning over both tribes while Reynolds saw to the business at Camp Supply. To Lee's advantage, both the Cheyenne and Arapaho demanded from the first that whites be allowed to travel to their robe-collecting sites. The military immediately protested that the Indians were already too far removed from its control. But not wanting to agitate the tribes, other authority carried the argument by permitting camp visits during a hunt. Therefore, beginning with the winter of 1870, Lee and, on occasion, Reynolds went individually to each camp unescorted while the tribes were on a chase.[16]

Hiring a reliable crew was Lee's next consideration. But finding men willing to visit Indians who during the spring of 1870 were involved in another uprising would be difficult. Even traders could not avoid the dangers. The lesson was brought home by an incident that began on the night of 18 May, when Camp Supply was robbed of two horses as well as a mule belonging to Lee. Thinking that the animal might have strayed from the compound, Lee sent an employee, Dave Weitz, to recover his property. However, when he also failed to return, a detachment was sent to investigate. The men had only to ride about three miles from the installation before finding the body of Lee's man stripped, scalped, and mutilated. The loss was particularly inopportune, as Weitz had been identified as one of four employed to work the new trade.[17]

Although the uprising lasted only one month, those at Camp Supply felt it was wise to keep a loaded rifle at hand at all times. Early June was the worst of the affair with almost daily raids on the garrison's herd of livestock. It was not discovered until weeks later that the principal instigators were bands of northern Cheyenne and Sioux who during a "medicine council" had urged their compatriots to avenge ". . . their beloved chief, women and children slaughtered by General [Custer]." Fortunately, most Cheyenne and Arapaho had rejected the plea out of hand.[18]

Therefore, on 3 July, when Darlington renewed Lee's bond to trade at the reservation, the Territory had begun the adjustment to an unsteady peace. The season also brought into the firm a new man, George Bent, who was hired as the company's interpreter. Bent's employment was particularly noteworthy in that he was the Cheyenne half-breed son of Colonel William Bent, himself a respected Colorado frontiersman. It would not be lost on the Cheyenne that the wife of the martyred Black Kettle, whose memory the northern tribes had used in their recent attempt to incite an uprising, was also Bent's mother-in-law.[19]

Yet a reliable crew was only one of several problems. Lee also had to establish the means to transport trade articles from company headquarters at Camp Supply, across 150 miles of unchartered prairie, to the Indian store at the new Cheyenne and Arapaho compound. A system was therefore devised whereby one wagon train of from six to fourteen vehicles, each using either a six-mule-team hitch or six to seven yoke of oxen (and hauling up to 12,000 pounds), would be used on the route south. The lead wagons would be packed with merchandise, making them the heaviest and largest vehicles of the group. The lighter wagons, stocked with the supplies needed only for that particular run such as spare parts, cooking gear, and bedrolls, would be positioned at the rear of the train. Lee also saw to it that the system was organized so that usually one man was responsible for the entire operation and, therefore, permitted to hire his own crew. Others needed for a successful haul would be a cook, a night stock herder, mule teamsters or bullwackers, and an assistant boss if the size of the train so demanded. Anywhere from ten to fourteen men would be called upon to make a run to the agency.[20]

The merchandise packed into these wagons would include literally anything and everything demanded by either the tribes or their agent. Among the first items freighted were in the category of Darlington's "subsistence needs" such as corn, lumber, and coffee. Also transported in July 1870 were buildings disassembled from the old headquarters at Camp Supply, including a warehouse, cattle corral, blacksmith shop, sawmill, and other structures that would constitute the nucleus of the Indians' new compound. Although the government was billed nearly $4,500 for this one haul, delivery probably would not have been attempted had Lee also not had elements of the U.S. Cavalry ride alongside his vulnerable wagons and crew. Certainly Lee had in mind an attack on a similarly bound train of another outfit less than two months previous in which one teamster had been killed and most livestock run off.[21]

Other merchandise packed into the first wagons—items which Darlington had called "trifling"—also revealed much of the partners' early business. For the winter trade of 1872–1873, Lee and Reynolds amassed an approximate $25,000 inventory of goods that varied from $845 worth of beads, bracelets, and chains to 317 shawls, 10 dozen handkerchiefs, and 44 vests. This merchandise was in addition to the approximate $4,700 invested in bolts of cloth, bracelets valued at $3,375, and 135 Indian saddles worth $2,029. Those Indians with a more fanciful taste could trade for boxes of tobacco, bags of coffee, or one of the 100 "New York City umbrellas." An inventory of 1873–1874 was more of the same—beads, blankets, vests, shawls, and cloth—with one notable exception. Also added to the stock were supplies of cartridges and pistol caps.[22]

Lee's ability to use the organization he had devised to service a particular demand was tested early. During the spring of 1871, Darlington faced a shortage of rations—specifically, flour—at the precise time the Indians were expected to move from their winter lodges to a camp near the agency. Darlington's crisis was immediate in that "this emergency occurred at the very time that many professing to know much about Indian affairs had predicted that our Indians were all going on the war path. . . ." Therefore, the agent could not have been more pleased to watch as Lee rode with a wagon into the Cheyenne and Arapaho compound.[23]

Darlington put his predicament to the young trader, and Lee, seizing the opportunity, offered his services at a substantially increased rate for pounds of flour shipped. Darlington had no choice but to accept, and within two weeks an ox-drawn wagon arrived at the agency loaded with 126 one-hundred-pound sacks of flour billed to Darlington at the charge of $564.[24] The crisis was resolved but at a price that also maximized profits for Lee. Again, all criticisms could be answered by pointing to the risks involved; in particular, a recent incident would have still been fresh in Lee's mind.

On the night of 18 February, as Captain William Kennedy prepared for an early ride north out of Camp Supply on the trail leading to Fort Leavenworth, he was interrupted by Lee, who that night had returned from a Cheyenne camp. Kennedy put aside his packing and listened with interest to the young merchant's account of the visit.

Lee began his story by telling how he had left Supply during late January in order to trade among the different camps. About seventy-five miles southeast of the post he had found a Cheyenne village where Greybeard's band was in the process of closing out the season's hunt. Although Lee was interested in acquiring as many of the newly cured robes as possible, the Cheyenne offered only those skins necessary to purchase certain items, notably stores of sugar and coffee. The difficulty was that the tribe was also involved in a "medicine council," and several Indians, particularly some visiting Kiowa, objected to the distraction. Consequently, Lee found it prudent to take his leave, and while returning to the safety of Camp Supply, he warned Kennedy that both the Cheyenne and the Kiowa would probably take to the warpath with a change in seasons.[25]

Although the report satisfied Lee's unspoken obligation to the military, he naturally took the threat—and the risk to his other interests—into account when dealing with men such as Darlington. What he did not know was that while ordering his freighters to transport flour to the agency, the military had also digested his information and was suggesting (or more correctly, demanding) a tour of Washington and other major East Coast cities by the principal chiefs of the Cheyenne and Arapaho bands. The hope was that while the chiefs were out of the region the tribes would forestall all thought of attacking government surveyors who were about to map a route through central Kansas for the Atchison, Topeka, and Santa Fe railroad. And the scheme worked.[26] But the then uninformed trader still

held the belief that war was imminent and conducted business accordingly. Lee's personal danger was even more acute if any one of
the competing interests with which he traded learned how he used
each differently. Therefore, he was keenly sensitive that all consider
him an ally, and with the Indians in particular he used every opportunity to ingratiate himself into their confidence. The ideal situation did not present itself immediately, but near the end of 1872 Lee
literally fell into the ready-made occasion.

The event began inauspiciously enough on 27 December as the
trader and a Cheyenne chief, Spotted Wolf, broke camp together,
stored their gear in the back of Lee's carriage, and started out for a
nearby trading site. The two had not traveled far when the rig suddenly lost balance and began to tip. Lee was able to jump, but the
Indian, caught by the fall, was thrown under the vehicle. When the
carriage was finally uprighted, Lee could see that the injured chief
was in need of better medical attention than he could administer.
However, as regulations did not permit Indians at the army's garrison
of Fort Dodge, the nearest doctor would be found at a new settlement
located near the terminus of the Santa Fe railroad approximately five
miles west of the post. Lee rehitched the team and drove north for
Dodge City.[27]

The trader brought his rig to a stop at the livery behind Fringer's
drugstore, where the carriage was left to the care of a stablehand as
Spotted Wolf was helped across Front Street to Charles Rath's general
merchandise store. Watching both as they walked from Fringer's into
Rath's building was the buffalo hunter Kurt Jordan, whose family
had been attacked by Indians that fall—and who had sworn to kill
the first red man he encountered.[28] Jordan turned and went inside
one of the Dodge City saloons, where he had no trouble in arousing
others to the threat.

Bob Wright, another post sutler visiting Rath, was the first to notice the commotion. He immediately motioned to Lee, and both
men grabbed the chief in order to hurry him out of the building. The
three raced across Front Street and burst into Fringer's drugstore,
where once inside they bolted the door shut. It was then noticed that
several boards separating the store from adjacent apartments were
loose. A few were pulled apart so that each could squeeze through an
opening; the wall was then refastened. Moments later the hunters
also broke into the building.

The three waited some time; then Wright hit upon an idea. Leaving the back room, he entered an alley and walked the short distance
to the livery, where he ordered one of Lee's horses saddled. Spotted
Wolf had been told that when the apartment door opened he was to

jump on the horse and ride as fast as he could out of Dodge.

Wright was at the back door and about to enter when he glanced down the alley. Staring back were the hunters, each with weapons drawn. Without anything said, the trader turned from the building and led the horse back into the stable. There he found a volunteer to carry his message for help to the Fort Dodge garrison.

Lee, Wright, and Spotted Wolf waited all afternoon and into the early evening for rescue. As none appeared, and with no relief now expected, the three devised their final plan of escape. When it was sufficiently dark the traders would again make it to the stable, where Lee's carriage would be hitched and moved to the rear door. Spotted Wolf was then to climb into the vehicle as all three wheeled out of town toward Indian country.

They did not wait long, and soon Lee and Wright made the dash from the room to the stable; as soon as Spotted Wolf heard the carriage roll to a stop, he also ran and jumped into the rig. The carriage happened to be loaded with buffalo robes, and the Indian buried himself under the skins. Lee then whipped the team to its fastest gait, but when they were only a quarter of a mile out of town, a cavalry detachment stopped the rig and insisted that it be escorted to Fort Dodge. At morning's light, however, the trader and chief wasted no time in continuing the ride south.[29]

The Cheyenne were not likely to forget Lee's part in the rescue; they also would not forget that it was Dodge City hunters who had threatened Spotted Wolf's life. Already "there . . . [was] a great deal of feeling among the Indians against these hunters . . . ," with the Cheyenne ". . . [burning] the grass from . . . [Camp Supply] to the Arkansas River for the purpose of running off the buffalo hunters. . . ."[30] Although the spark would not catch until 1874, Lee understood the importance of befriending members of both tribes with which he did business. These were the last years of the Indians' buffalo harvest on the High Plains, and he could not afford to jeopardize a share in that bounty.

During the winter of 1871–1872, the Cheyenne alone had cured as many as 10,000 robes, and the following winter both the Cheyenne and Arapaho had nearly 17,000 robes to offer in trade. By 1873 the collection of robes was so integral a part of Lee's business that a system was devised whereby small metal coins called "trade checks" were minted and given in exchange for robes, each skin valued at about ten coins or $5.00.[31] Accommodating the demands of either tribe (and those of the agent and the military) was absolutely critical to success.

But a growing threat to that obligation as well as to the bureau's peaceful settlement of the Indians on reservations was the constant disruption of a routine life by horse thieves and whiskey peddlers. Even as early as 1870, the Territory was considered ". . . so infested with horse-thieves and desperadoes that no Civilian [was] allowed . . . [at Camp Supply] without a written permit from the [Commanding] Officer. . . ."[32] However, little changed, and by 1872 permanent enterprises called "whiskey ranches" had sprung up along the road from Camp Supply to Fort Dodge and along the Chisholm Trail where it branched north from the new Cheyenne and Arapaho compound (see Map 2). Whiskey also came into the Indians' hands by a third route, over the rails of the Missouri, Kansas, and Texas line (the Katy railroad), which was then built to a southern terminus at Caddo. Yet by far the most notorious runs were those operated by New Mexican traders who frequently brought wagons into the Texas Panhandle from whiskey camps near the border of Indian Territory. Interestingly, during the spring of 1872, Lee and Reynolds also opened a drovers' outpost about eighteen miles north of the Cheyenne and Arapaho Agency on the north bank of the Cimarron River (also known as the Red Fork of the Arkansas) ostensibly for the purpose of trading with Texas cowboys. Any of the suspect stations was anathema to the Quakers.[33]

Consequently, men such as Lee, whose livelihood depended upon the Society's goodwill, realized the need to embellish their image. One of the more timely opportunities afforded to Lee and his partner followed soon after Brinton Darlington's unexpected death on 1 May 1872. Another Quaker, John D. Miles, was transferred from the Kickapoo Agency in Kansas to the Cheyenne and Arapaho reservation, and when he arrived during the last of May, he was accorded an unexpectedly warm reception. For this he had Mac Lee to thank; informed of the appointment, Lee had tactically alerted both Indians and staff to the pending visit. Yet although Miles put his acceptance by the tribes as the paramount concern, another factor that could not be overlooked—military cooperation—was unlikely since in May a mixed band of Cheyenne and Kiowa had stolen over 120 mules from a government station located near Fort Dodge.[34] It was a case of either arranging the immediate surrender of the animals or anticipating reprisals.

While Miles struggled with the dilemma, Reynolds was visiting Hoag at Muskogee in regard to pending fiscal contracts. During their discussions the trader happened to mention that several of the mules had "mysteriously" appeared at company camps located near Supply. Reynolds also led Hoag to believe that still other animals would be recovered from the Kiowa.[35] Thus, the crisis had an immediate resolution; but soon enough Miles would learn the price of cooperation.

During the first part of June, while Miles adjusted to his new appointment, two freighters were moving a Lee and Reynolds supply train out of Caldwell, Kansas, to a camp at Sewell's Pond Creek Ranch, located about twenty-five miles into the Territory. Sewell's was one of several way stations building along the old Fort Harker road, which, if followed to its most southerly point, ended at Fort Sill. Cattlemen used the same route, branching near the Cheyenne and Arapaho Agency, with their "highway" commonly called the Chisholm Trail.

Lee and Reynolds's men had pulled their teams to a stop for the night, with the livestock left to graze on the prairie near the ranch house. Suddenly, with darkness as cover, three white outlaws made a dash for the corral and succeeded in loosing many of the animals. The outlaws then rode for the mules of Lee and Reynolds's train but were repulsed. By 13 June, the freighters had worked the same teams to Turkey Creek, a distance of some twenty miles from Sewell's, and were again bedded down. But once more the camp was disquieted by another raid that was, as before, fought off.

The harrassed teamsters finally made it to the safety of the Cheyenne and Arapaho compound, where the incidents were reported to the Quakers. The demand was made that Miles take immediate steps to ". . . arrest all Suspicious characters and turn them over to the proper authorities."[36] And the partners saw to it that the pressure for Miles to react in force remained constant.

Five months later, on 6 January 1873, a half-breed Delaware Indian arrived at Camp Supply with three wagons in tow for trade among the Cheyenne and Arapaho tribes. Reynolds's reaction was immediate; he at once invoked the firm's trading privilege. Consequently, although Black Beaver explained that he had permission to do business, a protest was handed to the commanding officer at Supply demanding that the outfit be detained ". . . until the arrival of Agent Miles . . . as we claim that this party is an illicit Trader. . . ." What particularly irritated Reynolds was that he suspected the half-breed of attempting to use his Indian blood to gain access to the tribes when in fact Reynolds knew the man to be selling goods on behalf of a white competitor.[37]

Miles himself rode for Camp Supply as soon as he learned of the controversy; after discussions with all parties to the dispute, he asked for and was granted a military hearing on the matter. Following a day of testimony it was agreed that Black Beaver's wagons should be impounded and that the whole affair be referred to higher authority in Washington.[38] At the same time it was probably Reynolds who lectured Miles that "[although we] suppose the laws requiring the procurement of License and regulating trade and intercourse to be enacted for the purpose of enabling the various Agents to [control] the trade and provide permanent Traders, . . . at the same time they are intended to reasonably protect the Trader in his rights to his legitimate trade. . . ."[39] Unquestionably the understanding was that an agent render a decision favorable to the partnership. Anything less would have been viewed as a violation of law—and of trust.

Thus encouraged, the two traders continued with their unsolicited advice. During October 1873 Miles's attention was called to a situation in which ". . . The border men from Medicine Lodge & other creeks just over the line are inaugurating a most vigorous whisky trade & unless it is promptly attended to will be the cause of fresh trouble with the Indians. The Buffalo Hunters are also quite a number of miles into the territory and getting very near to the Indian camp[. U]nless they are sent out it would not be strange to hear of difficulties between them and the Indians. . . ."[40] Yet did either partner seriously believe Miles capable of preventing these practices and indeed, did they really want him to succeed? Their first consideration was uninterrupted business, and although many competed for the right to trade, only Lee and Reynolds were consistently reissued a license.[41] For past services nothing less was expected; what is more, the same probably held true for most suspect activities.

Lee's involvement in a whiskey trade may be inferred. It is known that by late 1874 the partnership was one of only seven outfits within the Territory to pay a revenue tax in order to "engage in the liquor traffic." Two years previously, a company drovers station had been located on that segment of the Chisholm Trail where every other outpost was tagged as a "whiskey ranch" and along which the Indian Bureau had no regulatory authority. Also in 1872 the partners were asked to add "native wines" to their otherwise excellent stock of domestic liquors maintained on the shelves at the Camp Supply store. Thus, although during late winter of 1873 the commander at Supply gave orders for a sentinel posted on the Kansas border to ". . . carefully search all trains and wagons passing the station . . . for intoxicating liquors," the command made an exception for ". . . trains in charge of a commissioned officer or trains belonging to Messrs. Lee and Reynolds. . . ."[42] Freed from search and with authority to have both liquor and a place from which to distribute the contraband, Lee and his partner at least had the opportunity to engage in an illicit trade. An 1873 incident suggests that the advantage was used.

In March, Benjamin Williams, the agency blacksmith, was sent by Miles to a Cheyenne village located near Camp Supply with orders to prevent the tribe from avenging a cavalry attack on marauding

Cheyenne. However, Williams found his job aggravated by a two-day "drunken spree" involving several chiefs, with the only interlopers in camp being a crew of Lee's teamsters. In fairness, Williams thought the liquor to have come from the ranches located near Medicine Lodge Creek, Kansas. He also reported that the partners' employee, George Bent, had been forced to hide himself from the Indians in order to avoid being flushed with alcohol.[43] Still, Medicine Lodge was many miles north of their position, and the *only* strangers visiting the campsite were employed by the army's sutlers.

As to trade in weapons, both Lee and Reynolds had requested authority to engage in the business from the first. However, by late winter of 1872 the bureau had authorized only sales of ammunition, and this was limited solely to the months of a buffalo hunt. Nevertheless, during the spring of 1874 an employee of Smith and Ford's trading company, also doing business at the agency, visited Lee, who was then trading on the plains, and confronted him with the charge that he and his partner were selling arms to the Indians. Lee was quick to deny the accusation and to say that ". . . he did not sell any Pistols and [did] not know of it being done."[44] But again not all the evidence bore him out.

George Fox and his partner had been sent to a camp on the Washita River by J. S. Evans, the post sutler at Fort Sill, to trade with the Kiowa and the Comanche for winter robes. Shortly after a site had been established, a Kiowa came into their tent and asked whether the whites had arms for sale. Fox said no. The Indian then proceeded to upbraid the hide dealer and to predict that Evans and Company was sure to lose all business unless weapons were included in the trade. The Indian then brandished a new Colt revolver and a belt of cartridges, both purchased, he said, "at the Cheyenne Traders."[45]

However, not everything was to the partners' liking. A lead article on page one of the 16 February 1872 issue of the *New York Tribune* accused them as well as others of bribing government officials for a sutler's position. Specifically, Brevet Major General W. B. Hazen, a man who had served on the frontier, charged that J. S. Evans and Company of Fort Sill had paid $12,000 a year for a tradership and that ". . . Lee and Reynolds paid $10,000 outright for the same exclusive privilege. . . ." The two were perhaps mollified, though, when Lieutenant Colonel John W. Davidson, by order of the secretary of war to report on Reynolds, returned a favorable endorsement. Subsequently—either that spring or early in 1873—Reynolds met secretly with J. M. Hedrick at Leavenworth, Kansas, to pay the last "annual" for the right to trade at Camp Supply. As Reynolds explained, ". . . my partner and myself talked over this matter, and decided at the time, when we ceased our payments, to take our chances. If we were removed, we would go."[46] Apparently they need not have worried, for months later both were still in business, and the problems of trade were again of the more usual kind.

In early December of 1873, as Lee was preparing for his seasonal visit to the Cheyenne and Arapaho camps, Miles, in the company of several chiefs, traveled to Dodge City in order to claim a remuda of horses promised them by President Grant. However, the livestock was found to have been erroneously routed to the Wichita depot. With a blizzard preventing an immediate return to the reservation, the agent was forced to find shelter in town, and he left the chiefs inside the Santa Fe depot while he sought lodging.

Inside the building were also whites who took offense at the waiting red men. As a practical joke one grabbed a handful of red peppers and threw them on a hot stove in front of which the Indians were standing. Contact with the irritant caused the chiefs to run outside and throw themselves into the snow. The whites found the whole incident immensely humorous. Miles, though, was enraged when he learned of the insult. Nevertheless, there was little he could do but calm the excited chiefs and take advantage of an empty boxcar made available for the night. The next morning they would leave Dodge and return to the agency; but a U.S. marshal, John Talley, had already promised an investigation of the affair in the hope of forcing such outlaws out of the region.

Not long after Miles's return to the agency, Reynolds came into Supply, having returned from camps of the Cheyenne and Arapaho, who were then collecting robes near the installation. At the garrison a topic of conversation was the ruse attempted by Miles and his agent, Talley, to flush outlaws from their suspected hideouts. The marshal could not have been in the field more than one hour before word passed that he was really a government detective. Reynolds reported to Miles and suggested a more discreet investigation. He then left the post and returned to the camps where Lee was still trading.[47] It is not difficult to imagine what goods the Indians now demanded in exchange for their robes.

CHAPTER TWO

Guns & Ammunition

O n 1 March 1874 Reynolds informed Lieu-
tenant Colonel John R. Brooke, recently assigned to Camp Supply,
that two Comanche bands had come under attack by the U.S. Cavalry
near Double Mountain Fork, Texas, and that twenty-three tribesmen
had been killed. A still more ominous message was relayed to the
same authorities by Lee, then at the Cheyenne and Arapaho Agency,
informing them that ". . . the Kiowa '[had] raised the pipe' to the
Cheyenne and advised them . . . to keep away from Camp Supply
[that] summer as they [proposed] to commence operations as soon as
their horses [were] fat and the grass . . . getting good." Like the Comanche, the Kiowa were spurred by recent deaths, in this instance
the killings of Chief Lone Wolf's son and nephew. The crisis was how
to keep the peaceful Cheyenne and Arapaho from joining up with
the more warlike bands although both tribes had their own complaints, particularly in regard to rationed food.[1] Neither of the traders'
warnings augered well for success.

Another group of men, Dodge City hunters, chose these same
weeks to plant themselves on the southern plains, and during early
spring a slow-moving train of men and equipment moved south from
Dodge City, across "No Man's Land," into the Texas Panhandle. The
outfit was bound for a site located just north of the Canadian River
where years earlier Colonel William Bent had opened an Indian trade
store as an adjunct to his outlet at Bent's Fort, Colorado Territory.
With Bent's effort long since abandoned, the Dodge City hunters
now hoped to reactivate the site—called Adobe Walls—as another
supply headquarters while they chased buffalo. A. C. Myers, owner of
the Pioneer Store in Dodge City and competitor of Charles Rath and
Company, had outfitted the expedition with approximately $50,000
worth of merchandise.[2] The fact that Adobe Walls was located approximately forty-five miles west of the border of the Cheyenne and

Arapaho reservation and that both would be competing for the same animals did not seem to bother the hunters. Once established, the men began in earnest the lucrative business of slaughtering buffalo. What disturbed men like Miles was that, although a confrontation between whites and Indians now hung precariously in the balance, no one in authority seemed bothered.

As the Dodge City hunters planned and executed their move south, Little Robe, principal Cheyenne chief, was establishing his own campsite on the Cimarron River just east of Camp Supply. While so occupied, the old chief momentarily let down his guard with a remuda of prized livestock; yet that was all "Hurricane" Bill Martin needed, for in that instant forty-three ponies were run off and the outlaw made for the safety of the Kansas border. Little Robe immediately took off in pursuit. Not far from camp he was joined by several young men, including his son Sitting Medicine. The old chief tried to dissuade the youths from riding with him into Kansas, even turning his own pony south in the hope that they would follow. Yet the young braves would not be turned back and continued with their ride north after the outlaw.[3]

Elsewhere, on the afternoon of 10 April, Captain Tullis Tupper, on patrol along the border between Indian Territory and Kansas, received word of an Indian raid near Sun City. He and his small detachment immediately rode east toward the community. As they approached the town's limits, they noticed a mixed herd of livestock in the same numbers as those reported stolen. Any doubt was erased when Indian herders were spied. The order was given to dismount, and after a brief skirmish all the animals were recovered and only two "Indians" wounded. Of the injured, one was James French (alias Frenchy), a white who on occasion lived with the tribes in order to trade whiskey. The other, however, was indeed a Cheyenne—Sitting Medicine, Little Robe's son.[4]

The raiding party had returned to Miles's compound by 16 April, and on 14 May, he could report Sitting Medicine nearly recovered from his wounds. But an immediate consequence was that many in the tribe now added this incident to their already aroused feelings and split into two bands, with one in support of the government camped near the agency and the other and larger force moved out to the plains.[5] To which voices the Cheyenne now listened would substantially determine the fate of Indian Territory in 1874.

By coincidence, W. M. D. Lee was conducting business at his Cheyenne and Arapaho store in March, when the crisis began to unfold. It must have immediately occurred to him that the situation offered several interesting business opportunities, and Lee must have used part of his time to ensure that these suggestions were heard by the tribe. During the following month, the trader could add his own grievance to the Indians' council. On the morning of 23 April, as George Bent walked out of his lodge to a nearby corral, he noticed that five of Lee and Reynolds's horses were missing. The trail seemed to indicate another rendezvous of "Hurricane" Bill Martin's gang, and most Indians camped with Bent wanted to give immediate chase. It was all he could do, Bent explained, to restrain his friends from taking to the warpath. Ten days later the partners' "stage ranch" was raided of another four horses.[6]

Not long after, on 18 May, two Cheyenne messengers rode into Miles's compound to report that three Indian youths had discovered a trail that also led to a remuda of stolen livestock. They had followed the markings, waited for the white herders to drop their guard, and then stampeded the animals. Once safely back in camp, the Indians were able to identify four horses as those stolen in April from Bent. But when Miles demanded that the animals be returned, the two Indians answered that "they [thought it was] very strange that after they [had] removed them from the white thieves . . . that they should be required to give them up, . . . especially as they had not yet recovered *one half* that had been stolen from them." What Miles did not know was that ". . . it was Cheyennes that stole the Stage Horses [from Lee and Reynolds] & those of the Agency, and that it was done . . . as a measure 'to get even'. . . ." Although he empathized with the tribe, the agent still insisted on the surrender of all livestock.[7] But the Cheyenne were in no mood to cooperate.

Instead, it was probably while the two Indians argued with Miles that other members of the tribe learned of Little Robe's stolen ponies being "exposed for sale in the streets of Dodge City." Indeed, the offer would have occurred at nearly the precise time that hunters were preparing to depart for Adobe Walls, and it is conceivable that several in the party rode Little Robe's stock into Texas. Less than one month later Miles would be reporting that "we have the names of some of the parties who run off the 43 head [of] Horses from Little Robe, and the locality where we may find a portion of it—but it is all a provocation as it will require *force* to get it and here we are powerless." Notably Adobe Walls was the single permanent camp of Dodge City hunters outside the borders of Kansas. But even then the Cheyenne promised that ". . . if the Dept. could recover and return to 'Little Robe,' 'White Antelope' and other Cheyennes the *greater part* of the Horses stolen from them by whites peace and confidence would at once be restored in the tribe." Although informed of the situation, the military refused to cooperate, noting that laws prohibited the army from aiding "in the executing of civil process." Therefore, Miles's warning that "the choice of peace, or raids, now rests in the *action* or *inaction* of the [Department]" fell mostly on deaf ears.[8]

Lee also found himself caught up in the situation, and uncharacteristically even he was unable to effect the Indians' usual cooperation. Still, there was business to conduct and certain commodities were yet attractive.

Ammunition was Lee's most notable trade during the first six months of 1874, and if the firm's sales are to be believed, March was the peak month in the business, a not unusual circumstance during an ongoing buffalo hunt. But by May, when hostilities looked inevitable, trade also slackened with sales of only a nominal "eight pounds of powder" and "eleven pounds of lead" sold to peaceable Arapaho.[9] Yet were Lee's reports accurate?

James M. Haworth, agent to the Kiowa and the Comanche, had a different opinion. "I cannot get any direct or [positive] information as to the sale of arms," he complained to the commissioner of Indian Affairs, "but am certain somebody has been doing it extensively as a great many of my Indians are armed with the latest improved Pistols and Guns. . . . My traders complain to me that they were . . . able to get only a small part of the Robes sold by the Indians of this Agency . . . about Five thousand Robes while . . . the Cheyenne traders [are] getting over thirty thousand. . . ."[10] A dollar estimate of Lee and Reynolds's suggested take would have come to nearly $150,000.[11] But at the time the partners were reporting only limited trade in powder, lead, and fixed ammunition.[12] Whether these small quantities were sufficient to purchase the thousands of robes alleged can only be conjectured.

Nevertheless, Miles was quick to defend Lee and Reynolds against Haworth's charge. "Our traders," he wrote, "had permission from the [Department] to trade *Ammunition* (not arms) to Indians of this agency, and I have confidence to believe that they have not openly & [purposely] violated a well known law or regulation."[13] To further demonstrate his confidence, on 14 May, Miles extended Lee's trade for another year. As the agent cautioned, "As far as the sale of Arms &c by the traders of this Agency to . . . [Haworth's] Indians I have to report that . . . [Lee and Reynolds] deny the charge emphatically, and request that J. S. Evans & Co. proceed to make good the charge."[14]

Lee, then, by this act of Miles, was able to fend off allegations of an illegal trade, but dealing with competing Kansas hunters would prove far more difficult. He had little complaint while the whites operated from a Dodge City headquarters and transported all supplies across two or three hundred miles of open prairie. In that situation he could meet the challenge, as his Cheyenne and Arapaho suppliers were better located to hunt. However, by locating a Texas settlement squarely in the middle of the herds, the Dodge City merchants now had the advantage. Army officials quickly sided with Lee's argument and adamantly opposed the Adobe Walls operation. As General Pope later recalled, the site ". . . was established by some persons doing business in Dodge City . . . , far beyond the limits of this department, [not only] to trade with the Cheyennes and Arapahoes, and such other Indians as might come there, but [also] . . . to supply the buffalo-hunters, whose continuous pursuit had driven the great herds down into the Indian reservation. . . ."[15] Yet because the government was committed to nonintervention in "purely civil matters," the army did nothing. Lee, though, might act, and a first step to rectify the imbalance was undertaken during late spring of that year.

Early in June, two employees, James McAllister and Amos Chapman, followed the trail of horse thieves southwest of Camp Supply for some distance. The outlaws could have escaped in any direction, but the nearest settlement—and the place most likely to have been visited by passing horse thieves—was located in Texas. McAllister and Chapman reined their horses south for the approximate sixty-mile ride to Adobe Walls.

As the two rode past the crude buildings at the outpost, they passed a rick of hides nearly one hundred yards long and ten feet high awaiting transport to Dodge City. Charles Rath, Bob Wright's partner, had by now joined the enterprise, and both he and his competitor, A. C. Myers, were at their respective stores, as were about seventeen other men.[16]

McAllister and Chapman immediately struck up a conversation and asked whether anyone had information pertaining to Lee's stolen horses. Not surprisingly, all answers were negative. Regardless, the two passed on a rumor heard at Camp Supply, namely that the Indians were determined to burn out every white outpost south of the Kansas line during the summer months. The hunters, however, showed little concern, as each was too involved in the bounty of the chase. Besides, as Myers was then boasting to an attentive Dodge City crowd, ". . . [although] there are one thousand lodges encamped within forty miles of his post . . . [he] never saw a set of men so eager for a fight—so anxious to exterminate the whole race of Indians."[17]

McAllister and Chapman wasted no time in returning to Camp Supply and recounting their visit to both Lee and Reynolds. Certainly the success of the Dodge city merchants in collecting hides was specifically called to their attention, as was the hunters' trade with Indians. Yet it also must be kept in mind that McAllister and Chapman were employed for the specific purpose of pursuing stolen livestock, and it seems unlikely that either man would have left Adobe Walls without first examining the stock corralled by the hunters. In light of the facts that Lee's trade centered on the procuring of buffalo robes and that the camp at Adobe Walls was an infringement on that privilege, some consideration must be given to the possibility that Lee might have suggested to the Cheyenne and Arapaho where stolen Indian ponies might be found. After all, Lee considered information such as the report given by McAllister and Chapman to be as useful a commodity as tangible supplies. In any event, the Indians soon made their feelings in regard to the matter perfectly clear.

The Comanche, with a following of Cheyenne, made camp during late May near the mouth of Sweetwater Creek where it emptied into the North Fork of the Red River. The Cheyenne pointedly ". . . collected on the Washita about 10 miles below the point of Custer's fight . . . at the call of Little Robe's son. . . ." It was also at this time that Isa-tai, a Kwahadi Comanche, "[made] his appearance as Medicine man, or prophet" and revealed that ". . . the Caddoes [and] Wichitas and other friendly Indians, who were following in the way of the whites, would soon go out of existence, and this would be the fate of the Comanche if [they] followed the same roads; that the only way for them to become the great and powerful nation they once were, was to go to war, and kill all the white people they could. . . ." Isa-tai also prophesied that he could ". . . [either] produce rain, [or] cause a drought; . . . [and] could so influence [the] guns of whites and soldiers that they would not shoot Indians." So that the tribes might believe his powers, Isa-tai next prophesied that a comet then appearing in the night sky would disappear within five days. When the comet vanished as predicted, the Indians were that much more convinced of the man's ability.[18]

Isa-tai next had the opportunity to make his visions known at the ritual councils of the Kiowa and other bands of Cheyenne. The ceremonies had been delayed until the return of Lone Wolf from Texas with the bodies of his son and nephew. Again the prophet restated his claims to great powers and demanded an attack on white settlements. But Kicking Bird, a principal Kiowa chief, voted early against the council and led away at least one-half of his braves. Many Comanche likewise departed. For others—notably Swan and Lone Wolf of the Kiowa and Little Robe of the Cheyenne—there was only one thought: war.[19]

Lone Wolf and Little Robe next disputed where and against whom they should begin the attack. The Kiowa wanted to avenge the Texas killings of Lone Wolf's son and nephew while Little Robe favored a strike against the horse thieves and buffalo hunters operating throughout the Territory and the Texas Panhandle. After it was pointed out that the government was more apt to defend soldiers than outlaws, the Cheyenne won the argument and war was voted against the white hunters and thieves.[20]

Although each chief had fanned hostilities in order to avenge a personal wrong (Little Robe, in particular, had not forgiven the outlaw "Hurricane" Bill Martin for stealing his ponies), something must be said of the Indians' more general grievance—the slaughter of buffalo then taking place on the southern plains. The Cheyenne remembered that no less a person than the president of the United States had assured them that ". . . improper white men and buffalo-hunters should be kept from their country at all hazards. . . ."[21] However, by early February of 1874 the Cheyenne were accusing Washington of ". . . [lying] to them, as there had been more [buffalo] killed by whites in the Territory [that] winter, than ever before. . . ." A special investigation by Miles had even found buffalo stands near the compound itself, where whites, after skinning the animals of their hides, had left the carcasses to rot.[22] The slaughter was not likely to endear these same white men to tribes who for months had complained of hunger.

No one was immune from attack once hostilities began, and one of the more eventful encounters began on Thursday morning, 2 July, about eighteen miles north of the Cheyenne and Arapaho Agency. The day held no greater promise for George "Monchy" Russell and the nine other men at Lee and Reynolds's drovers station than another hot day in an already month-long drought. Then, at an anonymous shout, each man put aside what he was doing and made a dash for the ranch house. Once inside, those nearest the porthole windows grabbed their "needle-guns" and took aim on the advancing party of about fifty red men. The skirmish did not last long, with one Indian killed and two ranchmen wounded. But the partners lost another three horses.[23]

About one-half hour after the first attack ended, a white runner came racing with breakneck speed from south of the Cimarron River toward the cabin. Close behind was a band of Cheyenne warriors, and all eyes watched as this one individual headed toward the ranch. Momentum threw the man through the door and inside, breathless but safe. A companion, Bill Watkins, was not as fortunate, for he had been chased down and scalped. As the men inside talked over the incident, the Indians quietly vanished.[24]

The following morning two Cheyenne braves rode into Miles's compound flaunting a ring said to have been taken from the man killed the previous day near Lee and Reynolds's outpost. The agent was infuriated but remained silent. Then, as soon as he was able, a message was dispatched to the commander at Fort Sill demanding intervention.[25] Although the request was an infraction of faith, Miles felt he had no alternative but to answer the threat with force. And there were other incidents.

In May, J. D. Holloway, son of the agency doctor, had been murdered by two Arapaho braves. Three days later another employee was murdered by yet another Arapaho youth. Although the three renegades were an exception to an otherwise peaceful tribe—in fact, all Arapaho, in the company of Whirlwind's Cheyenne band, were now camped near the agency—the current danger was real. Even Chief Whirlwind had warned on the night of 2 July that members of his tribe were ". . . camped in the vicinity of the Agency & the Stage Ranches along the cattle trail north . . . and that we [agency residents] would '*hear from them*' very soon. . . ." Miles understood the attack on Lee and Reynolds's outpost both Thursday afternoon and again on the morning of 3 July to be the opening salvos of that battle.[26]

Consequently, Lieutenant Colonel John W. Davidson's reply of 4 July, which denied aid because the agency lay within the Department of the Missouri and not the Department of Texas, jolted Miles to action. He talked the situation over with his employees, and together they agreed that they did not have the manpower needed to withstand a combined attack of Cheyenne, Kiowa, and Comanche. The regretful necessity was to abandon the reservation and ride north to the safety of the Kansas border. It was in the dark early hours of Sunday, 5 July, when those clustered inside the ranch house at Lee and Reynolds's station were awakened by the approach of riders. The men could not have been more surprised to find Miles at the head of a party of twenty-six civilians on the trail north. The agent and his fellow riders were bedded down for the night.[27]

Early the next morning, however, Miles continued his ride north along the Chisholm Trail toward Caldwell and past the several whiskey ranches—or outlaw hangouts—which had indirectly brought about the present state of affairs. After thirty-six hours, a tired but relieved agent finally approached the main street of the border community. Along the trail Miles had witnessed evidence of the current hostilities, including the burned remains of Pat Hennessey, his crew, and supply train; other civilians huddled inside the different stage houses and one freight train that had circled its wagons for protection. If anything, the sights steeled him to entrench military authority at the Cheyenne and Arapaho compound.[28] But neither the agent's party nor the stage ranches along the Chisholm Trail were the tribes' principal objective.

Approximately one week before Miles decided to abandon his outpost, the Indians attacked the Texas settlement at Adobe Walls. In a three-hour battle that began at dawn on Saturday, 27 June, Indians and hunters fought to a standoff, with four whites and an uncounted number of warriors killed. However, the skirmish did settle the matter of the prophet's influence: shortly after the attack began, Isa-tai suffered the indignity of having his horse dropped from under him by the marksmanship of the Indian scout Billy Dixon. Only with great difficulty were the Cheyenne able to save his life, after which Isa-tai was dismissed as both "a fraud and coward." By then the tribes had also surrounded the enclave, with the whites hard-pressed to continue the fight.[29]

For its part, the army again refused to be drawn into the predicament. Although Charles Rath, through the office of the governor of Kansas, demanded that cavalry intervene, General Pope dismissed the idea in one terse response: ". . . [It] is presumed that as soon as the Buffalo Hunters now defending these illegal trading Posts are willing to abandon the Goods, they can get away as easily as their messengers can. . . ." Rath had to console himself with twenty-four carbines on loan from the governor and brought south to the embattled camp by a hastily assembled Dodge City relief party of fifty men.[30]

Then, for two months, the hunters and the Indians tested each other with occasional sorties. For their part, the tribes planned a protracted siege of the outpost; two weeks after the initial battle, a teamster, J. Wright Mooar, took note of the tribes' ". . . hospital camps in sight of the Ranch . . . [where they are probably] waiting for reinforcements to make another attack. . . ." Indeed, the Indians were still attacking "near the place" as late as August. The hunters' response was to stake skulls on posts set up around the compound. Yet by late August "the men who had been living at Adobe Walls . . . [were] determined to abandon the place, on account of [the] almost daily annoyance and hostility of the Indians. . . ." By early September, the hunters were gone.[31]

Putting Adobe Walls in perspective to the general uprising, a rumor was spoken years later among Panhandle settlers that ". . . Lee & Reynolds . . . [had] hired Quanah Parker [a half-breed Comanche chief] to run the hunters out of Adobe Walls. . . . Lee especially [was] known to have done this. . . ."[32] And there was logic to the allegation. The settlement was an obvious challenge to the man's principal business: the procurement of robes and hides. Lee, therefore, might have assumed that his only chance to compete with an outfit that had unrestricted access to the herds was to force the Kansans into a retreat back to Dodge City. Indeed, who would care if an outpost of illegal hunters was destroyed? The Indians, particularly the Cheyenne, had everything to gain by defeat of a Dodge City crew who was slaughtering their only source of livelihood. Even the military had tacitly assented to this point of view. In fact, General Pope was later to conclude that "there can be no doubt, from the facts that have reached these headquarters from good authority, that the present difficulties with Cheyennes were mainly caused by the unlawful intrusion and illegal and violent acts of the white hunters."[33] McAllister and Chapman had warned the Dodge City operatives of the consequences should they remain in Texas. Is it also not possible, then, that either Lee or Reynolds suggested where Little Robe might find his stolen ponies? Thus, as the hunters refused the warning, an attack was inevitable.

Obviously such a conspiracy is conjecture. A convincing argument against the allegation is that in 1876 Lee and Reynolds combined resources with Charles Rath in order to hunt what buffalo remained on the South Plains. It seems very unlikely that Rath would have shown any interest in the enterprise had either partner earlier conspired to have him killed. Addressing the same issue, the Dodge City teamster J. Wright Mooar later said: ". . . [Lee and Reynolds] weren't interested in them stores [at Adobe Walls] but they sent their half-breed [Amos Chapman] to put these folks on their guard when they found it [the attack] was going to be done. . . . Rath and them [were] good friends. . . . Nevertheless, as Miles cautioned on 30 June, three days after the battle and before he knew of the attack, the Cheyenne" . . . [claimed] that these raids shall be confined to the exterminating of the buffalo hunters in the region and country of the border of Kansas where Little Robe's stolen ponies are supposed to be located. . . ."[34] If true, someone had convinced the tribes that the Texas camp was a likely place where Indian ponies could be found.

Still, while the Dodge City men agonized over their predicament, Miles continued with his efforts to obtain military protection for the Cheyenne and Arapaho compound. By 18 July, the agent had discussed the matter with Superintendent Hoag and General Pope, and while both appeared receptive to his arguments, an immediate commitment was not forthcoming. What was immediate was a demand by fellow Quakers that he resign for seemingly abandoning the Society's tenet of peace. For his part, Miles refused to be drawn into the controversy and planned for an early return to the agency.[35] As for the military, no matter what Pope's best inclinations were, he could not forestall pressures demanding that the army intervene. Therefore, on 26 July Secretary of War Belknap endorsed the general's reluctant decision to use elements of his command to put down the rebellion.[36] Consequently, the Territory's most dangerous threat to peace was brought under control.

In July Miles even learned of "Hurricane" Bill Martin's arrest at Wichita, Kansas; and in August Little Robe was welcomed back to the agency, the chief and his band escaping" . . . at night from the main Cheyenne camp . . . [although] compelled to abandon their lodges and most of their camp-baggage. . . ." Surrender by the more recalcitrant braves would be a slow process, however, and it would not be until March of 1875 that the last of the Cheyenne gave up the fight. A severe winter had more to do with an end to the rebellion than threat of military engagement. Once arrived at the agency, the tribe would be greeted by a new element: a detachment of the Sixth Cavalry permanently located near the agent's home.[37]

At Dodge City during these same days in August, a large force of men and equipment also assembled for the incursion into Indian country. The expedition consisted of eight companies or two battalions of Sixth Cavalry, commanded by Major C. E. Compton and Major James Biddle, and four companies of Fifth Infantry, for a total strength of 38 commissioned officers and 802 enlisted men; Brevet Major General Nelson A. Miles, Fifth Infantry, was placed in command of the whole. By August the expedition was bivouacked at Camp Supply preparing to march southwest into Texas and to strike at the rebellious tribes. It was not long thereafter that General Miles wrote of "a possibility of this campaign lasting during Autumn and winter," thus necessitating "the propriety of establishing a supply camp." By 15 September the general was committed to a winter bivouac at a site not yet determined but certain to be located in the Texas Panhandle.[38]

By late summer the prospect of military intervention also had a sobering effect on Indian temperament. Outlaws even dared the chance of apprehension by raiding Arapaho pony herds, and it was presumed that as soon as the tribes established their winter camps, whiskey peddlers would also resume their once-profitable trade. Times were so settled that Dodge City hunters even prepared to go back on the plains, as ". . . the Indians [had] not brought on a fight for over two months."[39]

Probably without a hint of deceit, both sutlers informed General Miles as he passed through Supply on his way into Texas that ". . . the strength of the Indians . . . [had] been greatly underrated, and that they [were] well armed with rifles of improved pattern, and provided with [an] abundance of ammunition. . . ." Consequently, the partners asked for protection of their "hay parties and teams." But at the time—the week of 12 through 19 September—most troops at Camp Supply were either detailed to relieve an embattled supply train or sent to rescue six men pinned down by the tribes at a nearby buffalo wallow. Yet although post strength was reduced to only seventy-nine enlisted men, troops were detailed to guard Lee's mule trains.[40] The partners reciprocated four months later when, with military freighters unable to resupply the wintering troops, the firm placed its considerable operation at government disposal.

In fact, Lieutenant Colonel W. H. Lewis, commander at Supply, had spent a substantial portion of his time during late summer and early fall bickering with General Miles over this one issue—the servicing of the government's Indian Expedition. Finally, the matter appeared settled when the troops were stationed at two base camps, one located on the Washita River in Indian Territory and the other on Sweetwater Creek in Texas. The difficulty now changed to one of weather: on 30 December a blizzard began that did not abate until mid-January of 1875. However, it was not until government freighters had lost fifty oxen to the freezing climate that Lewis finally opted to accept the help offered by his post traders. Three trainloads of supplies were immediately transferred to Lee's wagons, whose bullwackers now awaited a break in weather. That opportunity came on 16 January as an ox-drawn train moved out of the post bound for the government's new camp on Sweetwater Creek. With success of the first effort, other partner-owned trains soon followed.[41]

During these same months, trade at the Cheyenne and Arapaho store resumed, and Lee found himself involved in new projects such as contracting with the tribes to plant and harvest 250 acres of corn. In March the firm even submitted an application to renew its trade in ammunition. It was not until July, however, that a new liquor license was approved at Supply. Still, business was more attuned to the winter complaint that both condoned "ficticious [sic] standards of value" in the barter of goods, thereby cheating the Indians of the true value for their robes. John Miles at first explained that Indians had little understanding of "dollar and cents," but he was careful to add that "the traders [were] as ready as any one to bring their trade to a currency basis. . . ." In any event, as might be expected, "the outlook for trade the present season [would] not amount to much. . . ." A rebellion by the imprisoned Cheyenne on 6 and 7 April 1875, which resulted in many escaping north from the Territory, was a further indication of existing difficulties.[42]

Lee used the lull in affairs to visit his mother and sisters, who had moved to a new house he had purchased for them at Columbus, Wisconsin.[43] When recalling events, he must have reflected on the present turmoil and the need to find less volatile opportunities elsewhere. More importantly, the change would have to be made soon if profits were to be maintained.

On an early June morning in 1875, another man, Dick Bussell, led a crew of trail-weary buffalo hunters to the eastern plains of the Texas Panhandle, where they understood that the army was about to locate another installation. Not finding the site, they established a camp under a grove of cottonwoods near Sweetwater Creek while Bussell set off alone to explore the countryside. After walking only a short distance up one embankment, Bussell began to hear noises coming from over the rise. As he climbed, the sounds grew louder and the thought of Indians at once crossed his mind. Alerting his friends, Bussell stooped low in the grass and crawled the distance to the top of the hill. Then barely raising his eyes above the turf, he was startled by what lay unexpectedly before him: two military units (one infantry and the other cavalry) were unloading what appeared to be over one hundred wagons.

The other hunters joined Bussell at the top of the hill, made themselves comfortable, and watched as the soldiers continued to unload the train at the government's new fort. In the midst of all this activity a large white tent was also being raised above the prairie, and Bussell walked over to investigate. On closer inspection he found employees of a Lee and Reynolds crew staking down the canvas, with four or five wagons waiting to be uncrated as soon as the tent was in place. The sutlers' men even promised to open a bar by mid-afternoon.[44]

CHAPTER THREE

Buffalo Hides

By the end of September 1875, the command at Cantonment grew to include six companies of both Fourth Cavalry and Nineteenth Infantry, a total complement of 357 men. The installation was located approximately one hundred miles southwest of Camp Supply and nearly thirty miles west of Custer's battle site on the Washita. But attracting even more attention than the new post was a fast developing community of buffalo hunters situated about three miles down a hill and east of the army's position (see Map 3).[1]

White hunters had congregated on Sweetwater Creek where a store, several saloons, and one restaurant serviced the different outfits that had come to hunt in the region. Hide Town was the community's early name, which came into use by common reference. Bob Wright and Charles Rath together had opened an outfitting store in camp, while Lee and Reynolds remained in business on the hill near the garrison. As early as September the new settlement had sufficient notoriety for Indian agent James Haworth to report that "within the last few months a cantonment has been established on the 'Pan Handle' of Texas . . . near which I understand a new frontier town is springing up with all the accompanying vices of such places." Naturally, trade in hides was the town's principal commerce, with wagon loads of cured skins continually moving up the trail to the railyard at Dodge City.[2]

Dick Bussell and his fellow hunters were among those who had remained at Cantonment throughout the summer of 1875, and by early fall they had accumulated over one thousand skins. However, a problem arose when it was discovered that about two hundred of the hides had been hunted from the protected reserves in the Territory. Mac Lee resolved the dilemma by simply agreeing to purchase everything collected: he merely asked that the entire lot be hauled north of the cantonment, where in time his teamsters would purchase the contraband.

Following Lee's instructions, toward the end of November Bussell and his crew were unloading the last wagon of cured skins as another mule train moved up the trail from Texas toward Camp Supply. Only on this run Lee was accompanying his teamsters on the ride east. As the wagons neared the campsite, the train rolled to a stop, and Lee wasted no time in ordering a tally of Bussell's rick. The count came to fourteen hundred skins, for which the hunters were paid one dollar each, including those hides taken from Indian lands.[3] The idea of violating government orders by transporting contraband out of the region did not seem to bother the men so long as he was also exploring new inroads into the hide trade. White hunters were just too successful to be ignored.

At the same time, Lee had not forsaken his more established interests. Indian scouts had sighted buffalo on Beaver and Wolf creeks near Camp Supply, and both the Cheyenne and the Arapaho gave immediate chase. Within weeks of the advance, permits to trade at the isolated camps were also issued to both Lee and Reynolds and to a former clerk, Weller Hubbell. Hubbell's "independence" was more apparent than real, as all used Lyman Scott, a Leavenworth, Kansas, banker, as one of two sureties on each of their respective applications.[4]

With the wagons also went gifts of sugar and coffee, and by late November even supplies of powder, lead, and cartridges were sold, although ammunition was still restricted to specific guidelines. This at once drew the attention of General Pope, who "suggested" that the tribes ". . . kill what buffalo they need with bows and arrows. . . ." Therefore, Miles withdrew the authorization but not without protest. His complaint was of little consequence, however, as by late winter the herds had been driven out of the Territory by "[prairie] fires and hunters"; both the Cheyenne and the Arapaho ended the chase with only thirty-five hundred robes.[5]

For Lee the advent of the new year, 1876, held as little promise in other affairs. One of the more unexpected challenges began on 3 March nearly one thousand miles east of the buffalo camps. In the bay of the U.S. Senate, Congressman Hyster Clymer of Pennsylvania announced to the assembled legislators that the House of Representatives had that day enrolled five articles of impeachment against Secretary of War Belknap. The vote culminated three months of investigation that addressed the issue of whether the secretary of war had accepted bribes to appoint Calep P. March and John S. Evans to the tradership at Fort Sill.[6]

The accusation at once became the sensation of Washington, and as the notoriety came with General W. B. Hazen's published letter of February 1872, both Lee and Reynolds found themselves involved in the controversy. Yet, by the good fortune of having stopped payments to Hedrick, the two were able to deflect much of the criticism. Therefore, in April, when Reynolds was called to testify before Congress, he could offer his renunciation as mitigation to any misconduct. Lee also had earlier disclaimed all "post tradership bribes." Of course, both must have been aware that officers at Camp Supply had jointly advised their superiors in Washington that they ". . . had no reason to object either personally or officially to Messrs. Lee & Reynolds as post traders . . . [and] until these assertions [were] proven . . . that the public interest would not be served by their removal."[7] Thus protected, the partners could expect to weather the political storm relatively unaffected.

As for Belknap, the Senate's vote came on 1 August, and the ex-secretary was exonerated on each of the five articles of impeachment. The successful defense was that because of a prior resignation he was not a civil officer of the U.S. government at the time of impeachment. The Fort Sill trading firm of J. S. Evans and Company had had its license revoked months earlier.[8]

But while Reynolds wrestled with the issue, Lee busied himself with the more mundane matters of the partnership, and on 28 April he accepted an appointment as post trader to the Texas post now named Fort Elliott. This event occurred approximately one month before the company renewed trade at the Cheyenne and Arapaho Agency. If Miles had misgivings about relicensing the firm as a result of the scandal, he did not show concern. The application was processed as expeditiously as Weller Hubbell's the previous week. And for yet another year both firms listed brothers in the same Leavenworth, Kansas, banking house (Lyman Scott for Hubbell, Lucien Scott for Lee and Reynolds) as two of the required sureties on their trading bonds. The agent was more pressed to deal with northern Cheyenne who, during May, had escaped from the camps of Sitting Bull and Crazy Horse and were beginning to arrive at the agency. At the same time local Cheyenne, "fully realizing that the buffalo were fast disappearing," had requested "to exchange a portion of their ponies and robes for cattle, and in some instances for agricultural implements. . . ."[9] So Miles was consumed by his own problems and could pay little attention to the remote conflict taking place at the nation's capital.

Lee was also primarily concerned with local affairs, and other than organizing his newly won tradership at Fort Elliott, he set out to supervise the several military contracts that had been awarded to the

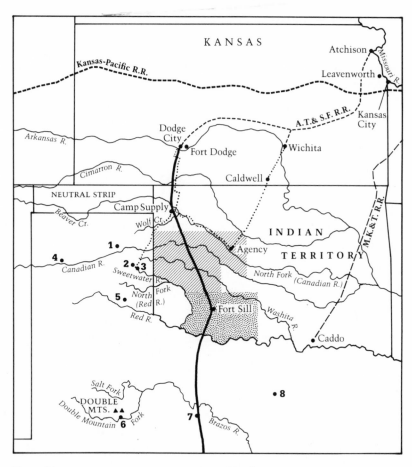

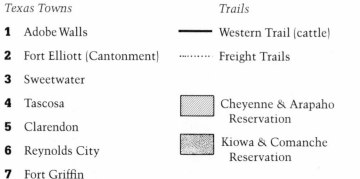

Texas Towns

1 Adobe Walls

2 Fort Elliott (Cantonment)

3 Sweetwater

4 Tascosa

5 Clarendon

6 Reynolds City

7 Fort Griffin

8 Fort Worth

Trails

— Western Trail (cattle)

········· Freight Trails

Cheyenne & Arapaho Reservation

Kiowa & Comanche Reservation

Map 3. Indian Territory and the Texas Panhandle, ca. 1877

firm. At Fort Elliott the last 150 cords of locally cut softwood for a $15,000 contract was delivered in May, and a similar arrangement was anticipated during fiscal year 1876–1877. The expectation of a contract to provide hay for the troops quartered in the Texas Panhandle caused Lee, for the sum of $1,200, to purchase the firm's first realty in that state: 1,960 acres located "twenty-four miles west" of the border with Indian Territory. There were similar contracts with the garrison near John Miles's agency.[10]

These several obligations caused Lee to allocate only short periods of his time to each installation, a situation made acute by Reynolds's continued absence. Some, like the commanding officer at Camp Supply, even began to doubt whether the senior partner would ever return. Nevertheless, Lee attempted to meet the demands of each interest, with his thoughts probably slipping to other ventures that might further expand the business. He and Reynolds had recently agreed to purchase a small herd of marketable cattle from a central Texas rancher and to move the lot to the open fields near Camp Supply. He probably also took more than passing interest in the talk of hunting the large herds of buffalo then roaming an area south of Fort Elliott and southwest of Fort Griffin. But even Lee came to the day when he put all business aside and returned to Wisconsin, where on 25 September he married the pretty twenty-nine-year-old Orlina Whitney. It was not until November, after an extended visit to the larger cities of the East Coast and Lina's safe return to her father's home, that Lee again returned to business. Shortly thereafter, on 4 December, Reynolds was relicensed as post trader at Camp Supply, and on 13 December Lee was relicensed as post sutler at Fort Elliott.[11] Ironically, in their most difficult year together, both men had actually augmented their already enviable position on the southern plains.

George Bent, a company employee, led the Cheyenne and the Arapaho on the next buffalo hunt beginning in October 1876. The party of nearly 2,500 Indians, under escort of 25 soldiers detailed from the renamed cantonment of Fort Reno, left the compound on 11 October to head northwest along the North Fork of the Canadian River toward Camp Supply. However, it was not until the first week in November that buffalo in any number were engaged, and even then the hides were "good only for lodge skins." Still, the first days of the hunt ". . . [had] been made with success and [to the] satisfaction . . . [of] both tribes. . . ."[12]

But, as in the past, good fortune proved elusive, and by mid-November the herds had moved west of the Territory into Texas.

With misgivings, Bent permitted the Indians to divide themselves into small bands while cautioning each to be on the alert for white outlaws. One gang had even ". . . [sent] word [to] Camp Supply [boasting that] they were going to steal ponies from these Indians."[13] Nevertheless, the tribes grew impatient of Bent's reluctance to ride beyond the reservation, especially when they learned that bands of Osage, Pawnee, and Caddo were chasing the same animals.

Despite these cautions, ". . . about mid-winter the pony herds of the hunting parties were 'raided' on by the common curse of . . . [the] country, horse-thieves, who kept-up their depredation with great vigilance and success until the last Indian had left the plains, leaving some of them without a pony. . . ." Under that circumstance, it was hardly the usual lift to morale when Lee showed up in camp, wagons in tow, expecting to discuss his customary trade. Although the Cheyenne and the Arapaho were successfully checked from avenging their losses, they also counted merely 7,000 robes between them. And when later challenged that the Indians were not adequately compensated, Lee, Reynolds, and Hubbell each countered that "we are now paying ten (10) 'trade checks' for a robe, the same we paid four years ago when robes were much higher in the market than now. While we are giving more goods for a check than we did then . . . if robes do not advance before fall, we are likely to lose money in the season's trade."[14] As they had done when earlier hunts failed, the partners looked elsewhere for business.

During December 1876 an unusually large wagon train of white hunters, buffalo skinners, and camp followers moved across the Texas plains. The outfit had started from Dodge City that fall bound for the twin peaks of Double Mountains near the Double Mountain Fork of the Brazos River. The organizers—Lee, Reynolds, and Charles Rath—were determined to establish a camp from which to hunt what buffalo remained on the southern plains. Travel was slowed by the mere size of the expedition, as nearly everything imaginable had been packed into the wagons, including a dismantled saloon and brothel with accompanying saloonkeeper and "some forty women."[15]

It took the hunters several weeks to maneuver through the prairie of north-central Texas, but in December the wagons finally rolled to a stop at a site ten miles south of Double Mountains; by mid-January of 1877 the camp, christened Reynolds City, was an active and prospering community. Although many continued to live out of the back of the wagons that had brought them south, work had also begun on a more permanent restaurant, mercantile store, and re-assembled dancehall and saloon. The operation was expected to handle as many as "1,000 Sharps Guns" or 1,000 hunters, with an understanding that ". . . Lee and Reynolds [furnish] everything in the way of supplies."[16]

When the hunters eventually returned from their buffalo stands, Rath's freighters stood ready to haul the dried hides out of Reynolds City to a company yard at Fort Griffin. W. C. Lobenstein of Leavenworth had his agents, A. G. Brook and James T. Hickey, posted at Fort Griffin and Fort Worth respectively, also prepared to pay top dollar for each cured skin. Lee's agent, W. H. West, was set to freight the partners' quota to the railyard at Dodge City. As no outfit imagined that it could satisfy the demand for hides on either the domestic or foreign markets, there was not the usual competition between the three companies.[17]

By spring 1877, those still in business at Reynolds City were in the final process of tallying the hunt, and by any reckoning the take exceeded all expectations. The estimates ran to over 100,000 buffalo killed, with the best evidence being the acres of staked hides laid out in all directions from the shanties. Lee, Reynolds, and Rath were each paying up to $4.50 for bull hides and $2.50 to $3.50 for the best cow skins. Once acquired, the hides were freighted up the trail to Dodge City or, in the partners' case, to the Cheyenne and Arapaho Agency. If delivered to the Indians, the skins were tanned at $2.00 or four "trade checks" a skin, where by winter's end Indian women had earned an unexpected $30,000.[18]

Of course, problems arose—not the least of which was the continuing disruption of peace by outlaws and horse thieves. Even in this, however, Lee and Reynolds did their part to reduce the chance of hostilities. That same year John Miles said of Reynolds that he ". . . manifested more than ordinary interest in assisting to recover stolen property & secure the arrest of thieves, & has thus far loaned . . . myself the means necessary to prosecute the work in the way of employing guides, subsistence, forage, &c. . . ." Interestingly, at the Texas camp, the survivor of a gunfight between two hunters was forced to abandon the compound. This man was Pat Garrett several years before the notoriety of another killing. The partners even continued to operate while a band of Comanche raided the campsite throughout late spring.[19]

What Lee must have realized was that as long as the reaction to any incident was kept in check, the firm would prosper. After all, the braves of both the Cheyenne and Arapaho tribes were content to have their women earn money by tanning the thousands of hides brought north to the agency. As Miles pointed out, "I think I can safely say that the Indians have appreciated the opportunity offered by the traders to earn the means to supply the deficiency in the rations to them, and I know there has never been so little complaint of hunger since my connection at this agency as the past summer." What other competitors failed to understand was that the Indians prospered while Lee and Reynolds's profits increased.[20] Peace had its dividends.

When Lee arrived at Dodge City late in July of 1877, he found the town astir because about nine hundred northern Cheyenne led by Chief Dull Knife had recently passed through the community en route to the southern agency. The town itself was in the early transition from a hunters' camp to a cattle town, due in part to the relocation of the Texas cattle trail from Abilene to a Dodge City terminus (see Map 3). In light of the change, Lee had petitioned the Cheyenne and Arapaho agent to move his drovers station from north of the Cimarron River to a "temporary tent" located near Camp Supply where the trail now crossed Beaver Creek; and Miles had approved.[21] Still, Dodge had not completely given up on the hide trade, and it was this business that now brought Lee into the city.

A result of his phenomenal success during the preceding months[22] was that he and Reynolds were said to ". . . do nearly all the business in this section of the world."[23] Consequently, both opted to open their own buffalo robe and hide outlets in Chicago and New York City.[24] Indeed, the number of hides shipped out of Dodge had grown to such proportions that Lee felt it necessary ". . . to apply for permission to erect on the 'government' reservation and on the . . . [Santa Fe] Siding below the Govt. Ware house a storage Ware house and yard sufficiently large to accommodate . . . [their] forwarding business. . . ." However, signs also pointed to a decline in the trade. In July Miles even predicted that "the Robe Hides furnished by traders (L & R) will soon be exhausted. . . ." The agent was properly concerned, for ". . . the Indians have with the funds derived from dressing Robe Hides for traders procured more sugar, coffee, Bacon &c (not including Beef) than has been issued from the commissary. . . ."[25] But for the immediate future Lee saw no end to the seemingly inexhaustible supply of skins.

Later, while reintroducing his Wisconsin wife to life at Camp Supply (her first visit being during late spring), Lee thus looked forward to still other successes in the business year. At Camp Supply the company had crews in the field putting up locally cut hay and wood; crews were similarly employed at Fort Elliott. In particular, of Lee's Fort Elliott contracts the local quartermaster made special note that ". . . there is no one in this country but Lee and Reynolds that have the facilities for putting in the hay in the time specified." And that was precisely how Lee would have it remain. As one journalist observed, ". . . it has puzzled some to know how it is possible for this firm to sell goods so cheap. . . ." But "the secret," he said, "is that . . . [Lee and Reynolds] make a very heavy purchase, pay cash and get good margins, and have their own wagon transportation from Dodge City to this point [Camp Supply], as well as having the benefit of special rates on railroad lines east of Dodge City. . . ." As a result, Lee and his partner were now tagged as "the boss traders of the southwest." In fact, trade was so lucrative that the army paymaster at Fort Elliott even borrowed money from company profits during July, August, and September in order to meet his "extra" duty payrolls for each month. Everything, therefore, suggested that Lee further limit himself to the affairs of hide camps and military posts. Yet both he and Reynolds refused to be shaken in their faith in the once-profitable Indian trade. Lee's only disappointment was that Lina, who had come in September to live at Supply, had returned to Wisconsin by December.[26] He perhaps only then began to suspect what adjustments this would require in his own life.

Yet while the couple talked out their differences, Miles authorized the Cheyenne and the Arapaho to ride again from the agency on another chase. The tribes left under escort of a military detachment with the unusual "prospect of a successful hunt." Large numbers of buffalo had been reported "in the territory and *this side* [southeast] *of Camp Supply*." But in the short time that it took the tribes to arrive at the ground where the herds had been sighted, "it was found that Indians from reservations east and south of [the Cheyenne and Arapaho Agency] . . . had already been at work, and buffalo but few in numbers. . . ." As a consequence, the herds had moved southwest of Fort Elliott. The local commandant, therefore, began to worry that Indians might raid area ranches, and as a precaution he ordered the tribes to hunt east of the Panhandle.[27]

Most heeded the order but to little purpose. By early December the Indians were ". . . out of rations . . . and in a starving condition." This situation caused Miles to petition Lee that ". . . if the hunting party from this agency is still in the vicinity of Camp Supply and destitute of meat that you issue them Beef on [the] hoof . . . for a sufficient time to place them at the Buffalo herds or at this agency. . . ." Yet, as Major H. A. Hambright, commanding officer at Camp Supply, observed, the tribes were "unable to move by reason of the poor condition of their horses." In fact, the Indians were "eating the flesh of Horses that [had] died. . . ." Although this development made the traders' cooperation critical, Lee and Reynolds refused the request to cut stock from their newly acquired herd until first presented with a written "certificate" that guaranteed payment.[28]

A crisis was averted only when Major Hambright, finishing a complaint of the situation to his superiors in Leavenworth, was interrupted by a clerk from the partners' store who instructed that ". . . an issue [of beef would] be made on . . . the [verbal] authority [alone]. . . ." Thus, on Christmas Eve, 20,500 pounds of beef were delivered to the Indians, which was closely followed by other distributions. So by February 1878 the government was indebted to Lee and Reynolds for nearly $3,400 worth of rationed stock.[29]

Lee himself was at Leavenworth in December contracting with the quartermaster of the Department of the Missouri for the use of freight wagons on the run between Fort Dodge and Fort Elliott when the dispute arose. He did not remain isolated long, however, and by 7 January, before riding off to Fort Elliott, he ". . . [promised] to send . . . a synopsis of the Indian situation down there as soon as it could be ascertained. . . ." Yet, as he learned, the once-profitable environment had changed. As Captain W. J. Lyster of Camp Supply wrote that same year, ". . . all the Indians who returned to this post last winter . . . realized . . . the buffalo was gone forever. . . ."[30]

To merchants like Lee this meant that the Indians would now be looking to the government for nearly all supplies. Even what little business remained, effective 1 January 1878, had to be transacted in cash rather than barter. Therefore, Lee also had to accept the inevitable—that his profitable trade was ending. A good indication of this fact was that by the end of the winter of 1877–1878, he, Reynolds, and Hubbell together had netted only 219 robes, with the tribes averaging no more than $3.00 a skin under the new cash system. Even the Texas kill was down from preceding years so that by mid-spring only 2,000 hides had been brought to the agency for tanning. Not surprisingly, Lee found himself also being asked to provision the Cheyenne and the Arapaho with many essentials that had to be freighted to the agency from a distant Kansas terminus. Even then, Reynolds found it necessary to travel east in order to prod officials in the Department of the Interior for payment, an obligation not met until June.[31]

However, both men did take some pride in the belief that they were helping the tribes adjust to a peaceful way of life. By August 1879 Miles could report that approximately $7,000 had been earned by the Cheyenne and the Arapaho in making bricks, chopping and hauling wood, putting up hay, and splitting and hauling rails—most of which was done to satisfy a contract for Lee and Reynolds. A project of special interest to Lee was an Indian mail service that ran between the agency and Fort Elliott and that gave twenty-five families their living.[32]

Therefore, Lee must have been particularly irate at a competitor's charge that although "there [are] nominally two traders at the agency they are really owned by one firm [in order to] . . . prevent competition. . . ."[33] Granted, Indian labor came cheap, and by using the Cheyenne and the Arapaho to work various contracts, Lee was satisfying his obligations at minimal cost. Still, without the contracts both tribes faced a far more desperate future. After all, Lee could as well have solicited whites to labor in the wood yards and hay fields as he did Indians.

Some excitement was caused in early September of 1878 when approximately three hundred northern Cheyenne were led away from the agency by their chief, Dull Knife. Even employees at Lee's store at Camp Supply were issued arms in fear that escaping Indians might attack the garrison. However, the alarm was unnecessary—the threat never materialized—and attention again turned to more usual events such as the unauthorized hunt in mid-November by Little Robe and a band of another three hundred braves. As the chief later explained to Texans settled near Fort Elliott, ". . . he had always eaten buffalo meat, liked it, and was not willing to go without it. . . ." In other words, he would not be denied his traditions, a fact appreciated by the Fort Elliott commander. Even the Comanche—certainly no friend of whites and in particular of white soldiers—were complacent enough during the hunt to invite elements of the U.S. Cavalry to ride alongside them on the chase.[34]

But a consequence of the Indians' reduced lot was that a trader's market for robes and hides had vanished, and Lee now found himself in the company of different forces—cattlemen and settlers—poised to further transform the frontier. Thus, when Lee and his wife departed Camp Supply for Fort Elliott during the first week of August 1878, they traveled with the satisfaction that others had assumed the burdens of the Indian trade. In fact, on 29 July George E. Reynolds, Albert's brother, was licensed as the only merchant at the Cheyenne and Arapaho Agency.[35] What profits Lee anticipated to lose because of the decline in business with Indians were now largely compensated by new inroads into an expanding cattle trade and military operation.

Lee increasingly gave attention to both enterprises. In particular, as evidenced by the winter demand for beef, an efficiently organized cattle trade could lead to substantial profits. Lee was quick to recognize an opportunity, and from the small herd of cattle first grazed near Camp Supply in 1876 he had expanded the enterprise: by the spring of 1878 company-raised beef supplied the garrison at Fort Reno.[36] It was cattle from this same herd that had fed the Cheyenne

during the preceding months, and now it was Lee's cattle that attracted attention during another crisis.

In late April John Miles faced the usual problem of inadequate
rations for the tribes camped near his agency. The shortage was
brought on by having only thirty-nine head of beef for immediate
distribution. Therefore, Miles had no choice but to approach Weller
Hubbell, then in service as Lee and Reynolds's foreman, and request
that fifty beeves be cut from their herd. Hubbell was receptive, but
he first set terms identical to those specified in the partners' contract with the military. Miles accepted, and in only a matter of hours
fifty top-grade animals were driven the short distance from a pasture
near Fort Reno to the agency pens. When by coincidence a government contractor arrived that same day with another herd of 153
beeves, it was immediately apparent that the LR-branded stock surpassed the quality of the competitor's animals.[37] If anyone needed
further demonstration, the partners again showed their ability to
better service a demand with no other obligation than maximized
profits.[38]

Criticism of Lee's new operation was immediate, and one competitor even charged that "the opinion is general that a large part of
the cattle were stolen from the Indian herd." This same individual
saw another evil in that Miles himself was thought to have invested
in the enterprise. Notwithstanding, by November 1879 Lee and
Reynolds had trailed nearly 2,000 head of LR beeves to Dodge City
for shipment to the slaughterhouse. And by July of that same year
Lee was also provisioning beef to the garrison at Camp Supply. Like
Hubbell at Fort Reno, James McAllister, a company freighter, was
tapped to be foreman of the Camp Supply operation. Certainly what
concerned the partners more than a competitor's allegations was the
real danger to their herd. During August 1879 alone, 50 head fell victim to an outbreak of "Texas fever"; but the balance survived.[39]

In military affairs the partnership also prospered. On 7 March
1878 Lee contracted with the army's quartermaster at Fort Leavenworth to provide 400 cords of softwood during the months of April
and May, for which he was to be paid $5,000.[40] The agreement was
followed by two other contracts whereby Lee promised deliveries to
the garrisons at Fort Supply and Fort Elliott during another six-
month period of 1,700 and 1,750 cords of softwood, respectively, for a
total compensation of approximately $40,000.[41] A renewal of the
Fort Elliott contract in 1879 promised Lee an additional $23,000. Yet
another deal signed by Lee in May 1878 obligated him to transport
military supplies between Dodge City and Fort Elliott. The firm also
held the contract for hay deliveries at Camp Supply. Of course, when

the government set out to construct a telegraph line or "electric girdle" around the Indians (extending from Wichita, Kansas, southwest to Fort Sill) in the summer of 1879, neither Lee nor Reynolds could pass up the opportunity. Therefore, of the $250,000 appropriated for the project, approximately one-half was allocated to the construction of a line between the redesignated Fort Supply and Fort Elliott, with Lee and Reynolds agreeing to furnish all telegraph poles at the Fort Elliott connection.[42]

For this greatly increased military trade expanded facilities were needed, and by spring 1879 one hundred men were employed at Fort Supply; "hundreds of men" were likewise retained at Fort Elliott. Both operations were well stocked, and of the Fort Elliott store a passing journalist observed in April 1879 that the partners now had ". . . several large buildings filled with clothing and groceries and hardware, and almost every species of merchandise in demand by military or civilians." A curious result of this increased activity was that to avoid a Dodge City tax on wagons moving south across the Arkansas River bridge, Lee outfitted all vehicles with wheels raised six inches higher than usual. So equipped, company freighters were able to roll across the river and thus avoid the Dodge City tax.[43] Success, though, had its burdens, as the trader again learned during the late spring of 1879.

Lieutenant Colonel John W. Davidson, appointed to the command at Fort Elliott, feared the inevitable confrontation between Indians and eastern Panhandle residents unless the tribes were turned away from another pointless hunt. Therefore, in June a band of approximately ninety Pawnee men, women, and children riding near the garrison were escorted to Indian Territory. However, no sooner had the Pawnee been maneuvered across the border than a messenger reported that a company of Texas Rangers, captained by George W. Arrington, had arrived at the fort with authority to engage all tribes in the region. Deciding that the troops also needed to be cautioned, Davidson rode for Arrington's camp in order to deliver the message personally.[44]

The colonel discovered that Arrington was already excited by an earlier encounter with a clerk at Lee's store who had also demanded the reason for the visit. The confrontation did not make Davidson's job any easier; nevertheless, he asked the same question. The captain's response bothered Davidson, for it appeared that the troops were indeed bent on engaging Indians, and that, to the colonel's mind, was precisely what he was determined to prevent. For his part, Arrington became convinced that the army was purposely avoiding all legitimate complaints of local citizens.[45]

As a result, during the next several days both men organized their own inspection of Panhandle affairs. Arrington went so far as to ride approximately one hundred miles southwest of Fort Elliott in order to interview homesteaders located at Clarendon who obligingly bolstered his allegations against the government. In response, Davidson ordered a company of infantry to the Texas border with Indian country in the event that Arrington and his troops should ride east in pursuit of red men. The Rangers added argument to their complaint when they took into custody a party of trespassing Navajo.[46] Therefore, Davidson, challenged in his authority, looked to those who benefited most from military and to one individual in particular.

Lee and his wife had arrived at Fort Elliott on Wednesday, 11 June, with intent to vacation at the garrison. But as the beleaguered colonel was the same officer who in 1872 had defended the partnership against congressional investigation, Lee now had an opportunity to reciprocate the earlier favor.[47]

On the day Arrington returned from scouting the Panhandle, he was greeted by county judge Emanuel Dubbs, himself greatly excited over an earlier argument with Lee's clerk, John Donnelly. Donnelly, also a county commissioner, had demanded that Dubbs convene an immediate session of the commissioners' court in order to formally petition the Rangers to leave the area. Donnelly told Dubbs that unless the troops rode out, Davidson was set to ". . . fire upon or arrest, imprison and iron Capt. Arrington's company of Rangers, in case he, Arrington, should fire into any of the Indians in the Pan Handle. . . ." He then threatened that if the judge did not convene the county government as requested, his employer was prepared to bring suit on all accounts due at the sutler's store.[48]

Arrington at once understood the import of the warning; he also realized that Lee stood behind the threat. Not trusting the man (who also ran the Wheeler County post office from his sutler's store), the captain went so far as to have all correspondence forwarded by way of courier. Some in Sweetwater believed that Lee routinely opened the mails before delivery. The mistrust was well placed, for three days later Arrington learned that Lee ". . . [was] getting up a petition to send to Austin to have us removed from the Pan Handle. . . ." In fact, three signators to the document were county commissioners—thus a voting majority—and men whom Arrington believed ". . . [Lee and Reynolds] have under their control."[49]

Therefore, although convinced that ". . . there was eminent [sic] danger of serious trouble between Lee & Reynolds and the citizens of the county . . . ," Arrington's options were limited. He must either leave Sweetwater as asked or place his superiors in the awkward

position of disputing with a U.S. officer and duly elected county officials. On 21 June Arrington chose his only practical alternative and
headed southwest out of Fort Elliott toward Clarendon, where he
understood bands of red men were still harrassing local inhabitants.[50]
Certainly neither Lee nor Davidson objected.

For Lee, this contest between captain and colonel brought into the
open an essence of character never so apparent. Challenged in a
matter for which he had personal interest, Lee demonstrated that he
could be a formidable adversary. This is not to say that the trader
acted without cause. As Lee's petition against Arrington stated, ". . .
[the Rangers] are here for the purpose of killing any or all Indians
that may be found within the limits of the 'Pan Handle' and . . .
should this body commit any such act they would only provoke the
Indians to a merciless & useless war. . . ." And lest the authorities
forget, ". . . it [was] but a few years since this country was the home
of the Indians who are now located on reservations very close to or
adjoining us. . . ."[51]

No doubt Lee was sincere in his defense of the Indian, and no
doubt he understood the importance of maintaining federal primacy
in the matter of Indian affairs. Indeed, a cause of the 1874 uprising
was the grievance that the government did little to stop unprovoked
raids upon Indian property. Arrington's mistake was not to heed Lee's
warning but instead to conduct his own investigation of purely local
affairs. At that instant, as perhaps other men at Adobe Walls had
discovered, the trader could answer a challenge with a surprise of
his own.

Other incidents, although minor, likewise interfered with the
usual conduct of business. In March two drunken soldiers shot it out
with each other in the company-run Fort Elliott saloon; and in August one employee clubbed another to death, again after a drinking
bout. Yet no single incident materially detracted from business, and
by 1879 Lee's military endeavors were perhaps the most lucrative of
all his enterprises. To acknowledge this successful transition from
the Indian trade, Lee and his partner had on Christmas Day 1878 offered free drinks to every man stationed at Fort Supply, ". . . for
which [they had] the thanks of every blue-coated uncle-sam in the
garrison." Even at Fort Elliott, with the recollection of past disputes
still fresh in mind, Lee and his wife Lina were able to enjoy a summer "hop" among the mixed company of military and civilians.[52]
The trader had come to relish these moments, although competitors
still forced him to keep a vigilant eye on other potential challenges.

During the spring of 1879, Lieutenant Colonel Richard I. Dodge
assumed command of another new cantonment on the North Fork of

the Canadian River approximately one-half the distance between Fort Supply and the Cheyenne and Arapaho Agency (see Map 4). The site was basically an unenclosed military staging area in the midst of a large, wooded ravine lying on either side of the wagon road between the two government facilities. And almost from the first, Indians were attracted to the installation, camping on nearby creek banks, determined that only they would dispose of the available timber. In fact, during April the Cheyenne had begun to rack wood for a local firm—Lee and Reynolds—although Dodge had asked James McAllister, Lee's crew supervisor, to stop.[53]

The partners' response was immediate, and by letter from Charles Campbell, acting Cheyenne and Arapaho agent, attention was called to the need for the tribe to earn money by working such contracts. As there was merit to the argument, Dodge relented and permitted the Cheyenne to rack more wood than necessary, with a stipulation that additional cords be sold only to the next year's contractor. But Campbell adamantly opposed the recommendation and ". . . ordered the [wood] cutting to stop as soon as he found it was not to the benefit of Lee and Reynolds." An incredulous colonel reported the matter to his superiors at Leavenworth, noting that "to an unprejudiced observer there would seem to be some connection between Lee and Reynolds and the authorities at the Agency."[54]

The controversy might have ended there had other activities remained undiscovered. Yet by the early fall of 1879 George Reynolds had learned that the cantonment's sutler was doing business with Cheyenne and Arapaho, and he demanded that the trade be stopped. Dodge again intervened, and to the several inquiries concerning the allegation he vindicated the sutler, even denying John Miles a mandated hearing. Therefore, the infuriated Miles conducted his own investigation, with the weight of his evidence not unexpectedly supporting the partners' claim. But the most intriguing aspect of the episode was the agent's vitriolic attack on Dodge himself, detailing how the cantonment soldiers had so abused an Indian prostitute (with the colonel's apparent knowledge) that the woman had died from "excessive sexual intercourse."[55] Obviously, Dodge had underestimated his adversaries.

Philip McCusker, a more frequent detractor of both Lee and Reynolds, had earlier been expelled from the Territory. Interestingly, he also was accused of subjecting an Indian woman to prostitution. Even Charles Rath, who as late as the winter of 1877–1878 had joined resources with the partners to exploit the buffalo trade, found himself during the summer of 1879 in competition with these same men. The difficulty was that this former hide trader had relocated at

Fort Elliott, where one endeavor was delivery of winter hay to the garrison, a contract usually awarded to Lee's crew. Rath soon complained that ". . . Lee and Reynolds are driving large herds of cattle on the hay grounds from place to place to destroy the grass to prevent me from [putting] up the hay. . . ." The army's subsequent interest in the matter apparently caught Lee's attention, for by October a Dodge City newspaper observed that ". . . [notwithstanding] the opposition . . . [Rath] had to contend with, he . . . filled his contract." During the summer of 1879, Lee also challenged the government's right to alter its mail run from Fort Reno to Fort Elliott thereby eliminating a source of income to several Indian families.[56] However, these challenges were only minor when compared to another dispute.

Fort Elliott and the nearby town of Sweetwater were both located in the politically unorganized Wheeler County, a district measured out to a perfect square of thirty miles, border to border. As were all counties in the eastern half of the Texas Panhandle, Wheeler was attached to Clay County and to its seat of government for administrative and judicial purposes. Local residents were thus required to travel approximately 150 miles to Henrietta—a small community located near the south bank of the Red River—in order to transact all government-related business (see Map 4). Moreover, under Texas law, the inconvenience would continue until 150 male voters of the unorganized county (each twenty-one years of age or older) petitioned the commissioners' court at Henrietta to organize a government.[57] Sweetwater resented the inconvenience; Lee, of course, did not.

As the resident partner of the largest commercial enterprise of the region, he had an obvious interest in keeping taxes at a minimum. And from 1875, when Fort Elliott and the adjacent hunters' camp took root, no one paid much attention to the authorities sent out from Henrietta to collect accounts due. However, during the fall of 1878 the status quo changed when about thirty individuals resituated themselves at a "new" Sweetwater located approximately one mile southwest of the fort. Taking note of this more permanent community, Clay County commissioners voted to assess liabilities on all cattle grazed in the county, thereby concentrating on the few individuals best able to pay—the ranchers and large property owners. Predictably, Lee felt singled out, and a response was immediate. A lawsuit was filed to enjoin Clay County officials from taxing properties held in the unorganized (and thus unrepresented) Wheeler County.[58] There the issue remained, stalled in the courts, until late winter, 1878–1879, when Sweetwater residents again muddied the waters by pressing for self-government.

While the locals solicited 150 voters to formally petition for county organization, ". . . a strong, and bitter opposition sprang up, against the wishes of the people in the matter, from certain corporations having large interests in Wheeler County and the balance of the Pan Handle."[59] Then came the struggle—from 13 March 1879 (the day Clay County commissioners accepted Sweetwater's petition) until 12 April 1879 (the day set aside for the election of Wheeler County officials[60]): "The attack was made and the fight fought . . . the cry of the opposition was 'Down with taxation at any cost!' . . . The cry of the people was 'Law and order with all its natural consequences.' The fight was a hard and bitter one. . . ."[61] However, on election day "the town . . . beat the Post Traders . . . and elected nearly all the ticket." An exception was the election of John Donnelly, clerk at Lee's store, to a seat on the five-member commission. Therefore, Wheeler County became the first self-governing entity of the Texas Panhandle, and first on the agenda, not unexpectedly, was an "occupation tax," proposed ironically by Lee's own employee. Another early act was to petition the governor for a detail of state Rangers to put down "a reign of terror" thought to exist in the Panhandle but which "the U.S. Military . . . absolutely [refused] to aid or protect . . . against any invasion or danger from these bandits."[62] It was Captain Arrington who responded to the call.

Although memories of the tax dispute quickly faded, Lee's opposition to county organization remained unobscured, and in June the Rangers still found ". . . the public mind fearfully agitated on account of the decided opposition of Messrs. Lee & Reynolds, Post traders, towards the organization of this county. . . ." As late as August, Lee was likened to a "bloodsucker" for opposing self-government.[63] It is no wonder, then, that the man looked elsewhere for a respite.

At the time, cattle raising was taking hold in the Panhandle, and on 17 December 1879 Lee and Reynolds joined the effort by purchasing 29,440 acres of prairie in Hartley and Oldham counties to form the nucleus of an LE (for "Lee") ranch. Apparently Reynolds was bothered by the immediate attention of his partner to the new scheme, for on 31 December he asked a company clerk, C. F. McKinney, to join him as an associate at the Fort Supply store.[64] But Lee was irrevocably drawn to the investment and to the new opportunities it offered.

CHAPTER FOUR

Three Brands

An encouraged Mac Lee registered at the Dodge House, a hotel in the city of the same name, on Friday, 10 May 1880. This was the second visit in only days to the west Kansas town, with most if not all business during the preceding weeks focused on the firm's developing cattle trade. A good-sized herd of New Mexico stock was already on the trail east to the Texas ranch, as was a herd purchased from Reynolds and Mathews, an outfit located in Central Texas; when joined, the two herds would be the nucleus of the LE ranch. The pride of the lot were 120 purebred shorthorns and Herefords purchased from Illinois, Missouri, and Canadian stock farms and freighted west at the expense of nearly $20,000, shipment of which was due in Dodge during Lee's visit. All animals would later take either the brand LE (for Lee's surname) or LR (indicating the partnership).[1]

Lee, of course, was not the first to be attracted to this remote corner of the Texas Panhandle. Comancheros had once used the land, distinguished by dry-bed arroyos and sandstone mesas, as trading sites with the various tribes of the southern plains. Yet these half-breed Mexican nationals were only impermanent intruders. Others, principally shepherds such as Casimiro Romero, Juan Trujillo, and Venture Burrego, next came to the region and clustered at small adobe homesteads located on either side of the Canadian River. Soon whites also staked out their claim to the land, and men such as Henry Kimble, Issac Rinehard, Jules Howard, and Lon and Jesse Jenkins came to live on the shaded riverbanks. By 1879 a community of about 150 individuals had settled at the far northeast corner of Oldham County in the thriving frontier town of Tascosa.[2]

Stockmen also could not resist the expanse of rich, short grass prairie and soon began to move herds into the region. Deacon Bates and David Beals, branding an LX, centered a herd of over 30,000 head on a nearby west-central range; Charles Goodnight, ramrod of the JA brand, ran nearly 12,500 cattle at his Palo Duro Canyon operation; George Littlefield established the nearby LIT while Ellsworth Torrey and sons branded a T to 8,000 head grazed in Hartley County. To the south and east of Tascosa were located Gunter and Munson's herds, branded either with a T-Anchor or GMS. And now Lee added his brands to this closed society, with Tascosa claiming itself as the center of the two-million-acre empire[3] (see Map 4).

Lee certainly must have recognized the many problems that lay ahead. One of the first challenges was to rid the countryside of itinerant, New Mexican rustlers such as the notorious William Bonney (alias "Billy the Kid"), who too easily stole from Panhandle herds. One method frequently used was the seizure of cattle that inadvertently drifted west of the Texas border, then herd the stock to Fort Sumner (or into Arizona), where they could be sold. Billy and his gang were believed to operate in this manner and not too far west of the newly acquired LE range.[4]

The first priority, then, was the hiring of responsible ranch hands, and in 1880 Lee promoted James McAllister from Fort Supply to boss of the Texas operation.[5] As the site for a permanent ranch headquarters, Lee purchased a Spanish settlement located on Trujillo Creek in Hartley County, approximately three miles east of the New Mexico border. As a consequence, several Hispanic families were uprooted from their comfortable adobe homes.[6]

But Lee was not inclined to give the shepherds much attention. He was more interested in crossbreeding different strains of cattle by which he hoped to upgrade the herds into more marketable animals. The first herds to be so used were the native stock brought north from Albany and the shorthorn, pure-grade bulls corralled at Dodge City.[7] No western stockman had ever attempted so large-scale a change in a breed while still expecting a return from his investment. Yet in one year journalists would be recording of the Panhandle companies that "many thousands of dollars have been spent by cattle-owners . . . to procure blooded animals for the improvement of their herds . . . ," and predicted that "eventually they will make this one of the greatest beef-producing territories of its size in the world."[8] During early 1880 no one, especially Lee, knew how accurate the conjecture would be; at the time, the venture seemed all risk—and primarily Lee's alone.

The 120 thoroughbred shorthorns and Herefords that arrived in Dodge during May 1880 were trailed as planned to the Texas range as other pure-grade cattle continued to be unloaded at the same city throughout that year. By Christmas, local newspapers were even inviting Dodge City residents to the cattle pens, where they could witness for themselves "the lot of hereford and Short horn bulls in the yards of Lee and Reynolds . . . worth a visit by all who admire fine stock." As citizens were reminded, it was Lee and Reynolds who ". . . constantly made additions of fine cattle to their herds . . . to which . . . [they had] added $60,000 worth of hereford and short horn cattle within the past year, bought from the best breeders in the United States and Canada." Indeed, the partners could even claim the "first thorough-bred hereford born in the [Panhandle]," an event noted at Dodge during mid-summer 1880. Therefore, it was no idle boast when in January 1881 Lee or his partner referred to the LE as "the finest stock range in the West."[9]

Perhaps with this claim in mind, Lee continued the practice of upgrading cattle. Thus in March 1881, while again registered in Dodge, he announced the trailing of still another herd of thoroughbreds to the Oldham County range. The breed would be joined to a combined herd of approximately six thousand yearlings, two-year olds, and three-year olds, also purchased in February from another Reynolds and Mathews herd. Actually, a circuit had evolved whereby all purebreds were first trailed from the Dodge City cattle pens to pastures near Fort Supply; then, after months spent adapting to the range, the head were driven to Oldham County and mingled with the native stock. By the end of spring 1881, an estimated two thousand beeves were on the LE, with another twelve thousand head being trailed north from Central Texas.[10]

It was now that Lee also decided to consolidate his separate holdings to the range of Oldham and Hartley counties. Therefore, in February 1881 the herds grazed at Fort Supply and on the Cheyenne and Arapaho reservation (between four and five thousand animals) were sold to J. L. Driskill and Sons of Austin, Texas. Then during late spring Lee astonished many by announcing the addition to his herd of an imported breed from Scotland. This was no ordinary purchase, for the thirty-nine head—stock imported to America by T. A. Simpson, a man associated with a noted Independence, Missouri, breeding farm—represented the first Aberdeen-Angus to be ranged west of the Mississippi River. It was later said that the cattle ". . . had scarcely reached their new home before the attention of W. M. D. Lee . . . was called to them, and he purchased the entire lot. . . ."[11]

Thus, it was with pride that Lee agreed to be interviewed by a *New York Times* reporter sent west to investigate the emerging Great Plains cattle trade. As the New Yorker observed, only "the big concerns rule the roost," of which Lee's interests certainly qualified. His enterprises now included ". . . a tract of land reaching from the line

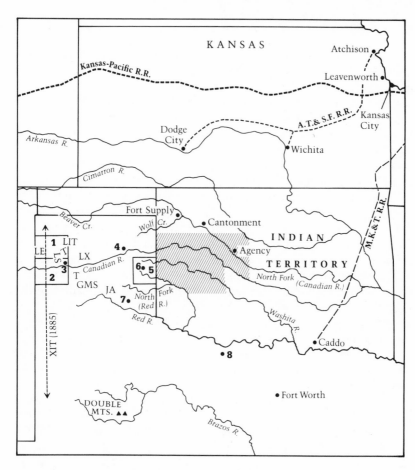

1 Hartley County **5** Wheeler County

2 Oldham County **6** Mobeetie (Sweetwater)

3 Tascosa **7** Clarendon

4 Adobe Walls **8** Henrietta

Cheyenne & Arapaho
Reservation

Map 4. Texas Panhandle, 1880

of New Mexico nearly to [the] town of Tascosa, on either side of the Canadian, and including nearly all the water drawing into the Canadian for a distance of about 50 miles." Indeed, Lee had outgrown the restrictions of one partnership and had begun a second venture with Lucien Scott, the same Leavenworth banker who, with his brother Lyman, had endorsed several trading bonds during the 1870s.[12] Scott had earlier become Lee's neighbor when on 3 December 1880 he had individually purchased 35,250 acres of Oldham and Hartley counties from Jot Gunter and W. B. Munson.[13] However, with no experience in the workings of a large cattle enterprise, Scott would have naturally sought the advice of men who could manage the investment for him. Therefore, he struck a loose partnership with Lee while adopting the firm name of the Lee-Scott Cattle Company and registering an LS as a brand. The venture was organized to work in tandem with the LE.

That Lee and his partnerships occupied land that was once the domain of Indians and buffalo held no attraction for the *Times* investigator. Lee was simply one of the few "cattle kings" whose ". . . royal domain . . . [would] soon be fenced all along its northern side, not to keep in their own cattle, but to keep out those that, during hard winters, drift down from the ranges as far north as the Arkansas River, and crowd the Canadian cattle." Lee, though, wanted to do more and promised not only to fence against drift animals but also to "stock up the range 'so that there will be no room for other people's cattle'. . . ."[14]

While they talked, another man, William Bonney, learned the resolve of these new Panhandle ranchers firsthand. Joe Poe and a posse of Wheeler County vigilantes rode for Lincoln, New Mexico, in March 1881 specifically commissioned to apprehend Billy and his gang for stealing Texas stock. As Poe recalled, "About the middle of that winter the cattlemen of the Panhandle . . . submitted a proposition to me to enter their employ, and as their representative, to cooperate with the authorities of New Mexico with the view of suppressing and putting an end to the wholesale raiding and stealing of cattle, which had [been] and was then carried on by 'Billy the Kid' and his gang of desperadoes. . . ."[15]

However, when Poe and his men arrived at Lincoln they found that the outlaw had been arrested and was confined to Sheriff Pat Garrett's jail. Nevertheless, this situation did not stop Garrett from listening to Poe's complaint, and both agreed to discuss the matter further when Poe returned from investigating brands in Arizona. When Poe returned in April, he discovered that Billy had escaped only days before from Lincoln and was last seen riding toward the foothills of the Rocky Mountains. Poe, Garrett, and a mixed posse of New Mexico and Panhandle deputies started out together on the trail leading north to Fort Sumner.[16]

Although there is no certain link to the idea that Lee encouraged the pursuit, it was both the LE and LS ranges that principally bordered the territory from where these outlaws carried out their most notorious raids. Garrett also was not unfamiliar to Lee, for in 1876 he had briefly hunted at the Reynolds City buffalo camp; and an even more significant involvement with the same man awaited him during the present decade. If Billy made one mistake, it was to assume that the long arm of this or any Panhandle stockman could not reach out for him while he was living in New Mexico. As Dodge City hunters and Texas Rangers had earlier discovered, Lee in particular could prove resourceful when provoked. Yet, in fairness, at the time New Mexican outlaws were not Lee's overwhelming concern, and Billy and his gang were but one of several problems affecting the man's two organizations.

The previous year, in May 1880, a prized LE bull was slaughtered at Fort Supply by migrating white "Oklahoma Boomers" passing through Indian Territory. What made the incident particularly irritating was that, although the violators had been apprehended, the government ruled that it lacked jurisdiction in purely civil matters and consequently released the perpetrators. Some such as Lieutenant Colonel Richard I. Dodge viewed the whites' claim to Indian lands as ". . . the quickest way to bring the race into something like a respectable degree of civilization. . . ." But others like the rancher Charles Goodnight were alarmed by the migration and, in particular, by the continued drive of South Texas cattle near the Panhandle herds. "Texas fever" was an incurable disease that fatally affected local stock, and Panhandlers quickly (and correctly) blamed the infection on the passing South Texas herds. Therefore, Goodnight and similarly minded stockmen organized a vigilante association to protect their investments.[17]

Lee could not overlook his neighbor's crisis, but as the LE and the LS were located nearly one hundred miles west of the conflicting interests, he was more involved with the local affairs of Oldham County, which Tascosa boosters had politically organized in December 1880. Lee probably did not have to be reminded that a majority of the five-member commission could now tax the over 60,000 acres held jointly by his two partnerships. An indication of that right was a judgment rendered by the Texas Court of Appeals against Lee and Reynolds affirming a lower court's decision that any Texas county—whether politically chartered or not—could tax its citizens. Therefore, Lee perhaps questioned Reynolds's recent acquisition of a Colorado gold mine when to him it would have been more appropriate to concentrate on their extended cattle operation.[18] Very likely Reynolds challenged Lee's seemingly inordinate attention to this very trade. Quite simply, the interests of one no longer complemented the other.

Thus, it was during the first days of summer 1881 that a startled LE cowboy watched as an infuriated Lee faced his partner Reynolds outside their Texas headquarters on Trujillo Creek. After a few silent moments, Reynolds began to curse, with the tall, blue-eyed Wisconsin Yankee giving as well as he received. Then, as quickly as the argument started, the two parted, each going off in separate directions. Whatever frayed bonds that still held the partnership together were in those few minutes severed.[19]

Although the practical dissolution of the twelve-year association was far more complicated than words spoken in anger, most properties could be easily divided. As a consequence, on 1 July George Reynolds sold all interest in the Cheyenne and Arapaho store to Charles T. Connell. And on 7 July three separate brands were recorded in Oldham County: the LR passed to Reynolds, the LS to Lee and Scott; the LE remained a joint venture until a more equitable distribution could be devised. However, at Lee's insistence the recently imported thirty-nine head of blooded Angus penned at Dodge City remained his separate property. The two military stores and all freight termini also passed to Lee (now doing business at Fort Elliott under the firm name of D. W. Van Horn and Company), with an anticipated yearly income of between $40,000 and $50,000. Lee could well afford the division, and by August a fence line separated the two interests with approximately 20,000 additional posts ready to mark off still other adjoining range.[20]

By now the idea to string a fence across the 185-mile breadth of the Texas Panhandle was also attracting other ranchers, and by the fall of 1881 different operations were involved in surveying a route that began at Indian Territory and ran west and north of the Canadian River. Each outfit—the Turkey Track, the LX, the LS, and the LE—organized crews to stretch a three-strand barbed-wire fence along the entire distance. An estimate of the cost to complete the scheme was put at nearly $250 for each mile fenced.[21] Even then, Lee used the opportunity to limit his own expenses by freighting to the various crews the thousands of pounds of wire that began to arrive at Dodge City during 1882.[22]

Earlier, with the end of the 1881 roundup and the sale of the last LE herds, Lee also gave full attention to the severing of his remaining ties with Reynolds.[23] An important move in that direction was the trailing of the purebred Aberdeen-Angus still penned in Dodge to a pasture near Fort Supply, which was completed by January 1882. Another maneuver was convincing Jim McAllister to remain with the LS, and by March the man was busy organizing an exclusive Lee-Scott crew. Even the freight livestock corralled at Fort Elliott were branded with new devices: S on the hindquarters of cattle jointly owned by Lee and Scott; L+ and L− on the hindquarters of cattle owned separately by Lee.[24] Thus prepared, on 15 April Reynolds was confronted in Leavenworth for the final exchange.

In payment of $75,000 and other promissory notes totaling an additional $187,000, Lee transferred to his former partner a one-half interest in realty with full interest in all cattle and improvements.[25] Then, with both signatures recorded, the twelve-year partnership was dissolved.

Lee's choice of Lucien Scott as successor to Reynolds made good business sense. As president of the First National Bank of Leavenworth, Kansas, and thus one of the region's better-known financial agents, Scott would be a valued ally. Born 30 June 1834 to a family of Illinois emigrants from Massachusetts, Scott had been reared in the Midwest. The man fondly recalled the early years when his father employed him as a clerk in a jointly owned riverboat company plying the Mississippi between Keobuk, Iowa, and New Orleans. Those were his days of glory until the elder Scott abruptly transferred him to an accounting room. Wanting no part of the shoreside end of the business, Lucien struck out on his own and established himself at Cincinnati, Ohio, where after several months of shrewd investing, he accumulated a $20,000 bankroll. Not long after, the family reunited and moved to Leavenworth, where during the late 1850s all involved themselves in the town's commercial trade. After several mergers and the elder's death, Lucien inherited the First National Bank. By then he had also married Julia Hoffman, a recent emigrant from New York City. Although noticeably shy, Scott remained an astute businessman whose interests extended not only to banking but also to investments in local Kansas railroads and a Leavenworth coal mining company.[26]

The Lee-Scott Cattle Company itself was titled to approximately 25,000 acres of eastern Oldham County, purchased by Lee from the State of Texas in March of 1881.[27] This acquisition was an addition to the 35,000 acres owned separately by Scott and the approximate 15,000 acres owned separately by Lee as his share of the LE split.[28] The company had also added to its holdings many of the sites controlled by the early Hispanic settlers, including the Trujillo homestead located south of the Canadian River near Tascosa, the small canyon at Sierra La Cruz, and the flats of Salinas Plaza. An additional 3,000 acres of unoccupied state land were patented by Lee in November 1882, while later in that same month another 1,280 acres were added to the ranch. The most significant transaction, however, came late in November with the sale of Ellsworth Torrey's ranch. In exchange for $400,000 the partners acquired 17,000 head of cattle, a remuda of 75 horses, all Torrey equipment, and, of course, the range itself. Torrey's headquarters was a prime acquisition as it was located only four miles west of Tascosa near the mouth of Cheyenne Creek where the stream fed into the Canadian River.[29] Thus, in slightly over twelve months, Lee and Scott were titled to an 80,000-acre ranch with adjoining but seemingly endless "free range."

The enterprise, though, would be useless without large numbers of marketable cattle, and Lee had been careful to continue adding stock as each section of property was acquired. During the spring of 1881, while answering the questions of the *New York Times* reporter, he counted only 2,500 head on both the LE and the LS. Yet at the same time another 3,000 animals were on the trail north from Central Texas for the exclusive use of the new Lee-Scott organization. They were purchased from Lee Mosty, a Wheeler County cattleman, at the cost of $50,000. Then, with the flurry of land purchases in 1882, the LS acquired an additional 17,000 head from Torrey. Therefore, by the winter of 1882, the range was stocked with nearly 22,500 beeves, the figure not taking into account either the calves born during the preceding years or the thoroughbreds held separately by each partner. In fact, when Scott first decided to invest in cattle, he had ordered that a well-equipped Hereford stock farm, called Ridgewood, be located just outside the Leavenworth city limits. "The young bulls from that farm were sent from time to time to the LS Ranch and in that way, and by culling out the poorest of the bulls on the ranch, the herd was gradually improved." Lee maintained his own purebreds on a pasture near Fort Supply, a herd grown to sixty head by the fall of 1882, with matured blacks also crossed with the hardy native stock.[30]

Yet, as with any new operation, problems arose. One was a lawsuit alleging that earlier in 1882 Lee and Scott, in joint venture with Towers and Gugdell of Kansas City (with L. A. Mosty as agent), had wrongfully appropriated 3,800 cattle. A compromise was eventually agreed to whereby the defendants promised $16,000 in damages while the LS retained its title to all cattle.[31] The agreement was also a recognition that without it an eastern Panhandle jury would have adjudicated the claim. Another irritant was the predictability of the five new Oldham County commissioners to vote a yearly increase in taxes. The assessments for 1882 included the funding of a new court-house and county jail and, in February 1883, an addition to the county ad valorem tax. Lee's hope was that the spring 1883 election of Lucien's brother-in-law, Charles Whitman, to the five-man board represented a friendly voice at the weekly meetings.[32] One outstanding problem, though, had been resolved with the completion of the drift fence across the length of the northern Panhandle. The few stockmen who voiced concern as to what might happen should the cattle bunch against the wires during a "blue norther" were stilled by the desire of most to keep unwanted livestock from the southern range.[33]

Therefore, by the spring of 1883 and largely as a result of Lee's efforts, the LS found itself in an enviable position. During the months since the break with Reynolds, the ranch had been built into one of the largest and potentially more profitable organizations of the Southwest. With the advent of a spring drive to "free range" on the Yellowstone River in Montana—an idea that was sure to challenge the stamina of an LS crew—the Lee-Scott organization might even refer to itself as an "empire."[34]

The purpose was to maintain the constant movement of cattle from the stock farms at Leavenworth and Fort Supply to the Texas range; then to drive the yearlings and two-year-olds from Texas to Montana; and finally to ship the fattened beeves from the Yellowstone to Midwestern cattle markets (see Map 5). Interference along any of these three critical arms of the LS triangle, with its legs crossing hundreds of miles of frontier, would have to be minimized. This is perhaps why Lee, in June 1882, sold his remaining interest in the Fort Elliott tradership, insisting that the cattle trade by itself was "good enough for him."[35]

Earlier, on 10 March 1883, by the vote of agents representing all western Panhandle ranches meeting at Tascosa, the annual drive was organized to begin in May. As planned, two crews of cowhands would move a mixed herd to a common point at Cheyenne Creek on the LS range, one having worked east from La Junta, New Mexico, while the other moved west from Adobe Walls. Oscar Schofield was appointed foreman of the Adobe Walls crew while Tom Harris, an LS wagon boss, was given charge of the second. Although McAllister had employed several inexperienced "nester kids," it was thought that these younger men would be more than offset by seasoned cowhands who comprised a majority of the seventy-five to eighty cowboys needed for the drive.[36] Now only the sweat of each was necessary to put Lee's carefully thought-out organization into operation.

Tom Harris, the LS cowhand, was otherwise disposed, however, and at his call twenty-four cowboys met secretly inside a dugout at Tierra Blanca to thrash out grievances against the larger companies. The issues narrowed to wages, and cowboys already salaried at thirty dollars a month demanded that the figure be increased to fifty. Cooks, likewise, demanded a monthly wage of fifty dollars; a boss, seventy-five. Then, to dramatize their cause, Harris and the protesting cowhands each signed a petition threatening not to work until their demands were met. Midnight of 31 March was set as a deadline, after which ". . . anyone violating the . . . obligations [would] suffer the consequences." The cowboys were reassured by the promise of Tascosa merchants to provide funds for any man who ran short during the April strike.[37]

Tom Harris then moved his protest to a campsite near the LS headquarters, where by late March about one hundred cowhands were camped alongside the banks of the Alamocitas Creek. Ranch foreman Jim McAllister was at first consoled in that several of the regularly employed men had refused to join the strike. Harris, though, had been careful to spread discontent among many of the younger hands, particularly the "nester kids," and it was this group of determined but volatile cowboys who threatened to impede the vital spring roundup. Some ranchers appeared unconcerned and talked of business as usual.[38] Yet McAllister knew better—even the ringleader was an LS employee.

The foreman's first thought was to compromise, and he offered a forty-dollar wage to the more experienced men. But Harris and his cowboys could not be persuaded, and while pointedly nudging their holsters, they promised that ". . . none shall come in and underbid them." It was all McAllister could do just to stall while a message of the crisis was transmitted to his employers.[39]

Lee was at Leavenworth on 31 March, probably involved with the final settlement of Reynolds's LE mortgage, when the warning arrived.[40] He at once put aside all business, caught the next train to Dodge City, and from there rode a two-mule-team freight ambulance down to the ranch. Perhaps out of deference to him or just not knowing how to deal with the situation, the striking cowboys were pleasant enough when the hitch finally rolled to a stop. Lee, however, wasted no time with pleasantries but instead went directly into the ranch house to be briefed by his foreman.[41]

Lee found that other ranchers had adopted their own policies to the situation. The LIT took the position that wages were already too high. Gunter and Munson's T-Anchor managers were also determined to stand pat and to fire anyone who participated in the strike.

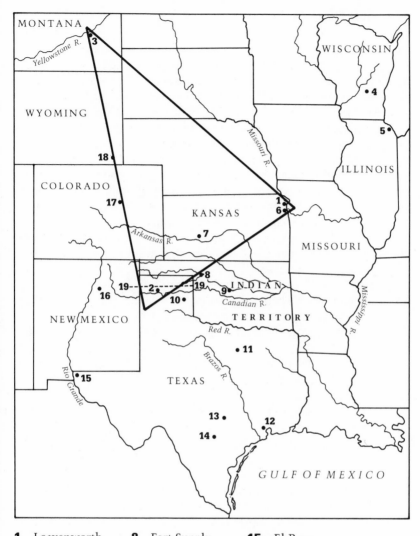

1	Leavenworth	**8**	Fort Supply	**15**	El Paso
2	Tascosa	**9**	C&A Agency	**16**	Las Vegas
3	Miles City	**10**	Mobeetie	**17**	Denver
4	Columbus	**11**	Fort Worth	**18**	Cheyenne
5	Chicago	**12**	Houston	**19**	Panhandle Drift Fence
6	Kansas City	**13**	Austin		
7	Dodge City	**14**	San Antonio		

Map 5. The LS Triangle, 1883

To this end a trap had been laid for their cowboys: should the strikers storm the ranch, a nearby storehouse had been mined with dynamite and a long fuse connected to the main house. The idea was literally to blow the protesters off the range. Lee, at least, could appreciate that McAllister had kept a calmer head. But that did not stop the rancher from criticizing his foreman for not agreeing to the demands and thus beginning the roundup on time. Later, he argued, the strikers could have been singled out and fired.[42]

Next morning, Harris was invited to the ranch house, and after a display of bravado by idle cowboys firing six-shooters into the air, the wagon boss confronted his employer. A cowboy later recalled that it was Lee who began the conversation.

"Tom," the rancher asked, "when you went to work here, who set the price of your services? Who asked you what pay you wanted to run a wagon for on the LS?"

"I priced myself at $75 a month," Harris answered.

"Have you ever asked for a raise? Why didn't you ask for some money if you thought you had to have it and were worth it?"

The cowhand responded, "I went into this strike to help the other boys, not to help myself, Mr. Lee."

"Tom, you know men and you know the cattle business, and you know what it takes to handle cattle. Do you believe every man here is worth $50 a month?"

"I guess there are some boys on the ranch who are not first-class cowhands, but they could soon learn."

Lee then spoke bluntly. "Tom, you know I've got several men who came up from Texas and never did anything but look a mule in the tail or drag a cottonwack. Now, Tom, I'll give you $100 to keep the wagon and pay you $50 for every man who is worth it, but you know there is quite a difference between a cowman and a nester kid."[43]

Harris refused the compromise, however, and Lee saw no alternative but to give in to the demands. And the cattleman was good to his word: those cowboys who worked the 1883 drive were paid the disputed wage, including a fifty-dollar salary to inexperienced hands. But as soon as the roundup ended, wages were immediately cut back to prestrike limits. Then anyone thought to have participated in the protest was fired from the crew and even blackballed from working other outfits. Lee went so far as to order that once a man had been discharged he was not to be fed.[44] Not surprisingly, the strike ended quickly.

Cowhands who perhaps did not trust the ranchers left the region immediately. Some, however, first drifted into Tascosa to take advantage of the promised free accommodations. When that credit ran out, they also left the Panhandle in search of new jobs. At the LS virtually an entire new crew was hired, many brought over from New Mexico, with some old hands such as Jim Mays and Al Popham promoted to the key positions of wagon boss. Harris, with a small but loyal following of strikers, settled west of the Texas line on a branch of Trujillo Creek in eastern New Mexico, ironically a past haven for other outcasts such as commancheros, whiskey peddlers, and Billy the Kid's gang.[45]

With the rebellion over, Lee next turned his attention to more personal matters. On 9 June 1883 he and his wife purchased a large two-storied home in Leavenworth, the house dominating the crest of a tree-shaded hill.[46] Appropriately, the site was located among the very best residences of this Missouri River community. Lucien and Julia Scott lived nearby in a large red brick house only three-quarters of a mile to the south, and not far west was the stone mansion of Fred Harvey, restauranteur to several major railroads. In fact, many of the best-known Kansas businessmen and politicians lived but a short carriage drive from this residence at the northeast corner of Sixth and Olive streets. But more than living among good neighbors, the new home convinced Lina, now four months pregnant, to leave her father's house in Wisconsin for a permanent residence with Lee. It would be a family that moved to Kansas.

In June Lee also tightened other bonds. Meeting with Scott in Oldham County on the twenty-first of the month, both men signed five documents that transferred all individual properties into the jointly owned Lee-Scott Cattle Company.[47] The old, loosely held venture of multiple operations separated by hundreds of miles of frontier was far too vulnerable. Therefore, by placing all related properties into one tightly held partnership, both were able to jointly and quickly respond to adverse situations. Problems, after all, were inherent to a frontier business.

One recent irritant was that Scott's brother-in-law had vacated his Oldham County commissioner's seat during the spring term. The departure came not only on the rumor of smallpox but also at a time when locals were debating tax increases. A result was Whitman's immediate replacement by a conveniently drunk cowboy, thereby permitting the Tascosa commissioners to up the assessed rates unopposed. Although the matter was later rectified by the appointment of McAllister to a commissioner's seat, the damage was done. "Texas fever" and South Texas cattle drivers also remained a persistent threat to all operations. Although Lee would not allow his LS crew to participate with Charles Goodnight's Panhandle Cattlemen's Association, he did have agents in Dodge City on 10 April 1883 when the larger Western Kansas Stock Growers' Association was organized. In November of that same year he also added his name to the charter of the American Angus Association.[48]

Even with these measures, other new challenges came to the fore. Enterprising cowboys had seized on the idea to corral unbranded cattle—usually newborn calves—with the hope of later claiming the animals as their own. This practice, known as "mavericking," would cut into the profits of the larger outfits unless an immediate deterrent was found. Outright cattle rustling, though, remained the most expensive nuisance. During the roundup just past, a young LS hand had chanced on a herd of stolen cattle being rustled out of Oldham County by Jesse Jenkins, a noted Tascosa saloonkeeper. The incident again demonstrated the value of good men, for McAllister immediately gave chase in order to determine if company stock was involved. In this instance the cattle belonged to another outfit. Lee, however, must have asked whose herd would be next. One report even had it that rustlers were finding safe employment on the LX, a close neighbor to the LS.[49]

Regardless, Lee must have savored some personal sense of accomplishment. Indeed, the dream of "empire" had finally been realized with cattle now moving unimpeded along the three principal avenues of business. Although on 27 November the birth of a son, Lucien, momentarily diverted his attention to family matters,[50] he had not raised the Lee-Scott organization to preeminence by letting personal affairs interfere for long. Challenges overcome in one season did not justify letting down one's guard, and Lee had an entire winter to outline appropriate responses to the anticipated challenges of 1884.

Lee and Scott spent the early months of the new year crisscrossing the midsection of the country, from Chicago to Austin, preparing for the year's roundup. Livestock on the southern range were said to have "stood the cold weather nobly," with estimates that the company might brand over 9,000 calves by the end of spring. Other ranchers were not as fortunate, particularly those cattlemen located near the border with Indian Territory, where individual owners were said to have lost as much as $40,000 each to an epidemic of "Texas fever." As a consequence, the issue of South Texas herds passing near the Panhandle would draw heated debates at the annual stockmen's associations. It was generally agreed that Congress should settle the matter by establishing a national trail, but no organization wanted the route near its own members' range. Lee took note of the issue, but another scheme challenged the orderly sweep of his spread. Local rustlers, operating as a syndicate, were blotching livestock with counterfeit brands and then releasing the stock to the open range. Their intent was to claim the rebranded head during the annual spring drive. Interestingly, one man caught rustling by a posse of deputized LS hands was the former wagon boss, Tom Harris.[51]

But Lee had taken steps to resolve even this problem, and by agreement with the governor of Texas, a small company of state Rangers was commissioned to patrol the western Panhandle during the roundup. More interesting was the "old friend" appointed to take charge of the outfit—Pat Garrett.[52] Although this mix of state Rangers and Tascosa-based outlaws begged a confrontation, it would at least keep the individual cowboy off balance while the companies went about their all-important business of herding cattle.

For Harris, the twelve months since the end of the 1883 strike were indeed eye-opening. The worst came during early winter when a posse of LS men led by Jim East, the Oldham County sheriff, crossed into New Mexico and arrested him as a horse thief. Yet actual confinement was short, and before long he was back in camp near the Texas border. The year, though, had given him an opportunity to refine the idea of another scheme. The plan called for cowboys not only to hire themselves out to the larger outfits but at the same time to purchase low-cost shares in a cattle syndicate. The organization would use the pooled money to buy and raise livestock; then, at the end of a five-year term, the outfit would be disbanded, the cattle sold, and all profits divided proportionately among its investors. Harris intended to head the organization while Jesse Jenkins, both Harris's brother-in-law and a Tascosa saloonkeeper, encouraged investments. By spring 1884 the idea was a going concern.[53]

Of course, western Panhandle ranchers were not expected to acquiesce, and their reaction to the scheme was immediate. When rumors of the operation surfaced, many threatened to fire any cowpuncher foolish enough to participate in the venture. As a consequence, the gulf between rancher and cowhand significantly widened, with its most outstanding breach occurring at the occasional meeting of Tom Harris's select inner circle. There men even drew lots to assassinate their more vocal opponents.[54]

Pat Garrett, Lee's personal answer to any who would interfere with the 1884 roundup, had arrived at company headquarters in Oldham County by the end of April. The lawman's first act was to request a "fugitive list" from Governor John Ireland, as ". . . things are going quietly now [and] the Rustlers are on a Stand Still waiting for developments[. They] seem to think there is something going on that is not to their best interest but I think as yet have not learned just what it is. . . ."[55] Therefore, by Garrett's own estimate, he had until 15 May, the beginning of the spring drive, to organize.

His first priority was to select a unit of special deputies, or state Rangers; two New Mexicans, Barney Mason and George Jones, were the first to enlist. Then, as the outfit was headquartered at the LS ranch house, local cowboys began to apply. By mid-May all but two of an anticipated force of twelve men had been deputized, with the majority being LS cowpunchers. Besides Mason and Jones, the cowboys who volunteered were Ed King, Lon Chambers, Garrett "Kid" Dobbs, Charles Reasoner, Bill Anderson, John Lang, and Albert Perry, the latter being a former cattlemen's detective appointed as the outfit's first sergeant.[56] Locals quickly tagged the men "LS Rangers."

After each was sworn in, the new recruit was put to work enforcing a recent proclamation. It seems that at the time Lee and his fellow organizers persuaded the governor to establish the force, they also convinced him that an 1881 executive order permitting certain frontier settlements the right to bear side arms should be revoked. Thus on 1 May 1884 the carrying of small arms was prohibited, and the first job of Garrett's men was to enforce the regulation in Tascosa.[57]

Local reaction to the new order was disbelief, to which Garrett merely pointed each man to the office of Sheriff Jim East, where the proclamation could be read. Even then a few dared to challenge the law, and two cowhands had to be forcibly disarmed. But most complied, although many showed their anger by walking Tascosa with empty holsters strapped to their legs. The dilemma was that to challenge Garrett was to violate a state order, and no cowboy wanted to spend years behind bars over a small point of honor. Their only practical option was to comply with the prohibition and to work the roundup without incident. On 19 May—four days into the spring drive—Garrett was able to assure his superiors that ". . . everything is quiet [and] I do not think [there] will be any serious trouble." Although Lee was occupied in Cheyenne, Wyoming, with the trailing of roundup cattle to the Montana range, he must have been pleased with Garrett's initial success. He would not be able to follow the herds north, as his prized Angus were being moved from pastures near Fort Supply to a recently acquired stock farm at Leavenworth.[58] Yet before leaving Cheyenne, Lee must have looked forward to an uneventful season.

Surprisingly, the 1884 roundup ended as it began, with the only notable event being an attempt on foreman McAllister's life. Waddy May, an LS cowboy, was discovered to have invested in Tom Harris's syndicate, and McAllister had ordered the man off the ranch. May did not take kindly to his dismissal, and before riding out he approached the ranch boss to argue further. During the confrontation May grabbed his six-shooter; however, another alert cowhand was able to wrestle May to the ground before a shot could be fired. The only consequence was McAllister's rattled nerves. Except for this one incident trouble was at a minimum, in large part due to the success of Garrett and his LS Rangers. Although Tascosa despised this special team of enforcers, no one dared to confront the only armed citizens in the county.[59]

While that spring most yearlings and two-year-olds had been separated from the larger herd and driven north to Montana, by early fall other stock had been collected for a similar drive to the Santa Fe pens in Dodge City. Remembering problems of preceding years, the companies insisted on working their spreads separately, with each outfit contributing hands to work a neighbor's range. The concern of "mavericking" was resolved by an agreement that "all [unbranded] cattle not belonging to . . . [a particular ranch would] be held for one week after the round-up [was] over and all calves [would then be] branded by the possessing company." Thus, by the third week in September the LS was freighting beef out of Kansas with the routine continuing uninterrupted until mid-November.[60]

Of the outstanding difficulty—the prospect of Harris's cowboys raiding Panhandle herds—Lee had still other ideas. One solution, put into effect in late summer 1884, was the parceling of several acres of land into small lots and deeding the same to loyal company men. By so doing, these same newly propertied citizens were qualified participants on a local grand jury and therefore able to indict. A similar measure was perfected in New Mexico with the purchase of 480 acres along the banks of the Canadian River in San Miguel County.[61] Not only was the acquisition a logical extension of the LS, but it also made Lee and Scott landowners in the same territory where Harris and his gang resided. Lee certainly did not intend that, once indicted, an outlaw would escape to the neutral ground of New Mexico.

But hostility between camps—the LS versus Tascosa-connected outlaws—grew more strained as winter approached. In one instance, during September W. B. Munson, co-owner of the T-Anchor, wrote Lee about the surge of outlaw activity and predicted that the LX would "probably put Tom Harris in charge of the range work." Munson sug-

gested that Lee meet with David Beals, an LX owner, and "put a stop
to this programme," which was a polite way of asking Lee alone to
handle a mutual problem. Munson probably knew that just to mention Harris's name would be like waving a red flag. Yet feelings in
Tascosa matched Lee's own frustrations. Even at Christmas, when it
would be thought that Garrett and his Rangers would be out of mind,
the town's most apparent reason to celebrate was that "the guardians
of the 'rustler,' [the] rangers, are quietly [lessening] in number like
the Pan Handle snow. . . ."[62] The wound inflicted during the 1883
strike still festered.

Camp Supply, Indian Territory, ca. 1868. Lithograph published in *Harper's Weekly*, 1869.

Cheyenne and Arapaho Agency compound. Lee and Reynolds's trading store is at left center, directly behind the barn-shaped structure. Photo courtesy Western History Collections, University of Oklahoma Library.

Arapaho in camp near Camp Supply, 1870. Photo by William S. Soule. Buffalo meat and skinned snakes are drying in the background. Lee made frequent visits to similar sites to collect buffalo robes. Photo courtesy National Anthropological Archives, Smithsonian Institution.

A white buffalo hunter's camp on Evans Creek near Buffalo Gap in the Texas Panhandle, 1874, with hides staked out on the ground and meat drying in the background. Lee and Reynolds were competitors of such outfits, a situation which led to the confrontation at Adobe Walls in 1874. By the winter of 1876, Lee and his partner were running similar hunters' camps from their enclave at Reynolds City, Texas. Photo courtesy Western History Collections, University of Oklahoma Library.

The only remaining structure of Lee and Reynolds's extensive operation: a picket shop building from Camp Supply, reconstructed by the state of Oklahoma at the Pioneer Museum and Art Center, Woodward, Oklahoma. Photo courtesy Sarah Taylor, Woodward, Oklahoma.

Fort Elliott, Texas, ca. 1880. Lee and Reynolds's sutler store was located approximately three-quarters of a mile from post headquarters (to the right of the photograph). Photo courtesy Panhandle-Plains Historical Museum, Canyon, Texas.

Front Street (main street), Dodge City, Kansas, 1879. The Dodge House, a
residence of Lee while in Dodge, is located at center right, next to the
Billiard Hall. At this date, Dodge City was in transition from being a
buffalo hide collecting site to becoming a cattle shipping terminus. Photo
courtesy Western History Collections, University of Oklahoma Library.

An LS fence-line crew in two wagons loaded with posts, ca. 1890. Lee was still in control of the ranch at this date. Photo courtesy Panhandle-Plains Historical Museum, Canyon, Texas.

LS cowboys branding cattle, ca.1890. Photo courtesy Panhandle-Plains Historical Museum, Canyon, Texas.

The Alamocitas LS Headquarters, 1884. Although the cowboys are unidentified in this photograph, it is probable that it is a composite of the LS Rangers, headed by Pat Garrett. The Rangers were organized in 1884 with twelve members. The greyhound in the picture was used by the LS to run down coyotes. Photo courtesy Panhandle-Plains Historical Museum, Canyon, Texas.

Lee's residence at Leavenworth, Kansas, which he maintained until 1901. Although the screened porch is a modern addition, the balance of the house is the same as when Lee acquired it. Photo from author's collection.

ABERDEEN-ANGUS CATTLE

— OF —

Approved Blood-lines and Superior Individuality!

— BRED BY —

W. M. D. LEE, LEAVENWORTH, KANSAS.

— MY HERD NOW —

NUMBERS 125 HEAD OF PURE-BRED "DODDIES,"

The foundation of which was the *first herd of Aberdeen-Angus cattle brought west of the Mississippi river.* In selecting these cattle in Scotland the importance of securing animals whose SUPERIOR MERIT would COMMAND FOR THEM FAVORABLE CONSIDERATION upon their introduction was duly considered, and the result was that for PRIME INDIVIDUALITY and SPLENDID BREEDING QUALITIES few importations have ever equaled this. At its head was placed the Kelly Victoria (Queen Mother) bull

HIS HIGHNESS 6th 2637 (2829)

[got by the Erica bull His Excellency 1355 (1271)], and his winnings in the show yard and the uniform and wonderful excellence of his get unite to prove him one of the FOREMOST BULLS OF THE BREED. Special attention is invited to the progeny of HIS HIGHNESS as will be seen in the two-year-old herd to be exhibited this fall (along with others from this herd) at the IOWA, NEBRASKA, and KANSAS STATE FAIRS, and the ST. LOUIS EXPO-SITION. The other bulls in use are DON CARLOS 2636, a son of HIS HIGHNESS, and the Dramin Lucy bull PRINCE WILLIAM 2793 by JOCK OF GREYSTONE 925.

I make a Special Offering of Twenty head of Young Bulls ready for Service and Twenty head of Heifers and a few Cows.

☞ Send for New Herd Catalogue.

W. M. D. LEE, Leavenworth. Kan.

Advertisement for the sale of Lee's herd of prized Aberdeen-Angus cattle, from *The Breeder's Gazette*, 1 September 1887.

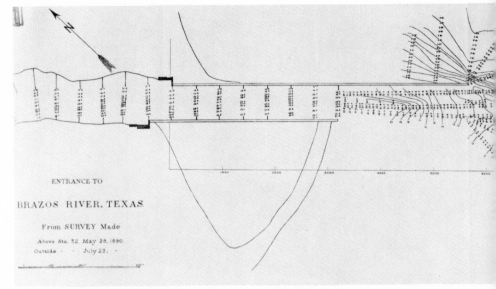

Planned jetties at the mouth of the Brazos River. The port of Velasco was located a short distance upstream. Drawing by chief engineer George M. Wisner, published in *Transactions of the American Society of Civil Engineers*, 1891.

View of the Brazos River, looking downstream to the Gulf of Mexico. The harbor of Velasco would be built from the point where the small river boat is anchored. Photo from *Transactions of the American Society of Civil Engineers*, 1891.

View of the west jetty and shoreline at the mouth of the Brazos River,
1890. Photo from *Transactions of the American Society of Civil
Engineers*, 1891.

Pile-driver, trestle, and brush mattresses at the outer end of the west jetty,
mouth of the Brazos River, 1890. Photo from *Transactions of the
American Society of Civil Engineers*, 1891.

Main Street, Houston, ca. 1910. The Capitol Hotel, where Lee resided when in Houston, is at the corner of the first intersection in the photo. Lee's Houston Transfer Company also did business along this main thoroughfare of the city. Photo courtesy Houston Metropolitan Research Center, Houston Public Library.

A roustabout works the newly pumped oil from one earthen pit to another at the West Columbia oil field, 1919. Photo courtesy Houston Metropolitan Research Center, Houston Public Library.

Two wagons pulling freight at the "new" West Columbia oil field, ca. 1919. Lee brought producers in on this same salt dome during 1907 and 1921–1925. Photo courtesy Houston Metropolitan Research Center, Houston Public Library.

Oil and sludge running from a well at the West Columbia field, 1919. Note the wooden holding tanks in the background. Photo courtesy Houston Metropolitan Research Center, Houston Public Library.

Capitol Hotel, Houston, ca. 1895, a frequent residence of Lee during the
1890's. Photo courtesy Houston Metropolitan Research Center, Houston
Public Library.

Lobby of the plush Brazos Hotel, Houston, Lee's last residence. Photo courtesy Houston Metropolitan Research Center, Houston Public Library.

CHAPTER FIVE

Showdowns

Lee began 1885 by severing himself from an old obligation: personal involvement as the Fort Supply trader. John Ferguson, a Leavenworth accountant, was brought in as the post's resident partner; both would continue to do business as Lee and Ferguson but without the rancher's overseeing hand. Lee then settled into winter at his new Leavenworth home, where he attempted something quite out of the ordinary—relaxing with friends and family. Typical of the weeks spent at home was the Saturday evening of 21 February. The Lees—both Mac and Lina—joined Leavenworth's society at Dr. and Mrs. S. W. Jones's progressive card party. It was a pleasant pastime spent among the very best company in Kansas, indeed perhaps matched west of the Mississippi River only by Denver and San Francisco society. Lina, in particular, enjoyed these distractions. At home Lee could engross himself in the comforts of beautifully furnished rooms with highly polished oak floors, stained-glass windows, and glazed fireplaces. Three servants—two young Swedish females and a black male—were retained for the domestic needs.[1] It was a genteel life that eased Lee's return from a frontier existence. For a time at least, others handled the obligations of business.

Perhaps the season's most elaborate scheme was conceived by Pat Garrett, who understood Lee's need to deal with would-be challengers before the start of another roundup. The idea was to surprise a gang of outlaws who were holed up in a line shack just west of the Texas border; as expected, the governor of New Mexico Territory had obliged with warrants ordering the arrest of three men high on the LS list of undesirables—Billy Gatlin, Wade (Waddy) Woods, and Charles Thompson. A heavy snow in early February seemed to offer a perfect cover for the planned raid.

Joining the Rangers at ranch headquarters as they prepared to ride west from Alamocitas were Oldham County sheriff Jim East and his deputy, L. C. Pierce. Nettie East, Jim's new bride, also came the short distance from Tascosa so that the curious in town might not guess her husband's purpose. She would spend the night before returning.

Shortly after supper, the twelve started out toward a rock cabin located on the Canadian River near Red Springs, New Mexico. As it happened, the hiding place was also an old homestead once used by the father-in-law of Ranger Kid Dobbs. It was not until 2:00 A.M., however, and after a forty-five-mile ride that the posse finally reached an old LE line camp on Trujillo Creek, where they stopped just long enough to warm themselves. The posse then continued west, following the Canadian.[2]

The cold ride progressed until the posse approached within four hundred yards of the outlaws' camp, where each dismounted and unholstered a gun. Dobbs next suggested that they position themselves north of the house which meant a run in the open around an exposed corral.

Bob Bassett happened to be outside, his arms full of wood, when from seemingly nowhere a man dashed ten feet in front of him. Startled, he dropped the pile and ducked inside the shack to warn the others. Tom Harris, also visiting, was the first to go outside.

"Are you fellows up here for me again?" he asked.

"No, we are not up here for you," Garrett answered. "But do you have Wade Woods, Charley Thompson, and Billy Gatlin in that house?"

"Wade Woods isn't in there, but Billy Gatlin and Charley Thompson are in there."

Garrett ordered everyone outside anyway, and nine men walked through the door. But the two wanted by the posse remained in the shack, where Gatlin's unmistakable laugh could be heard, and the Rangers settled back to await the last holdouts.[3]

After several minutes and with no movement from those inside the cabin, Garrett grew restless. Finally a door opened and Charley Thompson walked out. He walked straight to Garrett and East and, after a brief conversation, said that he was cold and wanted to go back inside for a jacket. Suspicious, Garrett first made him promise that once he had his coat he would return immediately to camp. The man nodded an agreement before disappearing into the shack.

The Rangers waited several minutes before the door again opened a crack and a pistol was aimed in their direction. Thompson, who was at the other end, yelled out to Sheriff East. "Jim, I told you I was going to give up, but I believe I'll stay with Billy and make a fight of it." East responded immediately, saying that it was foolish to stand alone; besides, Thompson was reminded, he, like Harris, might also beat the charge in court.

The cowboy started to cry. "Billy," he said, turning away from the Rangers, "I'm not going to lie to Jim East." Thompson then walked out of the building and surrendered. The Rangers now had only Gatlin to take into custody.[4]

Garrett finally reached the limits of patience and ordered Reasoner and King to the roof of the shack, where they began to wrench off supports. Three had been thrown to the ground before Gatlin finally called out, and it was the sheriff who again answered.[5]

"Billy, you'd better come out."

"No, Jim, I'm not going to give up."

East then told Garrett that he was going up to the house; that, alone, he might coax the man outside, as both had worked a range together several years back. Garrett did not object and East started for the cabin.

The door was still half open, allowing East to see the outline of a hat brim; the dim figure of a six-shooter could also be made out. East held close to the wall, motionless, hoping to catch the man inside offguard. That instant finally came, and taking advantage of the split second, he kicked the door open and shoved his cocked rifle into Gatlin's ribs.

"Lay 'em down, Billy." The outlaw did not argue but put his revolver on a cot as both walked outside.[6]

It was a cold day, and the exchange had frayed everyone's nerves. A fire was built, and bacon and coffee were put on a grill as the outlaws and Rangers relaxed before riding back to a Tascosa jail cell. The two did not remain confined long, however, as within weeks someone had slipped them a saw blade that enabled both to cut off their leg irons, climb through an open window, and escape.[7]

Undoubtedly the incident was called to Lee's attention; more significantly, Tascosa was again at the center of opposition to his LS crew. But when on Sunday, 22 March 1885, Lee finally stirred from the comforts of his Leavenworth home, he had traveled to the other end of the country—Miles City, Montana—seemingly unconcerned by the Tascosa challenge. On his mind instead were cattle losses trumpeted by the Leavenworth press, and it was not until he saw firsthand that damage was ". . . confined to pilgrim cattle that came late and went into winter in a weakened and demoralized condition . . ." that he put his concerns to rest.[8] Unlike other companies, the LS drove early, thereby enabling cattle to fatten on the rich spring grass along the northern trail. With the new season the company would cut another six thousand head from the approximate twenty-four thousand grazed in Texas and drive them north in the same manner.[9] It was not that Tascosa had been forgotten but rather that other problems were more critical.

In Texas, southern herds continued to trail near the Panhandle, and again the issue would be debated at the annual cattlemen's associations. What bothered most was that range wars were now real possibilities.[10] For that reason Lee, as a member of the Western Kansas Stock Growers' Association, along with members of four other organizations (including two from Indian Territory, one from Colorado, and Goodnight's outfit from the eastern Panhandle), attended a special meeting of stockmen held in Kansas City during the week beginning 20 April to discuss the crisis. Not surprisingly, the ranchers here also threatened to use whatever force was necessary in order to stop the drive of cattle through the Panhandle. The "suggestion" was that South Texas cattlemen either use the trail north from Fort Griffin to Dodge City or take their livestock up the more familiar Chisholm Trail.[11]

Lee, however, was only politely interested in the issue, as New Mexico rustlers, not South Texas drovers, were the most apparent danger to his LS range. Therefore, by early spring of 1885 another organization—the Southwest Live-Stock Detective Association— was established to patrol the lands west and north of the Texas Panhandle. Again Garrett would "manage" the organization from a headquarters reestablished at Las Vegas, New Mexico, while the LS phased its own force of lawmen into the new operation.[12]

What seemed critical during the spring was resolved by year's end, but not without incident. Stockmen of Texas and Kansas again met in Dallas on 15 and 16 May in order to air the controversy, and a compromise was finally reached. South Texas cattlemen promised to trail their herds to a common point at Doane's Crossing on the Red River and then proceed directly north through Indian Territory toward Fort Supply using the old Dodge City stage road. To be certain that no one was confused about the direction the herds should follow, the Panhandlers staked out a trail a mile or two in width to "guide" the drovers north. The compromise came none too soon, as one South Texan and his herd of longhorns had already been stopped by an armed patrol not far southeast of the LS range; and another, when told that his cattle could not pass through the Panhandle, swore to carry the dispute into the courts. The two were only the first of an estimated seventy-five outfits expected to trail through the region that season. Nevertheless, earlier agreements had their anticipated effect: it was soon noted that ". . . men of South Texas

[had] so far modified their intention of ignoring the will of the people of the Panhandle as to accept the [staked] trail."[13] Yet compliance created its own controversies, one of which troubled even Lee.

The South Texans, after crossing through Indian Territory and following the staked trail to a point north of the Canadian River, were unsure in which direction to turn their herds next. As a consequence, over 100,000 head stalled just south of Fort Supply, and a deputy U.S. marshal refused to untangle the confusion until both sides agreed to a route. To avoid the bottleneck, other cattlemen began to trail through eastern New Mexico, thereby passing near the LS range. Lee's immediate response was to demand protection from his newly organized association, and by early summer it was understood that "Capt. Pat Garrett and a posse of men [were] now on the ground, and [with] the authority of law behind them they [would] have but little difficulty in persuading these law-breakers to turn back."[14]

Those stalled near Fort Supply looked elsewhere for a remedy, and in early July thirty stockmen filed their complaints with a U.S. commissioner sitting at Dodge City. However, before the arbiter could rule, a telegram was received from the secretary of the interior ordering that the herds move on to a Kansas railhead.[15] Thus, a compromise was finally implemented and, after years of controversy, the issue resolved.

But other than the threat to his western range, Lee probably paid little attention to the affairs of Indian Territory. His sole interest in the country remained the profits derived from military contracts now supervised by his partner Ferguson. Lee's attention was elsewhere, and while visiting Montana in mid-September he found nearly 6,000 head of an unfamiliar brand pastured on his claim to the open range. A complaint was immediate, and the local stockmen's association promised to have the trespassers moved. However, in the brief time since Lee first pioneered the Yellowstone Basin, the region had become overstocked: 200,000 head now grazed on the land south of the river. Certainly what bothered Lee was that although the LS might hold off the new outfits for one season, what of the following year, or the next? In Texas he faced a different dilemma. The governor had sent agents to inspect ranch holdings in the Panhandle, where nearly 10.5 million acres (including sections of reserved school land or "free range") were found to be controlled by only twenty companies. One agent even recommended that ranchers "lease" these fenced enclosures at four cents an acre or forfeit the property. And while the proposal drew a heated response from many cattlemen, another event—as important but less noticed—literally swept

across the High Plains. The incident began when a crew of the XIT—
a new outfit to the Panhandle—broke camp without extinguishing
a fire. The constant winds of the region played at the coals until a
blaze caught and burned out of control, cutting a swath nearly thirty
miles long across the prairie. Learning that the LE had almost been
destroyed, A. E. Reynolds chided his neighbors and incidentally predicted that "a bad winter [would] put four times more cattle on the
range than it will support. . . ."[16]

Reynolds could not have known how accurate his words would be,
for not even the excitable Lee paid much attention to the range fire.
Apparently, like others, he saw it as just another problem to be
worked out in the long winter days ahead. Generally 1885 had been a
good year, and the ranchers uniformly drew back to enjoy their successes. But a hard freeze and then a blizzard settled on the plains
during early winter of 1886; and, although the fury had spent itself
by the first week of January, nearly everything was left snowbound.
Then, as Reynolds had foreseen, cattle by the thousands began to mi-
grate south from Kansas, Colorado, and New Mexico toward the
warmer climes of Texas. The animals, however, found their way
blocked by the northern Panhandle's drift fence; what ground that
remained exposed was denuded of its vegetation by the recent fire.
There the livestock huddled—without feed or shelter—and by the
thousands died, their carcasses waiting to be mutilated by scaveng-
ing wolves.[17] The full extent of the disaster would need time to be
understood.

The lull between roundups worked its usual strain on relations
between the LS and its adversaries, old and new. Tom Harris again
challenged McAllister to a gunfight from which McAllister wisely
turned away. It was supposed that the threat came in retaliation to
the foreman's purchase of a counterfeit T-48 brand that Harris's syndicate was allegedly using to rustle LS cattle. At the same time, Dave
Martinez, a company remuda foreman, found Gene Watkins, another
of the syndicate's renegades, stealing LS horses. When Martinez and
his brother next met Watkins at Tascosa's Dunn and Jenkins saloon,
the outlaw went for his gun, but Martinez, being faster, brought
Watkins down first. Jesse Jenkins, who also happened to be seated
inside the bar, immediately shot the foreman as two other men
killed Martinez's brother. Even Harris took an interest in the incident, as syndicate men were told to kill the Indian "Pisquash,"
whose sole offense was to witness the fight. It was later thought that
Watkins had been ordered to assassinate Martinez for uncovering the
earlier theft.[18]

The seeds of yet another controversy also took root in March when the Oldham County commissioners voted to build a 1,060-foot iron bridge, costing $22,000, across the Canadian River.[19] The marvel of the project was that it was literally a bridge to nowhere, barely connecting two hundred residents to the wilds of a Texas prairie. Lee, in particular, might have suggested baser motives, as the land on the south bank of the river belonged to the LS. But the rancher was in Kansas on the day of the vote and, therefore, had not been informed of what the county proposed. However, by now he was aware that his organization adjoined a new neighbor, an outfit with the brand XIT. This fact alone certainly gave him pause.

The new enterprise was a joint London-Chicago venture organized under a parent syndicate calling itself the Capitol Freehold Investment and Land Company, a creation of Lord Aberdeen of Great Britain, John V. Farwell, and his brother Senator Charles B. Farwell, both of Illinois. The venture had been sparked by a call from the State of Texas for a new statehouse; the syndicate had responded to the promise of title to three million acres of contiguous Panhandle property. The XIT ranch was subsequently established, and by early spring of 1886 approximately one-half million of the total acres promised were deeded. Lee's dilemma was outlined in a letter, dated 27 February, from an XIT foreman who suggested that the company ". . . should have a great range if we could get rid of Lee and Reynolds [the LS and the LE], & I expect they will realize before long that they had better go, or we will have to freeze them out.[20] A neighbor fated to build the world's largest cattle ranch did not portend well for those in its way.

Yet uncharacteristically the Kansan remained at Leavenworth, seemingly unconcerned by the new challenges. Weeks had passed where the most telling contests took place at a card table and achievements were measured by column space in a morning newspaper. "A delightful evening with the genial host and hostess [Mr. and Mrs. W. M. D. Lee] . . ." was certainly not the usual accolade of this frontier businessman. But Lee finally stirred, and on 18 March he departed Leavenworth for the open range of Montana to begin the more familiar business of inspecting his various enterprises.[21] Another roundup would soon take place, and as always he would be close at hand at a time most critical to his operation.

The night Lee traveled out of Kansas another crowd gathered at Tascosa's Dunn and Jenkins saloon. While standing outside the barroom, George Lote at first paid little attention to the men on horseback riding fast down the main street. Then one of the three broke ahead of the others and rode straight for the saloon. By the time Lote noticed that the rider was Ed King—an LS cowpuncher and former LS Ranger—King had unholstered a revolver and pointed it with dead aim at him.

"There is that [damn son-of-a-bitch] now!" was all the startled cowboy heard before turning back into the saloon. The next thing he remembered was watching King on his horse follow him through the door! Apparently the LS hand thought better of the move, for within seconds he, John Lang, and Newt Bowers (again, all of the LS) stormed into the bar—without horses—but with pistols drawn. Lote could not imagine what he had done to warrant the display and just stood there staring at King's unholstered revolver.

"Watch that door," King hollered over his shoulder to his two friends. The drunk cowboy then took a hard look at Lote and realized that it was not Len Woodruff, the Dunn and Jenkins bartender, whom he was chasing. Woodruff was himself a former LS cowboy who earlier that week had accused his old employer of mavericking four beeves from the small herd he and Teddy Briggs were grazing near Tascosa.

After being told that Woodruff had quit work early, King and his companions holstered their six-shooters and walked calmly out of the building as if nothing had happened.[22] Lote could only imagine what would take place should the two ever meet.

Lee, meanwhile, had arrived at Miles City on the night of 19 March and immediately put up at the McQueen Hotel. Saturday morning he walked the short distance to the office of the Niobara Cattle Company, where he joined other ranchers in a discussion of the pending Montana roundup.[23] Texas and controversy were perhaps the last things on his mind.

Yet at Tascosa that same Saturday night four of Lee's men—Fred Chilton, Frank Valley, John Lang, and Ed King—sat at a table inside the bar across the way from the Dunn and Jenkins establishment with Len Woodruff and a couple of the local boys at hand. Then someone again brought up the subject of mavericking, which at once had Valley on the edge of his chair. The LS cowboy had heard about all on the matter that he wanted to hear and stared across the table at Woodruff: he was tired of allegation, he shouted, and would not stand for it any longer! Woodruff and friends at once pushed away from the others and stalked out of the bar; the LS hands, however, did not move, as they were in town for their usual weekend fun.[24]

The night progressed as King and Lang watched a drunk Valley make a show of himself, at one time standing on top of a table to sing "Little Nell of Narragansett Bay." And a drunk Chilton was at Valley's side, egging him on. The sober cowboys finally decided that it was time their colleagues left town while the mood was still friendly. But not wanting to ride out of Tascosa themselves, they planned to hide their horses in the hope that Chilton and Valley would notice them gone, believe them returned to camp, and do likewise. It was between two and three o'clock on a bright, moonlit Sunday morning when King and Lang started for the horses hitched across the street.[25]

As the two neared the corner of the closed Dunn and Jenkins saloon, three men stepped out from the shadows. It was Woodruff, followed by two local gamblers, Charles Emory and Louis Bousman; each had drawn a weapon. King spoke first.

"What does this mean, boy?" As he talked, a hand inched toward Woodruff's unholstered gun. Emory, though, was faster and shot King in the face; the wounded LS cowboy was able to get off one round before collapsing to the ground. The bullet crippled Woodruff in the thigh, but while falling he managed to shove his gun into the fallen man's breast and fire. As the round exploded, Lang, now distracted to his left, turned and faced the raised barrel of a .50-caliber rifle with J. G. Gough (alias "The Catfish Kid") at the other end.

For an instant Gough stood frozen, his rifle taking dead aim at Lang. Next, as the LS cowboy went for his gun, the Kid fired, the round grazing Lang's arm. Both then turned and ran, with Lang heading as fast as he could across the street into the open saloon.[26]

"Stake me to another gun," he yelled to the bartender, Concho. "He killed Ed King." Concho at first refused, and while they argued, Valley and Chilton both at a poker table in the back room, overheard the shouts. They at once folded from the game and ran out of the saloon.

Chilton was particularly shaken. He ran up to the dead King, took the body in his arms, and started to rock back and forth, all the while crying and ranting. Then a movement down the street caught his attention.

Jesse Sheets, proprietor of a Tascosa boardinghouse, had been startled from his bed by all the noise. Curious, he walked to the front of the store and opened the door. Thinking it was Bousman, the LS cowboy raised his revolver, braced himself against a wall, and took aim. The shot cracked the night air and Sheets died instantly with a bullet through the skull.[27] Meanwhile, Lang had picked up King's .45 and run to the back of the Dunn and Jenkins saloon with Valley following. Once in position, both opened fire into a rear wall.

Unexpectedly a bullet-ridden door swung open as seven or eight rounds were pumped into Valley. At the same time, shots began to blast at them from behind. Caught in the crossfire, Lang turned and aimed blindly at where he thought the outside gun was hidden. After several rounds were unloaded, the shooting suddenly stopped. Chilton now rounded the corner of the saloon, and as he ran, he stumbled over his fallen friends. Shots again rang out, with Chilton taking three rounds in the back and one in the left side. Crippled, he tried to pull himself up for another effort, but was only able to get off one shot before falling to the ground, fatally wounded.[28]

As soon as the townsfolk thought the shooting was over, nearly everyone stepped outside with lanterns in hand. By then Sheriff Jim East had deputized a sufficient number of men to put down any further disturbance. He next set about to arrest those responsible for the killings.

Charles Emory was found lying in the street just barely alive; Louis Bousman and J. B. Gough were also arrested in town. Woodruff, however, was able to make his way out of Tascosa, heading in the direction of Teddy Briggs's shack, and a deputy was sent to apprehend him. The dead included Ed King, Frank Valley, and Fred Chilton—all LS men. The most tragic killing was that of Jesse Sheets, who left behind a wife and five children. County judge H. H. Wallace was sent to fetch E. C. Godwin-Austen, justice of the peace, so that an inquest could be held immediately. Others rode toward the LS with news of the incident.[29]

But at the ranch McAllister was already confronting a crowd of angry cowboys who had come up to the house, with Tobe Robinson acting as spokesman for the group. "This fight has been agitated for two years," Robinson recalled. "Four men are now murdered. If you want to do anything, now is the time. We will hang those men and we'll burn down Jenkins's saloon."

McAllister, however, thought better of the plan and turned a deaf ear. "I'm afraid Lee won't approve," he cautioned. "I don't want to do anything to get the company in bad. If you boys want to do it, I'll stay with you in money matters and lawsuits." Nevertheless, those taking measure of the foreman knew that a raid into Tascosa would be useless without him riding at their head, and they soon gave up the idea. Besides, the first order of business was the burial of three friends.[30]

Every man but one of the LS outfit rode into Tascosa on Sunday morning. Sheriff East and his deputies were naturally on edge, but they need not have worried. The cowboys stood silent as they watched four pine caskets lowered into graves on Boot Hill; they then returned to the LS. That same day a coroner's jury returned charges against Woodruff, Bousman, and Gough; Sallie Henry, a saloon dancer, was also taken into custody as an accomplice to the killings. The

accused refused any comment other than that ". . . it was a question
of annihilation of one side or the other, and they did the best they
could for their lives. . . ."[31]

Lee had arrived at Leavenworth from St.. Paul, Minnesota, on a
Wednesday morning coach, 31 March, and immediately caught the
next Santa Fe train bound for Dodge City. From there he started his
fastest freight ambulance to ranch headquarters. He actually had
little time to spend in Texas, but the one matter he had to settle was
whether the shootings concerned protection of company property.

He talked to his men, listened to all accounts of the incident, and
finally reasoned that the killings were simply the result of a foolish,
drunken argument. He said that if it had been a dispute over land he
would have spared no expense to prosecute all involved. Lee then returned north, satisfied that the crisis was over.[32] But the feud that
had begun with Tom Harris and the cowboy strike of 1883, that had
subsequently led to the employment of Garrett and his LS Rangers,
and that had so often flared into confrontations between LS cowboys and Tascosa outlaws had now cost three company men their
lives. Those old hands who knew the rancher best perhaps suspected
Lee's calm reaction.

For his part, Lee put Tascosa out of mind, and in Chicago on 5 April
he signed another agreement with Congressman Abner Taylor, general manager of the Capitol syndicate. The transaction stipulated
that in exchange for 106,707 acres of LS property located in Oldham
and Hartley counties (including Lee's share of the LE split), the XIT
would transfer to Lee and Scott over 71,131 acres all to the east of the
XIT tract and south of the Canadian River. This exchange meant
that for the first time the LS would be essentially one contiguous
body located entirely south of the Oldham County line; but, more
important, the arrangement resolved a potential confrontation in
which the LS appeared a certain loser. And by early May a content
Abner Taylor was cutting down old LS fences, including the drift
line, and moving a division of his XIT headquarters into Lee's former
ranch house on the Alamocitas. The LS would have to be satisfied
with a new headquarters relocated on Alamosa Creek. By August a
mutually agreed-to fence line separated both outfits.[33]

With other potential controversies, though, Lee was not as successful. In May Tascosa attorney J. R. Browning presented the Oldham
County commissioners with a petition of grievance against the building of the proposed Tascosa bridge. The document alleged that the
court had ". . . without legal authority entered into a certain so-
called contract with the Kansas City Bridge and Iron Company for
the construction of an iron bridge across the Canadian River . . ." or,

more to the point, that ". . . the price agreed to be paid for the said bridge [was] exorbitant . . . which would if paid unnecessarily burden the undersigned and all taxpayers of Oldham County. . . ."[34] Not surprisingly, Lee's name headed the list of irate citizens.

But the commissioners proceeded undeterred and even dared to add fifteen cents to a tax on personal property. A token adjustment was made on 9 August by reletting the contract to the King Iron Bridge and Manufacturing Company of Columbus, Ohio, for construction of a wooden span at the reduced cost of $18,000. The gesture would have only momentarily calmed Lee's anger, however, as two weeks later the same commissioners appointed an implacable foe, M. A. Dunn of the Dunn and Jenkins saloon, to a panel of surveyors empowered to lay out "a first-class road" on the south bank of the Canadian River.[35] The rancher looked elsewhere for allies, and he must have been gratified when his new friends at the XIT responded, "We have written to the King Iron & Bridge Co. as you suggest & also to M. Maud to join with you in any proceedings . . . to prevent the construction of this bridge."[36] For its part, Tascosa pushed ahead with the project.

With attention fixed either on bridge building or the recent shootout, it seemed impossible that the season's roundup would ever get under way. However, whether by custom or individual effort, company agents met in Tascosa on 15 April and voted to start herding livestock during mid-June. Although begun late in the season, the west Panhandle drive proceeded uninterrupted, and by the first week in October an LS crew was ready to start 2,200 head of beeves on their way north to Dodge City, all bound for the cattle markets. Other crews moved yearlings and two-year-olds up a different trail toward the Yellowstone range, with the last LS cowboys returning to Tascosa during the first week in November. In anticipation of the drive, Lee's Montana cowboys had earlier swept the countryside of its marketable stock.[37]

Lee did manage one surprise during late spring by firing his long-time foreman, Jim McAllister, but he was careful to do it before rather than during the cattle drive. Apparently the rancher had uncovered McAllister's secret partnership with a New Mexico stockman to run a small herd in San Miguel County. The LS foreman attempted to "sell" his interest in the seven hundred head to his wife, but undoubtedly the transfer was still reported. Then Kid Dobbs, who rode with Garrett as an LS Ranger, later recalled that "McAllister had a $2,500 interest" in Tom Harris's syndicate, a statement that, if true, more than justified the dismissal. In any event, James East, sheriff of Oldham County, was immediately hired as McAllister's replacement, and by late September the man was a resident at the new LS ranch house.[38] With everything else, Lee's disappointment must have been acute, and it is not surprising that he turned to another enterprise in order to recapture that sense of accomplishment.

Lee's herd of purebred Angus had been in the country more than five years and alternately pastured at Dodge City, Fort Supply, and finally at a stock farm located just outside Leavenworth's town limits. During these same years offspring from the herd had been used successfully to upgrade range cattle. However, this practice did little for Lee's reputation. Therefore, during late summer 1886 the rancher decided to correct the oversight by exhibiting his blacks at area stock shows.[39] The first competition entered was a local exhibit in Missouri.

In fact, Tuesday 31 August was the second day of the eighth annual St. Joseph Inter-State Exposition, where large crowds walked the grounds under a clear, warm sky. But the center of attraction was at the cattle arena, where over three hundred head were on display. Entered were shorthorns from Iowa, Kansas, Minnesota, and Missouri; Herefords, all from Kansas, with one lot belonging to Scott; and three holstein-friesian herds from Missouri. The Aberdeen-Angus were drawn from the farms of George Anderson of Oregon, Missouri; J. S. Goodwin of Belloit, Kansas; and Lee.[40]

At first the judges had difficulty in singling out the best of show from the polled blacks exhibited, but honors were finally declared. Of Angus bulls, first prize went to Goodwin's breed and second to Lee; in the competition of Angus cows, first again went to Goodwin, with Lee second; but in the final contest with Angus cows, Lee's entry took the blue.[41] It was a beginning, and Lee prepared his Angus for the next rung in competition—the Western National Fair at Lawrence, Kansas.

The exhibition that ended the second week of September 1886 proved to be all Lee could have anticipated. Although it was only the second time out for his herd, in almost every category it was a sweep. His Highness VI, imported in 1883 from the Angus farms of Waterside-of-Forbes, Scotland, took the blue as the outstanding bull (age, over three years); Anne 2d, a cow "wonderfully smooth, low and blocky," also took first in her competition; and of the six bulls shown in the two-year-old class, Lee took first and second with Don Carlos and General Scott, respectively, both sired by His Highness. It came as no surprise that Lee's herd was later judged "best of show."[42] There now remained but one hurdle, the all-important show at Kansas City.

As at the earlier St. Joseph exhibition, the second day of the annual Inter-State Fair at Kansas City held the promise of perfect weather.[43]

Yet it was the special events, in particular the over 365 head of prime beef and dairy stock, that attracted spectators to the top of the hill just south of the Kansas City depot. And by mid-morning on Tuesday, 14 September, many stood near the open-air cattle arena in anticipation of the day's events, the judging of Aberdeen-Angus. Four exhibitors were listed: Walter C. Weeden of Kansas City; A. B. Matthews of Kansas City; Joseph H. Rea of Carrollton, Missouri; and W. M. D. Lee.

Weeden's entry—Walter of Templeton—was the first to enter the ring, followed by Matthew's Baron Valiant, Lee's His Highness VI, and finally Rea's Model Prince. The judging quickly narrowed to Model Prince and His Highness, with the blue falling to Rea and the red to Lee. The Leavenworth entries recouped the disappointment, however, when the two-year-old Promoter took first in his competition. Then, of the five yearling bulls exhibited, Lee's Don Carlos and General Scott repeated their Lawrence sweep. Anne 2d of Waterside was judged the outstanding of her breed; and in the two-year-old ring a tie-breaking vote gave Lee's Matilda 3d the blue. Lee's yearling cows Lucinda and Welcome 3d placed first and second, respectively.

A different committee was empaneled for the sweepstakes, where five bulls were presented, and again competition narrowed to Rea versus Lee. But this time it was Don Carlos who entered the ring, and while the vote was again split, the umpire now cast for Lee. It was a unanimous decision that gave Lee's cow, Anne 2d, the win.[44]

An immediate bonus of Lee's new standing among cattle buyers was evident at the Kansas City auction held 29 October. He put five female Angus on the block that were quickly gaveled in for a total of $1,420; seven of his young bulls brought in another $1,445. But the accolade most relished came while attending the annual November meeting of the American Aberdeen-Angus Breeders' Association convened at Chicago's Leland Hotel. Although Lee was a charter member of the organization, the day marked the first time he was asked to sit as a director along with T. W. Harvey of Chicago, R. B. Hunter of Carrollton, Missouri, and George Geary of London, Ontario.[45] The recognition he desired had been achieved.

However, approval by established powers was more than fulfilling the need for acceptance; it was also adjusting to changed business practices. The frontier cattle range and the eastern marketplace were now each firmly tied to the other by railroads, and a stockman could ill afford to overlook the perception of his herd's quality as determined in the boardrooms of Kansas City and Chicago. Profits were based not only on being the first at market but also on the quality of the product, and Lee intended to meet both requisites. Therefore, with the success of his breed's bloodline momentarily assured, he began to work on the remaining obligation. Already, with the LS again showing the way, stockmen began to bypass the Dodge City terminus by trailing beef to the nearer railroad at Lamar, Colorado. Of course, each change was the practical response to closer railroad connections. During the spring of 1886, one line, the Fort Worth and Denver City, even published a map that proposed to diagonally bisect the Texas Panhandle. In that event, Dodge again would be that much more cut off from the region's trade. But no matter how demoralizing the changes were to the established communities, Lee and similarly situated businessmen were compelled to adapt. In December even the general manager of the XIT confided that "we are thinking of organizing to build a railroad . . . down through the Pan Handle . . . ," and inquired of Lee whether ". . . there [is] any road from Kansas City in that direction that does not belong to the Santa Fe or the Gould people."[46]

If Lee answered, that response has been lost. Yet only weeks previous, while LS cowboys were on the last leg of a drive to Montana and temporarily stalled at Luling, Colorado, the rancher offered each man some advice. They were to ". . . file on school land [free range] wherever they found it suited them and to go to work towards its improvement. . . . If any help should be needed, they were promised that it should be forthcoming . . . [He] recognized that the Grangers would soon be crowding it out, and he preferred to see his boys getting a chance of it, too."[47] A Tascosa cowboy remembered Lee's caution in slightly different terms. "Lee," he said, "came to town [Tascosa] and said . . . [the proposed Oldham County bridge] would [not only] hurt the stockmen but hurt them all alike because it would help develop the country and the stockmen would have to leave." In other words, the railroad and similar improvements must ultimately attract strangers to a land that he and others of his breed had given a lifetime to develop. A bridge, or a railroad for that matter, was an invitation to change a way of life. This was an immediate concern, for in October, M. A. Dunn's committee had appropriated LS property for a county road on the far side of the Tascosa bridge.[48]

Lee, of course, would appeal the decision, but what good was it to complain if change was inevitable? Even Scott had sold his Ridgewood farm in January for $95,000. The divestment was in keeping with the man's determination to "free himself as fast as possible from business cares" in order, he said, to improve his health. For Lee, the implications were ominous. Thus, perhaps wanting to relish his successes of the past twelve months and also needing to forget the problems, he and Lina departed Leavenworth on 19 December for a holiday in New York City.[49] It would be a new year before he again faced the challenges of yet another season.

The Lees returned from New York and were committed to the Leavenworth social circuit by 5 January 1887. Also greeting them was news of considerable loss of cattle on the Montana range. Lee perhaps took solace in reports that said damage was limited to stock ". . . brought over the [parched] trail from [the] Rio Grande and in their famished condition placed on ranges so fully stocked that only a phenominally [sic] mild winter could [have prevented] heavy losses." As in the past, the LS had trailed early and to a range used exclusively by the company; therefore, Lee probably discounted the reports. Yet unsuspected at the time, even these usually safe practices would be inadequate, and before winter's end nearly 75 percent of his herd would be destroyed.[50]

Lee spent long hours at Leavenworth socials—in fact, until the first week in May—before starting the yearly inspection of his different enterprises. Some time had been used to augment the nearby Angus farm and to promote the thoroughbreds by advertising in journals and at stock sales. In January alone, $2,835 was raised from just one auction. But on Monday, 9 May, Lee and his Texas foreman, James East, rode together from ranch headquarters into Tascosa. Unlike the preceding year, the Oldham County range had withstood the season admirably, the locals calling it the mildest winter in memory. Yet by now the rancher had also confirmed the reports of devastation to his Montana range, and the southern herds would be used to restock the north as soon as a Texas roundup could put approximately 4,500 beeves on the trail north. As Lee told an inquiring reporter, although "his company lost heavily of their through cattle on their Montana range . . . they [had] a large reserve to draw from and [were] in no way discouraged."[51]

While the rancher and foreman continued their ride into Tascosa it was evident that the townsfolk were unconcerned about the troubles of the northern range. Tascosa was prosperity itself. The town now boasted four mercantile houses, including one operated by Lee's old friend, Bob Wright, doing business locally as Wright and Farnsworth. Tascosa also counted among its many businesses a drugstore, two hotels, three millinery shops, three barbershops, two law offices, and one doctor's office. The public buildings included a county courthouse, jail, church, and two schools. But not everything was unfamiliar. The same four wild saloons—the Cattle Exchange, the Ranch Saloon, Equity Bar, and Dunn and Jenkins—still operated, each with its own claim to a thriving cowboy business. Tascosa also had its bridge across the Canadian River and, as expected, had built a connecting road through LS property.[52]

But the greatest excitement was caused by the prospect of the Fort Worth and Denver City railroad building through town. It was hoped that the juncture of steel rails at a Tascosa depot would establish the community as the area's premier settlement. Therefore, town residents were beside themselves when the line's right-of-way agent finally announced that the road would build to its borders. Lee could appreciate Tascosa's enthusiasm for railroads, which brought access and thereby reduced the cost of merchandise. An example was the approach of the Santa Fe's Southern Kansas spur, which during the spring of 1887 was driving from a newly established Woodward station, located about fifteen miles southeast of Fort Supply, into Texas. Even a third road, the Rock Island, was in May building through Caldwell, Kansas, on a route west toward Indian Territory and, eventually, across the Texas Panhandle.[53] Lee's problems, however, as he rode into Tascosa were not as remote as the approaching railroads but of more immediate concern.

Unlike the 1883 strike, it was experienced hands who now refused to ride on the spring roundup. Apparently the men expected trouble from Colorado grangers who had staked farms near the Montana trail, and the LS cowboys wanted no part of the threatened conflict. Needing cattle in Montana, Lee answered his men differently than before and replaced the older hands with more venturesome cowboys.[54] Anticipating that this might cause some to strike, the LS in cooperation with other companies posted a wage schedule mandating that experienced men be paid only their current wages while others draw the usual $25 a month. Neither Lee nor his fellow cattlemen would tolerate exceptions.[55]

When the rancher and the foreman finally reached the Oldham County courthouse that Monday, 9 May 1887, they dismounted and entered the building; the five assembled commissioners took immediate notice of Lee's presence. And upon the rancher's application, taxes erroneously assessed against personal and real property were favorably considered, as was an additional $250 payable to the LS as damage for the county road cut through company property.[56] But the question that perhaps crossed most minds was why Lee himself had appeared to press these seemingly insignificant claims. Then only those familiar with the past would have suspected the answer, and even they might have deluded themselves as to the rancher's purpose.

For his part, Lee soon returned to Kansas, and on 8 June he was at the Leavenworth depot for another trip out of the city, in this instance to Denver. Having made arrangements with Colorado's sanitary board for the passing of Panhandle herds through that state, he desired to be on hand when the cattle were actually transferred to other rails bound for the Montana range. The rancher barely made his connection when the first herd was started on the route north, and by late June another drive was on the trail out of Texas. By the close of the season over six thousand head of Lee and Scott's cattle had safely passed through Colorado and Wyoming. This particular movement of herds was watched with more interest than usual, for many saw it as the last great cattle drive across the nation's midsection.[57]

Apparently Lee himself was buoyed by the success, for he now spoke to others of the "good beef" expected from all quarters of the country. However, as this problem faded, another took its place: the southern range was burned dry by a scorching August sun. During August Lee also paid $1,800 for the privilege of grazing stock on previously "free range."[58] Then nearly every frontier stock grower shared a crisis—one in particular.

Throughout that spring and summer, many operations had begun the hard work of closing down, especially those outfits dependent on good northern pastures, with the Kansas and Chicago slaughterhouses suddenly overrun with beef. As a consequence, the August cattle trade tallied record low sales—stock was auctioned for as little as four cents a pound. Eastern financiers were particularly concerned and predicted the imminent collapse of the industry. The blame fell on high interest rates and the devastating Montana winter.[59] Lee might have added railroads to the list, as they were the obvious exponents of converting the western range into farm land.

A more personal alarm had been felt weeks earlier when, at the end of June, Lee stood alongside friends at the Leavenworth depot and bid farewell to Julia Scott, who departed the community for residency in New York City.[60] Thus, Lucien would be compelled to divide his time between the East Coast and his western enterprises. For Lee the departure merely underscored the dilemma in which he was left virtually alone to manage an "empire" suddenly riddled with problems. Still, and perhaps because of his frustrations, Lee took the time necessary to address one long-standing rebuff.

Having settled accounts in Leavenworth by 6 September, Lee and Scott started out together for the Texas ranch. The trip was short, perhaps taking no more than two days, and at Tascosa both went directly to their headquarters, where business was the principal topic of discussion. Time spent at the ranch meant that Lee would miss the state fairs and cattle shows of Iowa, Nebraska, and Kansas. Yet the

Angus had been groomed to stand on their own merit, and by month's end the breed had swept most of the honors from the cattle rings of all three states.[61] Still, Lee must have regretted that he had to confront less satisfying issues elsewhere.

One problem was the approach of the Fort Worth and Denver City railroad across the plains of the Texas Panhandle; in fact, on the date of their visit the line was only a few miles out of Tascosa. The Santa Fe had also built itself to a midpoint in the region, thereby establishing the new town of Panhandle, where construction was momentarily stopped. As was the case when the line had built around Fort Supply, the tracks had bypassed both Fort Elliott and Mobeetie (Sweetwater).[62] Yet the Santa Fe and the Fort Worth and Denver City were building to some undesignated intersection at which point a major community was expected to arise. Of course, Tascosa fancied itself as that future metropolis.

Stockmen such as Lee were more pragmatic and thought of the rails as little more than a means to transport farmers into the heart of cattle country. Even while Lee and Scott visited their crews, A. L. Matlock, an agent of the XIT, also stopped in town to discuss business, and likewise on his mind were the approaching rails. But this manager of the world's largest cattle operation thought differently than his peers, and within days of the Tascosa visit he was heard to promote the lines by observing that "with these . . . great roads . . . the farmer will seek that part of the state, and when he does . . . the syndicate will cut up the tract and sell to the actual settler. . . ."[63] If true, Lee might well have asked what chance the LS had to survive intact.

Obviously the frontier was changing, and, as was the case when Indians lost their source of buffalo robes, cattlemen now were forced to adapt to different circumstances. But the winter's hardships made a transition impossible for most, and the LS was one of only a handful of stock companies with the resources at hand to withstand such fluctuations. Yet both Lee and Scott must have asked themselves whether they were willing to make the necessary sacrifices of time and money. The answers were surely debated that week in September while both visited in Texas. Interestingly, R. E. Montgomery, the right-of-way and town lot agent of the Fort Worth and Denver road, also slipped into Tascosa one late afternoon while the partners were in discussion and left that same evening without disclosing the nature of his business.[64] Within a month most understood the reason for secrecy and, coincidentally, one of the decisions made that week at the LS.

By late October, the work gangs of the Fort Worth and Denver City railroad had laid tracks across the Frying Pan range in Potter County, passing through the recently settled Amarillo on the approach to Tascosa. The most startling revelation, however, came with the announcement that the Canadian River crossing would be moved about four miles west of Tascosa to the mouth of Cheyenne Creek— land owned by Lee and Scott. Tascosa was predictably outraged.[65]

Despite the outcry, a bridge spanning the Canadian River was up by 19 November as the crews moved northwest through Oldham County toward the New Mexico border. With the grading completed, tracks were laid to within five miles of the bridge, and the company expected to tie in on the north side of the river—at a new town of Cheyenne—by 1 December. A circular even appeared advertising 15 December as the day auctioneers would sell lots at this designated "great Panhandle city."[66]

Nearly three hundred visiting excursionists surveyed the new town in the late afternoon of 13 December, enjoying the comfortable weather and the carnivallike atmosphere. Another two hundred guests arrived the following day, which only served to heighten Tascosa's anxiety. Then, to the dismay of the older community, auctioneer J. H. Hosack opened lots to bids at 1:00 P.M. on Thursday, 15 December. And by nightfall Tascosa watched as the company tallied sales of over $20,000. The editor of the local weekly spoke for all when he wrote that he ". . . never believed, and still [doubted], that it ever was . . . seriously intended by the railroad authorities to build or to help to build a town at the site of the incipient Cheyenne." Rather, the decision was ". . . the direct outcome of a spleen that found its opportunity to dictate conditions there and to vent itself here. . . ."—or, more to the point, the pleasure of W. M. D. Lee.[67] Yet by 17 January 1888, the day when the Fort Worth and Denver City completed its tracks through Texas, and despite Tascosa's protest that law required all railroads to connect with a county seat, only Clarendon and Cheyenne were on the road's Panhandle map.[68] Tascosa had been bypassed—the fate most feared by a frontier town.

Lee was not at his ranch to savor the victory but instead, after the September meeting with LS personnel, had traveled north to Wisconsin, where he and Lina looked after her ill father. The visit was followed by one excursion to Austin and another to Chicago, with the remaining time devoted to family at Leavenworth.[69] This was just as well, for feelings were running rather high in Texas against him and his crew.

But whether it was Tascosa's threatened injunction or the frustration of unparalleled change within the cattle industry itself, on 20 January Lee rode into Tascosa and signed a document that allayed the town's worst fears. In exchange for 160 acres of LS property abutting the railroad and just south of the Canadian River, Lee received an equal share adjacent to the ranch. Although the property was formally deeded to three merchants, Tascosa was promised the land as a site for its coveted depot. Both parties stipulated that competing developments would be abandoned. Thus, the confrontation ended, and the community could uniformly sigh that "the agony is over. We are a railroad town. . . ." Tascosa now had to contend only with Amarillo, where one railroad had already constructed shipping pens and another, the Santa Fe, had surveyed the location for a possible terminus. Yet in all the excitement this upstart was overlooked.[70]

When Lee stepped off the train that returned him to Leavenworth during the first week in February, he cut a reporter short with only one comment. "Things are booming," he said, "because lots of farmers from the older states who are well fixed are going there to make homes." It was more an epitaph than praise. Even men such as Grenville Dodge of the Fort Worth and Denver City were noting that ". . . the Panhandle is not settling as fast as it ought to, nor as fast as people would like to settle it. . . ."[71]

With migration inevitable and the cattle market depressed (one-half million beeves had been delivered to the Chicago pens from the western range during August and September alone), it was no wonder that many looked elsewhere for relief. And Lee was no exception. As he wrote that fall to the editors of one journal, "I'm afraid we will see the grand rush of beeves continue till none exist. Everyone seems to be trying to see who can get rid of his cattle first. . . ."[72] The industry was collapsing, and Lee always held profits to be his bottom line.

Hardly anyone noticed the man's departure from Leavenworth on Tuesday evening of 14 February 1888, on a train bound for Central Texas.[73] But the stockman was determined to travel a course that again would change the nature of his own frontier.

CHAPTER SIX

Three-Masted
Schooners

On Thursday, 16 February 1888, Lee walked from his comfortable room at Austin's Driskill Hotel to join three others at the office of notary public A. B. Langermann.[1] The agreement they each penned was unique:

> Be it known that the undersigned Ira H. Evans, of Austin, Texas; Geo. W. Angle and Chas. W. Ogden, of San Antonio, Texas; and Wm. M. D. Lee, of Leavenworth, Kansas, hereby declare their intention of associating themselves together for the purpose of forming a Company . . . formed for the purpose of constructing, owning, and operating a deep water channel, from the waters of the Gulf of Mexico to the mainland at the mouth of the Brazos River. . . .[2]

The declaration was backed by a one-million-dollar investment.[3]

Deep water at the mouth of the Brazos River had long been a Texas dream. Stephen F. Austin first proposed the scheme in 1835, while Texas was still a province of Mexico, and a company was formed. However, for reasons left unexplained, nothing was accomplished and the project was abandoned. Then, in the early 1850s, a canal was cut through the narrow isthmus separating the river from Galveston Bay, a consequence being that the slowed current allowed silt to accumulate at the river's mouth; soon after, a sandbar became an impenetrable obstruction to navigation.[4] Yet while the potentials of a successful port on the Gulf of Mexico were staggering, as late as 1888 Texas still did not have an adequate outlet to the sea. On the contrary, most commercial businesses west of the Mississippi River and east of the Rocky Mountains continued to ship either through Chicago, New Orleans, or some distant Atlantic Coast port. But the feasibility of a Texas harbor had been studied, and three sites were most commonly mentioned.

In the southeastern corner of the state there was the bay formed at the mouth of the Sabine and Neches rivers, where Sabine Pass posed

a shallow six- or seven-mile obstacle. The small southern community of Beaumont on the northwestern shore of the waterway would
benefit most should a harbor be opened at its site. On the central
coast was Galveston Bay, also guarded by a pass at which considerable money had already been invested but to no avail. If, however,
Galveston did succeed, the modest-sized town at the head of the bay,
Houston, would benefit most. About 150 miles farther south lay
Corpus Christi, its access to the Gulf blocked by Aransas Pass. No
one gave much attention to deep water at the mouth of the Brazos
River (see Map 6).

As recent as the fall of 1887 the U.S. Army Corps of Engineers had
investigated the site, concluding that a harbor on the river would be
too costly and doubtful an enterprise for the government to undertake. Therefore, in January 1888 Congress endorsed Galveston as the
preferred deep-water port of the state.[5] Lee, however, saw matters differently. He had been convinced by the arguments of E. L. Cothrell,
chief engineer of a company that had opened the South Pass of the
Mississippi River to navigation, that a Brazos harbor was feasible.[6]
And there were similarities between the two great waterways.

The Brazos River, whose bed twisted several hundred miles from
the dry plains of the state's northwestern counties to the semi-
tropical settlements near its mouth, was the principal drainage system of Texas. Of the several Texas rivers only the Brazos spilled directly into the Gulf; therefore, like the different channels at the
mouth of the Mississippi River, an unobstructed current would enter the sea with considerable force. And a fast-moving current was at
the crux of Lee's scheme. In fact, two mile-long jetties were to be
stretched from the mouth of the river in order to clear the channel of
its bar. The feat was to move the tons of rock and other material
needed to build these jetties into an undeveloped region.[7]

The countryside southwest of Houston for a distance of approximately forty miles was little more than a flat plain of scrub brush
and bayous. Transportation was either by personal conveyance along
the barely passable Brazoria County thoroughfares or by rail on the
Columbia Tap line, which one traveler likened to ". . . travelling on
an ox cart over a stumpy road."[8] However, on reaching the small
town of Columbia, bordered on its western limits by the silt-rich
Brazos River, the traveler's environment changed. Vegetation now
grew profusely, with willows, cottonwoods, and moss-laced oaks
forming an almost impenetrable wall along either bank of the river.
This was the land of Texas heroes where in a small cabin at West Columbia—the forgotten town immediately across the Brazos—Texas
established its first government. But in 1888 residents along the

lower Brazos thought only in terms of seasonal sugar cane and cotton crops, with occasional interest in cattle raising.[9] Columbia, though, was only the first stop on the circuitous route to the proposed harbor.

From Columbia small steam-driven side-wheelers churned the muddy Brazos daily past wood-lined banks toward the county seat of Brazoria, a distance of some fifteen miles. The traveler would be able to stop only briefly, however, at this isolated community before the boat again built up a head of steam and started its last leg on the journey downriver. By now a first whiff of saltwater would be noticeable as the boat glided along the ever-widening stream. When the east-bank village of Velasco was reached—some four hours after leaving Columbia—the river had tripled in width to nearly 1,200 feet, with no observable vegetation on either bank. Three miles farther downstream—about five and one-half miles by boat—came into view the west-bank town of Quintana, located at the point where the Brazos emptied into the Gulf of Mexico.[10] It was here that Lee proposed to build his jetties and, at a yet-to-be-determined site, to construct a world-class harbor.

The logistics were enormous. Hundreds of workers and tons of material would have to be transported from the barely accessible upriver communities to this isolated point on the Gulf. Even if that were accomplished, the natural obstructions, particularly the sandbar at the mouth of the river, offered little encouragement. For years government engineers had experimented with jetties at Galveston's harbor—at the cost of many millions of tax dollars—without success.[11] Yet Lee believed his plan would prove the exception.

Perhaps it was a vision of literally controlling the largest international market in the South that spurred him on. As matters now stood, all farm and ranch exports were expensively processed either through the Atlantic Coast or at the ports of Chicago and New Orleans. Therefore, Lee probably felt confident that farmers and ranchers would use a town built closer to their areas of production and thus more accessible to international markets. But the scheme was probably as challenging as it was intriguing. Could he, the son of a Wisconsin settler, who had traded with Indians and herded cattle hundreds of miles across frontier America, succeed where his betters had failed? For whatever reasons, on 22 February 1888 Lee filed the charter of the Brazos River Channel and Dock Company with the Texas secretary of state signifying his intention to do business as a deep-harbor contractor.[12]

By Monday, 20 March, there was considerable activity at the mouth of the Brazos while Lee himself registered at Houston's Capitol Hotel.

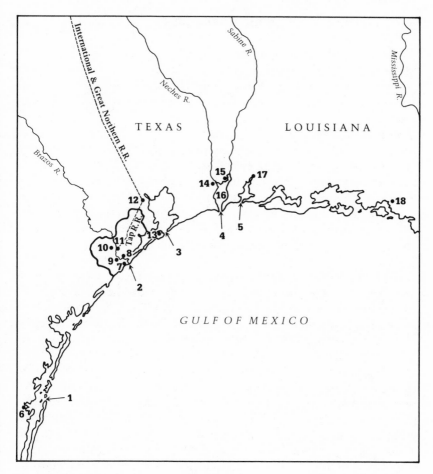

1	*Aransas Pass*	7	Quintana	13	Galveston
2	*Mouth of the Brazos R.*	8	Velasco	14	Beaumont
3	*Galveston Pass*	9	Brazoria	15	Orange
4	*Sabine Pass*	10	West Columbia	16	*Sabine Lake*
5	*Calcasieu Pass*	11	Columbia	17	Lake Charles
6	Corpus Christi	12	Houston	18	Morgan City

—— Brazoria County

Map 6. Coasts of Texas and Louisiana, 1888

Two weeks before, he and John Ferguson had contracted with Guy M. Bryan, Jr., a local banker and plantation owner, for the option to purchase several hundred acres of land near the mouth of the river at $5.00 an acre. Another 4,500 acres had been acquired the day preceding his visit to Houston. But even these sizable acquisitions were only a fraction of the total needed. As contemplated, the Brazos River Channel and Dock Company would own merely a narrow strip of property, 300 feet, along either bank of the river while the Texas Land and Immigration Company (an old chartered operation earlier acquired by Lee, Ira Evans, and others) would retain title to additional parcels of land. The plan was for the land company to sell lots as work progressed while the parent organization retained title to all other properties; thereby, control of the development would be assured.[13]

With this framework established, Lee took a leave from the river camps for visits to Leavenworth and Chicago. But he left the day-to-day operations in the able hands of two men who accompanied him to Houston—George Angle and George Wisner. Angle was a transplanted Pennsylvanian who from the early 1860s was variously occupied as a deep-ocean sailor, a New York investor, a railroad engineer, and most recently a San Antonio cattleman. Angle had agreed to act as general manager of the project while Wisner took on the responsibilities of chief engineer. There was little that could be done anyway until Congress reviewed the company's request to control a potentially navigable river. Senator Richard Coke and Congressman W. H. Crain, both of Texas, had agreed to promote the development with their fellow legislators. Therefore, everything was stalled until the decision was made.[14]

A Brazos River bill was placed into the hopper of the House of Representatives on 1 May, but it was not until 27 July that members gave their hesitant nod to the measure. The bill was next carried to the Senate, where on 1 August Richard Coke maneuvered it to passage without opposition. By 7 August both the speaker of the House and the Senate's president pro tempore had signed House Bill 10165, thereby passing it to the president for review.[15] But President Cleveland had expressed his reservations concerning the proposal.

Backers of the Galveston project had earlier argued that it was fiscally unwise to endorse a private, competing development only miles from the government's own investment and that conceding any constitutional privilege to a private outfit—in this instance, control of a navigable river—was always a bad precedent. Still, Cleveland had to balance these arguments against other considerations, not the least of which was that Senator Charles B. Farwell, part owner of the Capitol syndicate (XIT ranch), had spent nearly one hour at the White House personally lobbying on behalf of the bill. As Farwell explained, "Senator Coke [came] to me one day . . . and declared that unless I went to the president and told him of the importance of the work undertaken by the company the chances were good for a veto. I told the senator that it was not a common thing for a republican to go to a democrat and ask favors. . . ." But the president listened, and on 19 August a message was received by the speaker of the House noting that ". . . the bill . . . has become a law without his signature."[16]

Thus a major obstacle was hurdled, and it must have been an encouraged Lee who weeks later escorted all directors and company officers from Houston to an awaiting railroad coach for the inland journey through Brazoria County. The November visit marked the first time all shareholders had traveled together to the mouth of the river, and Lee would have used the opportunity to explain more fully his means for accomplishing the near impossible. Apparently some other difficulties had come to light, for during congressional debate the company had voted an additional outlay of one million dollars.[17] But Lee was committed to the scheme, and, not wanting loose ends, he began to sever all contacts with the cattle trade.

The first inkling of what was contemplated came near the end of July when residents of Miles City, Montana, took note of a sale of all LS stock and the transfer of company employees to Texas. In August advertisements even appeared in western journals announcing the imminent sale of Lee's herd of prized Angus. A first attempt to auction the lot at the Lincoln, Nebraska, state fair was cancelled when buyers did not arrive in the numbers anticipated; however, the sale was not stopped until twenty-one head had been sold for nearly $7,000. The next offer was far more profitable when, on two mornings in mid-November at Des Moines, Iowa, the balance of the herd—ninety-six animals in all—were auctioned for a total of $25,900. Lee must have regretted the loss but noted, "I have engaged in an enterprise on the Gulf of Mexico that will occupy my entire time for two or more years, and where it will be impossible for me to take my herd of 'doddies'. . . ."[18]

Shortly thereafter, on Christmas Eve day, both he and Ferguson contracted in Chicago with Gustav Wilke for construction of all facilities. Wilke, who was also the Capitol syndicate's contractor for building the new statehouse of Texas, agreed to begin his labors within ninety days, his first priority being to scour a channel twenty feet deep and one hundred feet wide at the mouth of the river. A working harbor was promised within two years, which, if not realized, required that all improvements revert to Lee. For these services, Wilke was paid $650,000 and an additional $200,000 in bonds, most pro-rated to set increases in channel depth.[19]

Wasting no time, on the morning of 9 January 1889 Wilke arrived at the Houston depot and immediately traveled south on a Columbia Tap coach. He was joined two days later by George Angle and Lee. Detractors of the project, such as Galveston's boosters, still doubted "whether the main object [is] to increase the value of land in the neighborhood or to establish a seaport. . . ." But even they had to concede that "nothing remains to be done but to go on and improve likewise. . . ."[20] General sympathies were more akin to the encouragements expressed by the editors of the *Houston Post*, who in their 17 January issue wrote:

> . . . a deep water harbor at the mouth of the Brazos has been definitely and absolutely decided upon. There is no longer any doubt about the matter. The contract has been let, all the preliminary arrangements for the great undertaking are being rushed through, and the work will be speedily commenced and carried to completion as rapidly as an army of laborers, unlimited means, and the most accomplished engineering skill, can do it. . . .[21]

The *Post* even went further and predicted that "by the triumph of this grand scheme, now an accomplished fact, Houston becomes the great city of Texas, with prospects and possibilities of soon becoming the leading business center and commercial metropolis of the South."[22] Whether the prophecy held true depended in good measure on Lee's untested skills.

George Angle accompanied the former stockman to Houston from the Brazos development on Tuesday night, 22 January, where they had hardly settled into a suite of rooms at the Capitol Hotel when both were confronted by a local reporter. Angle obliged with an interview.

"Do you really expect to see a new city at that point?" he was asked.

"You will see a city there the largest on the Gulf Coast," was the reply, "and it will spring up more rapidly than any city ever did in this country before. . . ."

"When do you propose to sell out some of your town lots?"

"Why, my dear sir, we could have sold them all long since if we cared to do so, but we have agreed not to place a foot of land on the market until the harbor is built and deep water is secured."

Other questions were asked, but neither Lee nor Angle probably paid them much attention until near the end of the interview.

"Where is Colonel Abner Taylor?"

Angle tried to evade the answer by responding, "I see by the papers that he is in Austin."

"As a matter of fact, is he not one of the projectors, if not the actual contractor, in this undertaking?"

Angle laughed. "He may have an interest in the project, but further than that I do not care to speak. All I need to tell you is, there is ample money at the back of those who have the work in hand, and it will go ahead from the jump without stop or hindrance."[23]

A full explanation of the last question—whether Lee had gone to the Farwell and Taylor syndicate for backing—was revealed on 27 March at the second annual meeting of the Brazos River Channel and Dock Company. Both Senator Charles B. Farwell and Congressman Abner Taylor were seated as two of an eleven-man board of directors.[24] Little attention, though, was paid the matter, as the curious were more interested to find space on crowded Columbia Tap coaches and the few river steamers plying the Brazos in order to witness the beginning of the state's first deep-water port. Finally, on 18 March, a spade was turned, and Gus Wilke promised that ". . . before January 12 [1890] large ocean steamers [will] safely cross the bar." It was a bold statement considering that the channel barely measured four and one-half feet deep.[25] Yet it was a start. Indeed, seemingly the entire state was soon caught up with the project.

When Thomas J. Hurley, a Farwell man and the dock company's new secretary, registered at Austin's Driskill Hotel on his return from the opening ceremonies, he was confronted by another reporter eager for still more details. "It is like a mining excitement to see the people rushing for the Brazos," Hurley offered. "As the railway and steamboat accommodations are insufficient, they are going in with wagons of all descriptions, many floating down on flatboats. With all the meager facilities for getting in material, thirty large buildings have been erected inside of thirty days, with scores of people camped on all sides in tents. . . . [Nowhere] outside of a great mining camp have I seen so much activity. . . ." Curious, the reporter asked if it was also true that J. D. Rockefeller had made a substantial investment in the scheme, but Hurley said no.[26]

At the Gulf itself, with crews moving machinery and material into place, an outline of construction began to take shape. Two jetties were still key to the project's design. Rows of five pilings would first be hammered sixteen feet into the sand, one post separated from the other by approximately eight feet of water, with another sixteen feet separating each row. As the rows built out into the Gulf, brush mattresses would next be tied to the posts and sunk by adding tons of rock. Once the foundation broke the water line, concrete blocks would "cap" each wall; only then would construction be complete. The plan called for one jetty to be separated from the other by merely 640 feet in order to constrict the Brazos into a narrow sluice. Upstream, wing dams would be built out from the riverbanks in order to direct the current through a confined waterway.[27] Then, if nature favored the project, a navigable channel was expected to result.

By the second week in April a pile driver had begun work pounding wooden posts into the offshore mud, followed by crews who submerged the first mattresses at the base of each row. By the end of May, two hundred tons of rock were also ready to be ferried out past the shoreline and dumped on top of the mattresses. It was a hard and slow job, but the effort continued uninterrupted so that by July an east wall was nearly three thousand feet into the Gulf and the west extension out approximately four thousand feet. The crews intended to be finished with all construction by fall. Although this was not to be, in September George Angle noted that "we now have nine feet on the bar at mean low tide . . ." and predicted that ". . . next spring we will have a steady channel twenty feet deep. . . ."[28] The remaining problems appeared to be merely logistical, and even those were slowly being resolved.

As anticipated, the Columbia Tap and the few available river steamers were inadequate to the job of transporting material to the site. Therefore, company officials voted to build their own railroad and barge system. A railroad, at first called the Brazos and Northern, would service the project from Houston, and men went into the field on 1 June to establish a route that would cut through Brazoria County. By late August, a surveyor's report had been prepared and submitted to Austin for state approval. By then the company had also purchased a refitted steamboat and five barges from a Galveston shipyard.[29]

Another problem was how to accommodate the company's several hundred workers. At first crews were housed in tents staked near the site; however, as lumber became available, hastily built shanties were erected as were more slowly assembled houses. A consequence was that the village of Quintana saw its population swell from about fifty residents at the beginning of 1889 to over seven hundred citizens; the same was true for the upriver community at Velasco. Of course, the usual boomtown establishments such as saloons and merchandisers were attracted to both settlements. Even another town, Angle, was established by local businessmen at a site about ten miles north of the river, conveniently beyond the dock company's control.[30] But Lee probably did not object.

In May, with construction under way, Lee's attention now turned to the problem of long-term financing, and for this he traveled to

Chicago and a meeting with Taylor. The congressman wanted to defer costs with a bond issue and suggested the Boston investment house of Potter, Lovell, and Company to underwrite the sale. Partners in the firm, notably Walter Potter, had proved useful in past dealings with the Chicago-based organization. A complication, however, was that at this time Potter was departing Boston for London and would not return until late summer, a time, Taylor noted, when American businesses also closed for a holiday. Taylor was worried that should the company authorize a sale now, Potter might be tempted to trade the instruments while in Europe. In any event, Lee promised delivery of five hundred bonds by 20 May and the remainder by the first of June; timing of the sale, if any, was left to Taylor's more expert judgment.[31]

By mid-August the Chicago congressman was frantically corresponding with Lee, for Potter, contrary to instructions, had indeed taken it upon himself to sell the newly delivered instruments on the London exchange. At first Taylor considered sending Hurley across the Atlantic, but the congressman reasoned that ". . . Potter could put him off probably with a nice breakfast. . . ." Therefore, Lee, then in Boston, was asked to make the trip himself because ". . . your interest would require that you should go to the bottom of everything, and when you [were] told they would accomplish certain things you would be able to demand of them the basis of which they form their opinion. . . . [A] breakfast would not have any influence on you. . . ."[32] But Lee had other matters on his mind and could ill afford the necessary one or two months out of the country. The problem was of the syndicate's making and therefore remained the syndicate's to resolve.

What most concerned Lee became apparent on 1 November, when construction at the Brazoria County site stopped. Meeting with Wilke at Houston's Capitol Hotel in early December, Lee called attention to their agreement and demanded reasons for the stall. Unpersuaded by Wilke's explanation, Lee announced his intention to exercise an option under the terms of the contract and assume control. The decision was ratified in Houston on 10 January 1890, when Lee, as president, paid out $90,000 in cash and $210,000 in bonds for Wilke's full surrender of the agreement. However, the exchange was nothing more than formality, as Lee had already ordered that work resume.[33]

When questioned by a *Post* reporter on the matter, Lee answered that "Mr. G. W. Angle, Resident Engineer Wisner and myself are going to the mouth of the Brazos to-morrow to receive the property from Mr. Wilke. We will have a full force of men there, commencing with next Monday, when we will employ every man we can find, and the more we get the better pleased we will be." By mid-January Lee was back in Houston promising deep water within three months. Toward that goal, Charles Clarke and Company of Galveston was contracted to freight one thousand tons of rock a week to the harbor as Lee also made a commitment to be present "a good deal of the time."[34] The near collapse of the project made his promise essentially a public obligation.

Yet optimism was warranted in light of the immediate surge in activity at the mouth of the river. By 11 April over ten thousand cords of brush had been cut and were waiting to be sunk into the jetties, as were fifty carloads of rock parked on a spur near the Columbia depot. Untangling the congestion would be the job of the company's new jetty superintendent, Fred Brock, who arrived at the riverside camps that same week. With the Brazos now rising, it was hoped that the current would finally clear all obstructions from between the two walls. Even more significantly, the site had quite suddenly taken on the appearance of a port.

The *Lead Rivers*, an inbound steamer from New Orleans, had docked that day so that its boilers might be cleaned before continuing on to Tampico, Mexico, while a nearby Galveston steamer, the *Whitewater*, discharged passengers and equipment. A company steamer, the *Seminole*, had also arrived towing barges of rock and brush in its wake as the sloop *George H.* worked its way through the narrow entrance to a makeshift wharf.[35] It was precisely what Lee had promised when he took charge.

Two men in particular were impressed. Charles Goodnight and H. B. Stoddard, both well-known cattlemen, had spent nearly two weeks at Velasco inspecting the harbor as a potential site for a refrigerated beef-packing plant. Yet progress on the channel was so much more advanced than either anticipated that both joined in a statement on the subject when interviewed in Houston. "The question of deep water on the Texas coast," one said, ". . . will be settled in a very short time. . . . Thirty or forty more good working days will enable them to cross the bar with a line of their jetties . . . and together they are forming there a harbor of great capacity that will compare with any in the world. . . . The indications now are, and we firmly believe this will be the first deep water port procured on the Texas coast. . . ."[36] As the cattle trade was very much in Lee's thoughts when the project began, the praise must have been gratifying.

Therefore, it was a confident Lee who rode the deck of the revenue cutter *Dix* on 19 May as it eased over the fourteen feet of water marked above the bar. On board were representatives of the Missouri, Kansas, and Texas railroad who could not help but to be impressed as an enthusiastic shoreside crowd cheered when the cutter turned its bow upriver in order to dock at a company wharf. This was the first steamer of its class to enter the Brazos and the first to sail so far inland. Indeed, Lee was so buoyed by the feat that he now accepted Taylor's offer to promote the scheme in Europe. Consequently, near the end of May he departed Leavenworth with reservations on a White Star ship bound for London, and on 4 June Lina received a telegram confirming his safe crossing of the Atlantic.[37] The once-improbable harbor was almost a reality.

Lee was absent for over two months, and when he returned to the mouth of the river he found that significant progress had been made. Three tugs were now being used to haul material to the jetties, where sixteen hundred cords of brush and twelve hundred tons of rock were placed on the walls weekly. As a result, the east jetty was nearly complete, and the west wall lacked only three hundred feet to its full extension. Even a new company-run town near Velasco was planned.[38] Therefore, Lee must have read with disbelief a late August report sent from Boston that the syndicate's underwriters Potter, Lovell, and Company were nearly bankrupt.

But evidence of a collapse, although sketchy at first, continued to mount. At one point it was even speculated that over $2 million of syndicate money was involved, with $700,000 said to have been lost by Lee, Taylor, and the banker J. Otis Wetherbee alone. No wonder, then, that ". . . Taylor [was found] sick in Washington with two doctors attending him. . . ." Lee, although "excited" by the news, held his composure long enough to board a train bound north to the congressman's Washington office. Once at the capital, "when asked what effect the Boston failure would have on the harbor improvement, . . . Lee said it was impossible now to foretell. . . . He was [there] for consultation with his coadjutors, and would be able to tell better after the conference."[39]

Neither man later recalled their assuredly tense conversations, but by the time of Lee's departure for Boston, Taylor gave reassurance to an anxious financial community that he was ". . . willing and able to pay every piece of paper he [was] on that Lee and Ferguson [could not] pay." The outstanding defaults were then estimated at $300,000, for which Lee anticipated "some counter suits against Potter, Lovell & Co." The situation, however, demanded only one solution, and on 8 September, having returned to the harbor, both Lee and Ferguson applied for receivership. Two days later a U.S. district judge granted the petition, with George Angle and Frank Caldwell named as receivers. The court's order specified that the two ". . . prosecute with diligence the construction and completion of said jetties . . . ,"[40] but Lee had to surrender all personal control of the scheme.

There was some consolation when, on 15 September, Walter Potter and Wallace D. Lovell were taken from their Boston offices and transported to a city court where both were arraigned for embezzling another company's funds.[41] Yet even that allegation was dismissed when parties to the suit accepted an out-of-court settlement.[42] The arrangement probably satisfied those eager to silence speculation concerning the Brazos project's solvency, but it did little to vindicate Lee.

Instead, the Kansas merchant was forced to stand aside and watch as legal expenses grew to include $11,000 in attorneys' fees and $27,500 claimed by the receivers. His most heartrending day was Saturday, 29 November, when both he and Lina sold their community interest in the LS to Lucien Scott for ". . . $1 . . . and other various sums received. . . ."[43] For the moment he could do nothing more than observe as years of hard work dissolved.

One of the more culpable parties to the collapse, Charles Farwell, was far more confident of his position. Accompanied to Houston in March 1891 by Taylor, Angle, Wisner, and Lee, he did not attempt to avoid the *Post's* staff reporter.

"It is a good scheme," he answered to a question that touched on his involvement with the project, "and will certainly be a success. . . . It pleased me very much, and I shall invest in the company and push the enterprise as much as I can. . . ."

And when, the reporter asked, would town lots be offered to the public?

"I cannot say . . . ," Farwell responded. "We are now grading the streets and laying off the town site, and it will be some time this summer before the first sale of lots is held. . . ."[44]

Farwell's use of "we" certainly did not go unnoticed. Indeed, barely one month later Lee also hesitantly answered a reporter's questions.

"I have just visited the river," he said, "and the water in it is very high. This is what we needed to scour out the channel across the bar. We have sixteen feet now, and when the high water in the river subsides it will have been increased to twenty feet. Of this I am as certain as that day will follow darkness."

He then addressed the subject of a new town. "We shall proceed at once with our new hotel, which will cost $50,000, and it must be completed within ninety days. The jetties will be raised and the caps put on as soon as possible, as the work of securing deep water is practically finished."[45]

Actually Lee had not addressed all particulars: a reinstated Gus

Wilke had negotiated the construction of a four-storied, two-wing hotel at the "new" company town of Velasco. To the question of when property would be sold, Lee answered, "It will not be later than July. Our hotel will then be finished, and we will be at work on the railroad extension."[46]

The hotel was not opened in July as promised. However, the syndicate's infusion of money gave the stalled project new life, and even the moribund Columbia Tap began to schedule daily excursions from Houston to waiting steamers bound for Velasco. Once arrived—and the trip still took a tedious eight hours—the visitor docked on the east bank at a site about three miles north from the mouth of the river where the outline of several town blocks had been meted out by newly graded dirt streets.[47]

Most work now centered on raising a syndicate office building at "new" Velasco, with a mountain of lumber, over 650,000 feet, lying nearby waiting to be used for docks, wharves, and at the company's promised hotel. The jetties were also nearly complete (both needing to be capped), with each extending more than one mile into the Gulf.[48]

Yet Lee was not one to fool himself. As he wrote his longtime friend W. B. Munson, "We have been forced to place part of our property on the market reserving alternate Blocks for a Public Sale to be held in October. . . ." Toward that end twenty or more buildings were under construction, and negotiations were in progress that, if successful, would tie Velasco to New York by ship.[49] Therefore, enthusiasm was justified if guarded. But the inescapable fact was that without Farwell's backing the project could not have survived. It had been years since Lee was beholding to any man, yet that was his current—if unpleasant—circumstance.

All indications, though, pointed to success, and an important endorsement came on 7 July when the secretary of the treasury telegraphed the U.S. customs officer at Galveston that "in view of the fact that the water over the bar at your port is not of sufficient depth for vessels of certain draught, such vessels, although foreign, may be allowed to go to Velasco." Almost immediately large-masted ships made for the Brazos harbor, and by the end of July the first ocean-rigged vessel, the *Vidette*, inbound with nine hundred tons of coal from Philadelphia, docked at a company wharf. Soon the river on both banks was ". . . an array of shipping . . . [with] three-masters, square riggers, sloops, lumber schooners, tugs, steamboats, all lying along the wharves. . . ." To acknowledge its status, the company proclaimed its deep channel as "a fact, not a promise . . ." and Velasco as "the only harbor on the Texas coast. . . ."[50]

Accordingly, attention now turned from the jetties to upgrading portside facilities. A contract to build more permanent docks and wharves was let during the first week in August as simultaneously the company moved from its Quintana offices into a new, two-storied building at Velasco; Lee was assigned one of the ten first-floor rooms. Advance sales of selected lots were also brisk, with a cumulative total of nearly $300,000 paid by mid-summer. But the job was not finished, and as one resident observed, "There is no first class place here—nor any place else for that matter where deep water can be had to build a town. . . ." Still, he continued, "[Velasco] is a better layout than Galveston. . . ." And with "people . . . pouring in from all other *would be* Deep Water places," with crews working hard to repair an unexpected break in the jetties, it was little wonder that many looked with pride on the development. As Lee himself wrote, "We are a lively place for *only* 8 weeks [of] existence. . . ."[51]

The boom continued, and by fall all manner of businesses and homes had been built. Velasco's population approached nearly fifteen hundred residents. The company's most touted addition, the one-hundred-room Hotel Velasco, finally opened on 5 October and lived up to expectations with its spacious rooms centered toward the Gulf of Mexico. However, the best news came earlier, on 21 August, when the Brazos River Channel and Dock Company passed out of receivership and back into Lee's hands.[52]

As might be expected, then, it was an enthusiastic company president who during the first week in November escorted Brazos visitors through the jetties and up the coast to the nearby Surf Side Beach. Lee could point with satisfaction to the seventeen and one-half feet of water now under the boat's keel, which easily slipped over the bar. He could also point out to his guests the pleasant strip of white sand that the syndicate hoped one day to develop into a South Texas recreation site. For that reason an electric steetcar line had been graded from the center of an even larger road, the Velasco Terminal Railway, which was finally organized in July. Capitalized at $600,000, the line had a ten-member board that included Lee, Ferguson, Angle, and Taylor.[53] The plan was that once the Velasco road was connected to Houston, either the International and Great Northern, the Santa Fe, or the Katy would tie into the system and thereby anchor Velasco to the important commercial centers of the Midwest.[54]

Ground was broken for a depot on 26 October, three months after another crew had staked out a grade to Houston. It was not until early November, however, that contracts were let for water stations and other small roadhouses along the line. Meanwhile, a dockside pile of railroad ties had grown into the thousands, while on 8 November residents watched as the *Mollie Mohr* towed one locomotive and several rail cars to a Velasco slip. The equipment was on loan to the Velasco from the International road, and had been moved on barges downriver from the Columbia Tap depot. About the only material not on hand were steel rails, and Lee expected delivery of even those very soon. The delay, though, mandated another postponement of the advertised property sale until December. The harbor remained an expensive but impractical investment without its complementary rail system.[55]

In that regard, more than fifteen hundred miles to the east, two large steamships, the *Brixham* and the *Czarina*, had set sail in mid-October from Philadelphia loaded with the rails that would link Velasco to Houston. It was not anticipated that the transfer would be of any great duration. Nevertheless, as the *Brixham* rounded Cape Hatteras off the coast of North Carolina, it encountered heavy seas that slowed passage considerably. The *Brixham* met with further delay when it encountered the English freighter *Chatfield* adrift, its propeller and shaft broken. After towing the crippled vessel into port, the *Brixham* discovered that it too was damaged and sailed for repairs at the Norfolk, Virginia, shipyard. Strangely, however, no one bothered to communicate these difficulties to the syndicate's officials.[56]

But even if they had been informed, company officers at the mouth of the Brazos River were probably too busy to give much attention to the crisis. Carpenters, stevedores, and real estate hucksters were swarming into Velasco while ships of every size and type, from scows to three-masted schooners, lined the banks near the new town. One day in particular stood out.

On Tuesday, 16 November, a large crowd gathered near the wharves at the corner of Third and Avenue C, where a tall and rather proud Yankee stood out from all the commotion. Next to Lee was a large bale of cotton, rolled into Velasco that day by Uncle Si, a farmer from nearby Oyster Creek. It was the first bale to be delivered to port officials, and several suggested that a collection be taken to buy the bale as a souvenir of the day. Uncle Si would not hear of it. He had personally guided Lee through these parts two years ago, before any of the newcomers had arrived, and he was determined that his cotton would be sold to no one but Lee. The contractor then ceremoniously handed the man a fifty-dollar gold piece while promising to enshrine the bale as a memento of this first in Velasco's history.[57]

For Lee, 16 November was not a bad day, all told. The last of his railroad construction cars had that day been moved to dry land; plans for another hotel, the Surf Side, had been announced; and work on an artesian well for the present hotel had started. With the land company having passed out of receivership in October and its assets fixed at approximately $2 million, Lee's usual confidence had returned. If he did not actually own the project, he was at least in control. This was especially satisfying, as literally all roads now led to Velasco. Indeed, the syndicate had contracted with several large railroads offering reduced fares to the harbor in anticipation of the December sale.[58] The only missing element remained Velasco's connection to the main lines.

But for Captain John Sheldrake, the forty-one-year veteran at the helm of the *Brixham*, it had been a voyage in which one problem compounded another. After leaving the Norfolk dry dock, he had headed his ship south down the Atlantic Coast, where it almost immediately sailed into another gale. From that moment high winds and violent seas dogged its wake until it finally turned west through the Florida straits. A lighthouse passed on starboard (the last American station) was the first hope that calmer waters lay ahead. Then, only twelve miles out of Key West and in the dead of night, the ship unexpectedly ground to a stop. It had hit a reef known locally as the Western Dry Rocks, and a large hole had been ripped in the forward watertight compartment. Worse yet, the *Brixham* was locked to the reef.

At dawn, while Sheldrake and crew puzzled over how to free the ship, a flotilla of eighteen schooners began to encircle the vessel. The ships were manned by crews who called themselves Key West Wreckers, and they demanded the *Brixham*'s surrender. It took considerable persuasion, but Sheldrake was finally able to convince these nineteenth-century brigands that it would be possible to strike a deal. They wanted booty; therefore, he suggested, why not take some of the cargo? This would also serve his need to lighten the ship.

After lifting thirty-three bars of iron and twenty bundles of fishplate from the hold—a total haul of some sixteen tons of metal—the wreckers finally set sail. The *Brixham* was also loose of the reef. But it again had to put into port for repairs.

With some trouble it steamed into Key West to drain the flooded compartment. After two days of attempting to get a borrowed pump to work, the unit was disassembled, only to find it clogged with forty pairs of women's stockings—cargo, Sheldrake thought, no doubt stolen from another ship. When the water was finally bailed, the captain found an eight-foot hole bashed into the hull of his ship. A crew of "honest wreckers" was hired to patch the damage; but within hours these same men stopped work and demanded a wage of six thousand dollars. With the rejection of a compromise salary of thirty-five hundred dollars, Sheldrake felt obliged to remain in port until the matter was settled by an impartial authority. It was not until 19 November that a telegram was received at Velasco informing Lee that the *Brixham* had been dry-docked and that the *Czarina* was also undergoing repairs at the Charleston, South Carolina, harbor. The man's reaction can be imagined.[59]

The message, however, would have been welcome news to another group of men meeting behind locked doors at Denver's Windsor Hotel. Members of Galveston's deep-water committee had been debating the advent of a harbor at the mouth of the Brazos River, and it was no secret that the bay community cherished the privilege of deep water for itself alone. As a Houston newspaper explained, Galveston's boosters ". . . [had] lobbied and spent money freely in Washington to prevent the Brazos River Channel and Dock Company from permission to make a harbor . . . and when it passed, it set to work and let fly a fusilade [*sic*] of lies about the possible depth of water . . . , the progress of the city and the health of the community. . . ." Now, while bemoaning Velasco as "no more than a plaything," a committeeman at the Denver meeting proposed another congressional lobby to stall Velasco's "grand sale."[60] But Lee and his fellow investors could no longer be put off.

It was a few minutes before 10:00 A.M. on 16 December when officials of the Brazos River Channel and Dock Company finally entered a large tent and mounted the platform reserved for the occasion. Accompanying the party were Senator Farwell and Congressman Taylor. Before the auctioneer could gavel the crowd to order, Taylor stepped up to the podium and indicated that he wanted to speak. He was greeted by cheers. "I can only talk business to you today," he began, ". . . [and] I direct your attention to the fact that the men who undertook and succeeded in this enterprise are not only of mature experience in business, but are men . . . who have never failed in anything they started out to do. . . . They came here to succeed, and you see for yourselves that they have done so beyond any question. . . ."[61]

Then, having completed his introduction, the auctioneer stepped forward and brought down a gavel that opened the sale. The first lot offered was Number 12 in Block 14 fronting on Avenue B and South Second Street. It opened to a call of $2,000 and quickly rose to $3,000 before it was knocked off to Dr. S. W. Fields, a local physician. Milling in the crowd was a familiar face, that of Robert M. Wright, who must have felt a personal sense of amazement. Twenty years ago he, a Cheyenne chief, and the organizer of this project had waited out a crowd of drunken buffalo hunters in the back room of a Dodge City residence.[62] Now, at slightly before 11:00 A.M., Lee was dedicating the first operational deep-water port of Texas. For both, it had been an eventful two decades.

By late afternoon over $100,000 in sales had entered company ledgers. However, enthusiasm waned and officials looked for something unusual to renew interest in the venture. The captain of the schooner *John B. Butterick* overheard the complaint and suggested that potential buyers be invited to an excursion on the Gulf. The offer was seized, and authorization for the sail came within hours as word spread quickly that the tall ship would leave port on a free tour.[63]

Early Thursday morning, 17 December, a cold north wind could not keep over three hundred people from congregating near the docks where the *Butterick* was moored. Then at precisely 8:00 A.M. the tug *Seminole* docked beside the three-masted ship; by 8:30 A.M. both were coupled and turned toward the jetties and the open sea. The Gulf had calmed as a hearty breeze blew from landward; the captain expected an uneventful sail.[64]

The *Seminole* did not signal the excursionists' return until noon. Coincidentally, the *Butterick* sailed through the jetties just as the syndicate's artesian-well crew struck water with a thirty-seven-foot geyser shooting skyward. Even the company's landlocked railroad engine greeted the return with a high-pitched whistle. Whatever excitement had been lost was now rekindled.[65]

When the sale reopened at 2:00 P.M., the scheduled auctioneer was "too ill" to continue, and in his stead O. W. Crawford, the company's advertising agent, came to the podium with gavel in hand. In slightly more than one hour Crawford nailed down approximately $165,000 worth of business. The distinction of high bidder went to J. A. McClennan of Chicago, who promised to locate a $50,000 grain elevator at the port. Watching it all from the sidelines was a tall, quiet, blue-eyed man who, much to the crowd's disappointment, ordered the sales closed for the day. But it was only a temporary measure, and the auction would continue as long as there were buyers and available lots.[66]

Capping the week's events was the sighting of the *Brixham's* stacks on Tuesday evening, 22 December, as it turned to move through the jetties and up the Brazos River. The *Czarina* anchored five days later. The final touch, though, did not come until a month later, when at precisely 4:00 P.M. on Wednesday, 27 January 1892, Lee stepped forward to bring a hammer down on the last spike to complete the Velasco Terminal Railway. With the swing a loud spontaneous cheer went up from most spectators, signaling that the port was finally linked to Houston and the harbor opened to international trade. Lee had literally given the final blow to a month of activities during which nearly $1.5 million worth of property had been sold and more than three hundred new buildings promised. Even more important, the development had already attracted $800,000 in exportable merchandise. There remained only one last detail, and on the afternoon of 1 February Lee boarded a railroad coach bound for Austin.[67] Cattlemen were meeting at the state's capital, and Lee had earlier accepted an invitation to announce completion of the scheme to his old associates.

However, he first indulged himself in the comforts of Austin's plush Driskill Hotel. For once even the curiosity of local reporters did not bother him; in fact, Lee welcomed the publicity. "I could not resist the temptation," he said, "to come here and shake hands with my old friends and assure them that I was still working in the stockmen's interest, inasmuch as I have been somewhat instrumental in giving them an outlet to the markets of the world for their livestock and livestock products. My opinion is that a deep water port on the coast of Texas is the hope of the livestock interest of the Southwest. . . ." Lee was in a rare mood that day as he continued with the interview. "Velasco is today the only port on the Gulf coast where there is enough water to handle such vessels as are required in this traffic and will be the only one for years to come," he boasted, "if indeed it is not the only one that will ever be secured on the Texas coast. . . ."[68] At fifty years of age and in the prime of his years, it was a very special hour for this former Indian trader and Texas cattleman.

CHAPTER SEVEN

Tugs & Barges

H. C. Rouse, chief executive officer of the Missouri, Kansas, and Texas Railway Company, had it within his power to realize Velasco's grandest dream: that of becoming an international port of trade. Consequently, Lee obligingly spent three long hours on Sunday, 27 March 1892, escorting his guest among the wharves, jetties, and rail facilities at the site.[1] And there was much to commend Velasco as the Katy's principal terminus on the Gulf.

During February the first trains began to arrive from Houston over the newly completed railroad. This event coincided with another arrangement—one between European steamship companies and syndicate officials to open a line of ocean freighters across the Atlantic. Wilke had negotiated the deal whereby an initial test of the service would be undertaken by the steamship *Austerlitz*, which had already left Halifax and was due at Velasco's docks during the first week of April. The ship would load the approximately five thousand bales of cotton now stored in a company warehouse before starting its return run to Liverpool. Anticipating success, the company had contracted to build six barges for servicing the new trade. Lee even talked of organizing another railroad—tentatively called the Velasco, Henrietta, and Kansas City—which would tie in with the Rock Island, the Fort Worth and Denver City, and the Katy at another terminus near Henrietta.[2]

But as to connecting its main line with Velasco, the Katy still waivered. As J. Waldo, company vice-president, put it, "The road may be built to Velasco or Galveston or to both. Mr. Rouse, chairman of the board of directors, . . . is the only one authorized to finally act in the matter. . . ." Yet Rouse gave no indication of that decision while inspecting the Brazos with Lee. What bothered the man was locating so important a terminal at a site wholly controlled by another company.[3]

In contrast, foreign investors were more optimistic of Velasco's future, and the *Austerlitz* arrived in port as anticipated on 6 April. The docking came only one day after Congress approved the harbor as a subport of entry. Then, on the morning of 23 April, after 5,400 bales of cotton and 400,000 pounds of cottonseed were loaded into its hold, the flag-bedecked steamer again sailed through the jetties to begin the return leg of the run from Great Britain.[4]

A consequence of a successful passage was that on the fifth and sixth of July, shipping agents in Liverpool, Bremen (Germany), and New Orleans affixed their signatures to commercial documents guaranteeing trade between Velasco and European markets. On behalf of the syndicate Lee signed an agreement that promised fifteen steamships for the Atlantic crossing to Texas. Immediately after the signing, Lee departed New Orleans for New York, where rumor had it that John D. Rockefeller would pen another deal to route ships from the East Coast to the Velasco docks.[5]

Each contract added to the excitement felt throughout company ranks, bolstered by the Terminal Railway's first annual report. Filed in June, it showed that in only five months 3,588 tons of assorted merchandise had been shipped over the new line. With cattlemen still touting Velasco as a place to locate a refrigerated packing plant and the Katy rumored to be extending its rails to the harbor, it was no wonder that little attention was given to the opinion of a few that "the d——d Syndicate appears to be entirely out of funds. . . ." More obvious were the active solicitations of steamship broker J. Moeller inquiring about harbor depth and warehouse capacity; the hiring of Charles Clarke and Company from Galveston to organize stevedores; and the formation of a longshoremen's union. Doubts concerning the syndicate were forgotten by late September, when the steamship *Blue Star* left port loaded with 3,000 bales of cotton and 2,100 tons of oil cake, all bound for Europe. The ship was followed into port by two other vessels, each scheduled to be loaded with similar cargoes for the Atlantic voyage. The wholesale value of the products stored in the holds of all three ships was said to total nearly $300,000.[6]

But on occasion Lee must have privately wondered if everything was as it should be. Indications of a problem again surfaced in November when several property owners petitioned that ". . . the pledges made by the syndicate . . . be carried out in good faith and that a first-class city . . . be built." The complaint—pointedly carried only by the Galveston press—was eventually answered by syndicate agents who noted that "the only boom or what could be called one was made by the speculators in Velasco town lots . . . [but it] was short-lived, as all such booms ought to be."[7] Surprisingly, the retort satisfied most.

However, while inspecting the site in February 1893, Lee also found work at the harbor slowed. Therefore, despite bad weather, crews were pushed day and night to lay the last mattresses before an expected rise in river depth. The hope was that a swifter current would clear the mouth of silt. Maintaining a channel was critical, for during the preceding months another seven ships had left port with more than $750,000 in cargo. Yet even this sizable trade still did not work to Velasco's advantage with the vital trunk railroads. Again in March the project's organizer left his visiting wife and son at Hotel Velasco in order to escort still doubting Katy officials along the banks and bends of the Brazos.[8] Although no one publicly addressed the subject, enthusiasm had waned.

C. B. Farwell, during an April visit, did his best to project optimism. To a reporter's questions he good-naturedly responded, ". . . I have just as much confidence as ever in the success of the deep water project. The proof of it is in the fact that I am putting more money in down there." But the man's confidence was partly a facade, for at the annual stockholders' meeting held only days earlier an important change had taken place. Abner Taylor was voted president of the organization, with Lee demoted to the vice-presidency.[9] Although obscured by Farwell's promise of additional funds, the move underscored the dominance of the syndicate's agents in the project.

Still, Lee had hopes of international trade rescuing him from the downturn in affairs. During the months of May and June 1893, another six steamers arrived at Velasco, each to be loaded with cotton. Furthermore, another international agreement worth $1.75 million was ready to be signed. Such details must have offset even the most pessimistic reports, including the June accounting by the Terminal Railway which, although boasting a substantial increase in business (14,000 passengers; 29,000 tons of freight), reflected net revenues of only $9,000. Along with the line's meager earnings also surfaced a report that the International and Great Northern had acquired a thirty-day option to purchase the line. For days Lee attempted to suppress the story, and he was barely saved embarrassment by a timely dispute between the International and the Katy over acquisition of a Galveston-to-Houston service that ironically touted Velasco as the alternate port of trade. Still, all differences paled beside the simple fact that only Velasco had deep-water capability. As the British captain of the steamship *Stelia* noted while loading cotton oil for transport to Hamburg, "The Mouth of the Brazos is certainly the great port of this part of the coast."[10]

But Velasco's syndicate was a diverse entity needing constant outlays of capital. Indeed, since the collapse of Potter and Lovell's brokerage firm in 1890, the Brazos River scheme was a particular drain on resources. This is perhaps why in 1891 even Lee opted to sell lots months before the harbor was finished. Yet revenues received were merely a stopgap, and by the summer of 1893 "the only work done [at Velasco] was in the repair of the jetties, and this only to a very slight extent." Syndicate men were even observed doing the unthinkable—borrowing—"no doubt to tide over the present money stringency. . . ."[11] Quite simply, by 1894 the company was financially strapped.

Consequently, a retiring Mac Lee returned to Velasco during the first days of October from visits with stockholders in Boston, New York, and Chicago. To questions put to him by an inquisitive reporter he answered, "Before I left the East the reorganization of the companies developing this port has been completed, and money is now in our hands to carry out our original designs as quickly as possible." He added that "while completing and capping the Brazos jetties with all speed, dredging will be carried on and the remaining shallow places will thereby be deepened to over eighteen feet at low tide. . . ."[12] Again, the import of the statement was probably lost with the revelation that still more capital had been found to sustain the investment. But sacrifices were inevitable.

Throughout December, unfamiliar businessmen began to arrive in Velasco, where each asked to individually probe and inspect the development. Then on Tuesday, 18 December, the strangers secluded themselves inside a Velasco office where notes were compared. The predictable outcome was that ". . . the men who put the money into the enterprise now [took] hold. . . ." Lee was able to hold his position as director of the land company, but he could no longer sit as a board member on either the Terminal Railway or the parent Brazos River Channel and Dock Company.[13]

Abner Taylor aptly put his finger on the problem. "The trouble heretofore," he said, "was that too much was undertaken at once." That Velasco had the distinction of being the state's foremost harborage did not pay the bills, and it was perhaps a discouraged Lee who passed through Houston en route to Leavenworth, Kansas, on 22 December.[14] For the only time in his life, a challenge was not met.

On 9 February 1895, almost seven years to the day from the start of the Brazos project, Lee again registered at Austin's Driskill Hotel, his spirits somewhat rejuvenated. The charter of the Velasco Construction Company would be filed in two days, thereby enabling him and three others to organize a new Gulf transport and shipping line.

But for the first time a company of which he was a principal investor would be formed without his name entered as either a director or a company officer. There were anxious moments when a dredge leased from the Mexico Central Railroad capsized while being towed to the river, drowning four passengers and a crew of five. However, the barges *Lee, Ferguson,* and *Kossack* continued to haul the tons of rock consigned to the new company. Then, when the Brazos receded from its annual rise, another dredge was put to work moving silt from between the two walls. Lee even found the time to travel to the small harbor at Orange, an outlet used by East Texas lumbermen, in an attempt to charter a tug. Although he was not able to come to terms with local owners, the visit gave him an opportunity to investigate this rival to Velasco's monopoly.[15]

Orange was located approximately one hundred miles east of the Brazos River on the elongated sixteen-mile Sabine Lake, with the city of Beaumont its closest neighbor. As recently as October 1894, Sabine Pass promoters had announced their intention of creating a harbor at the narrow seven-mile neck where the lake emptied into the Gulf. As at Velasco, it was hoped that jetties would eventually open a navigable channel to shipping. The work was barely eight months along when Lee arrived; yet its early progress certainly did not go unnoticed. Assuredly it took his mind from more personal affairs at Velasco, where syndicate officials had stripped him of all remaining interest in the scheme.[16]

Still, Lee's immediate priority was the acquisition of a tug, and after three days at home, in September he and his wife departed Kansas for New York, where he expected to broker for a vessel. Three weeks later Velasco was introduced to the ninety-foot tug *Stella,* purchased at a cost of $15,000 and promised as "one of the largest and most powerful towing vessels in the Gulf. . . ." It was soon apparent why Lee was so persistent in the acquisition, for with the *Stella* he had the leverage needed to demand a renegotiation of his Velasco contract. Therefore, almost immediately he visited the mouth of the Brazos camps and ordered all towing and dredging stopped. Then, to dramatize the issue, as soon as the *Stella* moored he dispatched it on hauls other than those syndicate-related. Indeed, in October his entire "fleet" of tugs and barges weighed anchor for Morgan City, Louisiana. And for the next few months the vessels were used to tow bargeloads of lumber from the East Texas mills to freighters docked at Galveston.[17] The less than subtle message was undoubtedly understood by those who now controlled Velasco.

For his part, Lee was content to trade at other ports, and on 2 December even Velasco Construction had its name changed to the broader-sounding Gulf Towing Company. If syndicate officials were not yet alarmed, they surely must have frowned on the December meeting between Lee and a Sabine Pass contractor who had plans "of selling out to him." As there remained only one-half mile of rock and capping to complete the Sabine jetties, even Galveston now acknowledged the upstart as "her greatest rival as the seaport of Texas. . . ." But perhaps as disturbing to the syndicate was that in November another site had been located only miles inland from the mouth of Sabine Lake and, using the name Port Arthur, had announced its intention of laying out a competing deep-water port.[18] Therefore, if Lee and his company took on the work at Sabine Pass, two additional harbors might open to challenge the Brazos investment.

Apparently Lee had such a scheme in mind, for in December three barges and two tugs were mortgaged for $10,000. Perhaps it was only coincidence, but earlier a Sabine Pass contractor had estimated that a $12,000 investment would complete the work.[19] The syndicate, therefore, had to decide whether to meet Lee's terms or face the likelihood of other developments sharing his expertise.

On Christmas Day of 1895, rumors circulated throughout Velasco indicating that Lee and the syndicate had agreed to a contract that would complete the jetties. Speculation was brief, for on the following day it was confirmed that "the Gulf towing company's plant, consisting of the tug Stella and several barges, which [had] been at work at Sabine Pass and Calcasieu [Louisiana, had] been ordered [to Velasco] . . . at once . . ." On 31 December Lee and members of the syndicate even rode the *Stella* together for an inspection of the nearly complete facilities.[20] However, the point had been made. As the *Houston Post* editorialized on 27 December, "Velasco is to be congratulated not only on the resumption of work, but that the contract has been placed in the hands of such men as compose the company of Lee & Ferguson. These gentlemen have the practical experience, and the required amount of energy and business management to make any of their undertakings a success. . . ."[21] The entire episode was reminiscent of past disputes with buffalo hunters, Texas Rangers, and outlaws.

Still, the year of forced absence from syndicate boardrooms gave Lee the incentive to continue with his tug and barge system, in which profits could be made just by playing off the jealousies of competing ports along the Texas and Louisiana coasts. Therefore, stripped of his obligation to protect Velasco's monopoly, in February 1896 Lee contracted to build an east jetty at Calcasieu Pass which, when finished, would open Lake Charles to the deep-water trade. A similar deal was also penned at Velasco in February, and in April

Lee acquired the rights to complete the jetties at Sabine Pass.[22]

The day of greatest personal satisfaction, however, came on 10 April as Lee watched the last blocks put into place on Velasco's two walls. Of course, any real sense of contribution to the project's success had been robbed from him by East Coast bankers; even more discouraging were reports that the syndicate was bargaining with Massachusetts senator Henry Cabot Lodge for government control of the facility.[23] Yet Velasco had its deep-water channel.

Nonetheless, Lee must have been anxious to distance himself from the scheme. Therefore, he and his crews immediately traveled approximately 150 miles east along the Gulf Coast to Calcasieu Pass, where equipment had been relocated and the men prepared to start work at a different site.[24] The same contractor who once boasted that Velasco would be the region's only deep-water port was determined to disprove his own claim.

At Calcasieu an east jetty already extended 7,300 feet into the Gulf, but portions of the wall had slipped into the channel, causing an accumulation of mud and debris. This, in addition to a sandbar at the mouth of the waterway, made navigation from Lake Charles to the open sea almost impossible. Lee examined the locale while visiting the site during March 1896, after which he probably agreed with an earlier estimate that repairs might total as much as $500,000. Apparently unconcerned, however, crews were ordered into place and work begun, although a Louisiana senator ominously favored another location as an international port of trade. An additional problem was that the congressional bill to fund construction also contained a provision to repurchase Velasco's improvements, a measure adamantly opposed by President Cleveland.[25]

Overriding his veto, Congress released $80,000 of an appropriated $315,000 for immediate repairs of the Calcasieu jetty. Thus financed, the Gulf Towing Company worked throughout that summer to finish a single wall, and by late August another crew had begun work on a second extension. Only when Congress began to tighten the appropriation did Lee stop work.[26]

The man faced similar difficulties at Sabine Pass. When Lee arrived at a construction camp on 28 May, he found that a twenty-four-foot channel had already been dredged between two walls and that only an estimated six thousand tons of granite needed to be hauled into place. As a result, ships regularly docked at the new town rising near the mouth of the pass. Even Lake Charles businessmen freighted the approximate fifty miles to this East Texas harbor and would continue to do so until a deep channel had been opened through the Calcasieu narrows. During late spring of 1896, Port Arthur, Sabine's nearest competitor, was only a few wooden shacks cramped near a recently built three-storied hotel.[27] Therefore, when the Sabine Pass operators completed their channel, they might properly consider themselves the most likely rival to both Velasco and Galveston.

But again Congress equivocated, and the Sabine works were placed on a "continuing contract" whereby funds could be spent only when government agents certified a need. Thus, while overriding the president's veto, barely $75,000 was made available for construction. Yet of this sum a large percentage probably went into the coffers of the Gulf Towing Company for its work at the site. However, by mid-September, with both walls extended nearly two and one-half miles into the Gulf, work was halted as officials debated the next stage of development.[28]

Lee was caught in the predicament. But since there was little he could do, he packed up and traveled north for a vacation with his wife and son. When he returned to the coast in November, the government was still equivocating. In fact, an engineering team had arrived in Beaumont at about the same time as he, and they were only then beginning to survey the needs of both the Sabine and Calcasieu passes. Thus delayed, during early December Lee even traveled to syndicate offices at Velasco in order to convince another team of government surveyors to purchase the works. All the while his barges were kept busy hauling lumber from the Orange and Beaumont mills to ships harbored at either Sabine Pass or at Galveston.[29]

Contracts were awarded in January 1897, with Charles Clarke and Company of Galveston tapped to work the west Calcasieu jetty. And in May, the government announced that Christie and Lowe of Chicago would undertake the development at Sabine Pass. At first Lee might have shown his disappointment, but then he did not have far to look for other business. His tugs and barges could haul all the lumber they could handle from the Beaumont, Orange, and Lake Charles mills. More important, earnings in the trade were excellent. Although the rate was $2.00 per one hundred feet of lumber shipped (as compared to the railroads' $3.50), the lower scale gave nearly all business to companies such as Lee's. While the competitor was urging the state's railroad commission to correct the imbalance, Lee used the momentary advantage to his profit, even selling the *Stella* to Christie and Lowe. He apparently decided that the lumbermen could as easily tow barges to the Galveston and Sabine Pass docks as could his own vessels.[30]

Yet problems still arose. During mid-summer of 1897, the re-christened *Lucien W. Lee* (formerly named after the father) stuck fast in the shallows of Sabine Lake. Its owners bemoaned the fact that the government ". . . will spend millions to deepen a harbor and refuse the paltry sum required to take a few scoopfulls of mud. . . ." A September hurricane devastated the Texas coast, after which an outbreak of yellow fever panicked the same communities. However, even now Lee profited, for while his barges went relatively undamaged, the weather left his competitors' equipment dry-docked for months. By October, Lee was so sure of business that he made another of his infrequent visits to Leavenworth, where more personal matters pressed for attention.[31]

Although there is nothing to suggest that either parent was embarrassed by an abnormality of their fourteen-year-old son, Lucien's deformed spine and retarded growth must have strained both adults. Therefore, when the healthy nine-year-old Selina Harris stepped off a train at Leavenworth's depot, a relieved Mac and Lina must have found it hard to contain their feelings. They had agreed to adopt this unwanted and mistreated child, who was probably escorted west from Poughkeepsie, New York, by a close friend during an October 1897 visit.[32] The similarity of names was probably never broached; instead, for the balance of that year both parents acquainted the healthy child with her new home.

Lee, however, eventually had to resume business, and on 15 January 1898 he was observed passing through Beaumont en route to the Sabine Pass works. In his absence the area had quickened its self-promotion as the preeminent deep-water facility of the state. But the visit was cut short when Lee apparently turned all his attention to family matters. He remained at Leavenworth until June, when he reappeared at Beaumont in order to supervise the repair of company barges. Not until March 1899 did he stop over long enough to be interviewed on renewed interest at Velasco. "The new work can be made a part of the old," he said, "which is still good. . . ." And perhaps consciously overlooking past difficulties, he went on to say that "had one bank not given out just when it did, Velasco would have had deep water ahead of Galveston. . . ." The explanation was as good as any; it certainly stilled his own memories of the scheme. His principal concern now was merely to stay active in a trade that rarely seemed to need attention. Therefore, by April, a decision had been made to transfer all business to Houston.[33]

Rooming at the Capitol Hotel, Lee again associated himself with his old friend John Ferguson, who had moved into the nearby Hotel Bristol as both took charge as new owners of the Houston Transfer Company, one of the city's freight and passenger services.[34] However, there was barely time to get his feet on the ground before an urgent message drew him home—Lina was seriously ill.

For weeks he nursed his wife so that during August 1900 they both could travel to the mountainside retreats at Las Vegas, New Mexico, where Lee hoped the region's hot mineral waters would speed her recovery. Apparently the remedy worked, for the Lees returned to their Leavenworth home on the last day of September with Lina much improved. Lee, anyway, was convinced of her good health, and on the evening of 11 October he left Kansas to resume business in Houston. It must have been a jolt, then, when on 10 December he received word that his fifty-three-year-old wife had died.[35]

Because of a confusion in train schedules, a shaken Mac Lee arrived in Leavenworth one day later than expected. The delayed services were kept simple, with the Reverend F. N. Arkin of the Episcopal church officiating at the Olive Street residence Lina so enjoyed. Then, as friends stood near, the tall Yankee placed his wife to rest in a temporary vault at Mount Muncie Cemetery. There had not even been time to arrange a suitable burial. Five days later Lee boarded another train out of Leavenworth bound for Houston; it was a stunned man who traveled by rail to what over the years had served him well: business. It was the one thing he could be certain would take his mind from the tragedy.[36]

The next visit to Leavenworth did not come until spring. On 25 May 1901 Lee again stood at graveside for the formal burial of his wife. The site finally selected was at the base of a shaded rise not far from the graves of both Lyman and Lucien Scott. But again, as soon as he could, Lee put everything behind him. The immediate plan was that he and Lucien would travel to New York, where the boy would undergo surgery in an attempt to correct the deformed spine. While Lee remained at Lucien's bedside throughout the ordeal, in August, with his son recovering, he moved to sever the last bond holding him to Kansas.[37]

On 4 September the two-storied Leavenworth home was sold. The day was warm and pleasant, a fond memory for Lee's last day as a resident of this Missouri River community. Then, during the next several months, he returned to Houston while the responsibilities of family grew. Important to the adjustment was the intervention of Lee's youngest sister, Lillian, an unmarried woman in her mid-fifties who lived with her mother in Wisconsin. It was Lillian who apparently came to Lee's aid and brought the children to Columbus. Thus it was from Wisconsin that Lucien left for college, and it was to Lillian that the boy's expenses were paid from Lina's estate.[38] Selina also must have come under Lillian's care.[39] Yet in March 1905, two months after Lucien had moved to Houston, Lee sold his ownership in what was now the largest transport company of that city in order to retire from all business affairs.[40] Apparently he had decided to enjoy the years remaining to him with his son and adopted daughter. But if experience told Lee anything, it was that so simple a life was not his fate.

It was near 7:00 P.M. on Wednesday evening, 17 May 1905, as Lucien rode to the Houston intersection of Main and Rusk streets. As he bent forward to adjust a spur, his right foot kicked the flank of the horse and caused the animal to rear back and throw the surprised rider to the pavement. Stunned bystanders immediately ran up to the unconscious boy and carried him to a nearby house. It took a doctor fully ten minutes to revive Lucien, who was then placed in the care of a Houston infirmary. Three weeks later, the boy died.[41] John Ferguson, Lee's lifelong associate, died nine months later.[42]

The time came, then, when Lee had to face up to the deaths of a friend, a son, and a wife. In late July 1906 he and Selina departed Houston for Wisconsin, where nearly one-half century before he had begun his life on the frontier.[43] The wounds would need time to heal.

CHAPTER EIGHT

Salt Domes

Houston's principal commercial artery along Main Street to the intersection at McKinney Avenue near the Grand Central depot was a wall of three- to five-storied red brick buildings. Tucked into the canopied facades were banks, retail stores, and nickel arcades, as horse-drawn carriages vied with open-topped automobiles for right-of-way along a street already congested by an electric transport system. During the preceding decade Houston had flourished so that now, for the first time, its 209 factories employed more wage earners than Dallas, and in only a few months the city would rival Galveston as the state's foremost port of trade. A man who had contributed to the upturn of Houston's affairs, Mac Lee, and his daughter returned to the city during the first week of September 1906, crossing from the railroad depot to their apartments in the four-storied Brazos Hotel. First on the agenda was the enrollment of Selina at St. Agnes Academy—a finishing school for young girls.[1] With that done, Lee had his own schedule to attend to.

What he was about became evident on Thursday, 27 December, as Lee, Frank N. Bullock, and Frank J. Clemenger (the latter two of Brazoria County) signed the charter of the West Columbia Oil Company. The three—with I. Malley Eastman and C. S. Gordon, both of Beaumont—bound themselves to prospect for oil on the West Columbia ridge in Brazoria County. Specifically, where the company proposed to drill was on 143 acres leased from the estate of Governor James Stephen Hogg following an agreement that had been negotiated in October. Three other leases on adjoining lots had also been acquired.[2]

The particular site was a domed rise about thirty feet above sea level located on the west bank of the Brazos River barely three miles northwest of Columbia. Previously Bullock had explored the field; however, each of his two Equitable Company tests had to be abandoned. Then, between 1902 and 1903, two other outfits had drilled into the same formation without success. Characteristically Lee appeared unconcerned by past failures as a wooden derrick already marked the West Columbia site[3] (see Map 7).

By late January, progress momentarily slowed while a crew awaited delivery of pipe to case a hole 300 feet deep. "Those who engaged in this business . . . ," one West Columbian noted, "are determined upon success . . . of which they entertain no doubt." Others were as encouraged. "They, as well as the best informed people of this section, believe that oil, with an abundant flow, will be the result of this venture. . . ."[4] But again the risk was all Lee's.

For over one month West Columbia's crew carefully worked its first test to a depth of 780 feet, with early samples holding out the promise of oil. But as the drillers were bound to another contract, the rig had to be temporarily shut down and moved. Work resumed in April only to have the hole abandoned in salt water at the 1,112-foot mark. Undiscouraged, the drillers moved the 83-foot derrick another one-half mile north as the crew renewed its job of twisting pipe into the shallow sands. While they labored, Lee, Bullock, and Clemenger negotiated for additional leases that effectively closed the field to other prospectors.[5]

By Friday afternoon, 10 May, an 8¾-inch bit had been maneuvered through 480 feet of earth, the last 12 feet being solid rock. A last length of pipe to be used that day hung from the derrick ready to be swung into place when, unexpectedly, the ground near the wellhead began to rumble. Then, as if lifted by invisible wires, the pipe and casing blew out of the shaft. In that instant the rumble became a roar, and what had been locked in the sands for millenia spewed into the air, rising 25 feet above the rig: mud, rock, and fragments of petrified wood all exploded to the surface. It was a gasser, not exactly what had been expected, but very close.[6] It took only a spark from the rotary boiler, at midnight on the same day, to turn well No. 2 into a 40-foot flame that instantly consumed the derrick and all equipment. Even forced steam from a quickly assembled fire unit was unable to extinguish the blaze, and it was not until the early hours of the following morning that the flames died out of their own accord.[7]

Two days later, three excited men assembled near the banks of the Brazos River. Besides increasing the capital stock of their West Columbia company to $16,000, Lee, in agreement with Bullock and Clemenger, also planned the immediate redrilling of the blownout well. Consequently, a new 84-foot derrick was standing over the now chocked-off gasser with additional equipment in place. A blade welded to the end of the first length of pipe soon reopened the hole,

1	Brazoria County	**8**	Humble	**15**	Orange
2	Damon	**9**	Houston	**16**	Newton County
3	West Columbia	**10**	Jefferson County	**17**	Deweyville [1917]
4	East Columbia	**11**	Beaumont	**18**	Sour Lake
5	Angleton	**12**	Port Arthur	**19**	Vinton
6	Velasco	**13**	Sabine Pass	**20**	Lake Charles
7	Harris County	**14**	Orange County	**21**	Jennings

Map 7. Oil Fields of the Texas–Louisiana Coast, ca. 1911

and by mid-May a bit was again down nearly 500 feet. As the men continued to twist the stem deeper, for a second time the derrick began to shake. But unlike before, warm crude now exploded high above the rig, and within minutes the ground was literally covered with thick, black oil that quickly filled the nearby earthen pits. West Columbia had its first sustained producer, with an estimated flow of between 300 and 400 barrels a day.[8]

Lee at once traveled from Houston to Columbia in order to witness the strike, the noise from which could still be heard more than one-half mile away. Yet the best estimates of his crew were that the present gusher would choke itself out with a larger pool still to be tapped some 200 feet deeper. Consequently, two additional derricks were raised nearby. Before the men could resume work, however, a storm slammed into the area and wrecked most of the equipment, including the derricks. At the same time well No. 2 stopped flowing. But as fast as the wreckage could be cleared the men set to work rebuilding the company's third test about 200 feet northwest of the damaged site.[9]

They were forced to delay drilling again when the bit broke loose in the shallow depths. Yet all were encouraged by the crude which still bubbled from around the hole of the damaged test. The company literally inched through the sands, hoping to claim whatever deposits still lay hidden. Even with these precautions, Lee's roustabouts were unable to bring in a second strike, and finally in August, after 200 feet of work, the test was abandoned. Not disheartened, they set up another derrick and began drilling on a fourth well.[10]

Meanwhile, Lee—or Captain Lee, as he was now called—had moved from Houston to a rented home known as the Chilton Cottage in East Columbia, the town's name having been changed in order to distinguish it from the West Columbia field. Lee's relocation came at a time when his operation had also caught the attention of others, and there was even talk of laying out another town adjacent to the new site. Yet he must have realized that "nothing big [would] be done until the present [well reached] the stage of the one that blew out." The difficulty was that no one even knew whether a primary pool existed. Nevertheless, a crew renewed its efforts on a fourth derrick, with work progressing at the usually slow pace; results were also the same. Thus in November, after three months of labor, the company abandoned the test after losing still another bit. By now several outstanding leases were due to expire which, considering the lack of success on each, forced Lee to reconsider the entire scheme.[11]

East Columbia slumbered through the winter of 1908, and it was not until April that the county began its annual ritual of plantings and harvests. Lee was among those who awoke slowly to the new season. It was perhaps with a degree of cynicism that some noted the pretensions of the downriver settlement at Velasco, where locals again talked of deep water. Much had changed since the days of Lee's involvement, however, not the least of which the destruction of almost every building in town during the devastating hurricane of September 1900. If he looked back wistfully on the experience, it was because he had not retained some interest in certain aspects of the development. Recently natural gas was found seeping up through the shaft of the artesian well drilled for the occupants of Hotel Velasco.[12] No one in the early 1890s slightly imagined that minerals were the natural treasure of the region.

Even now, in 1908, about the only excitement in East Columbia was the one town automobile raising dust down the main street. Rumor had it that Lee was about to order work resumed at the West Columbia site, but a flooding Brazos River soon silenced that notion.[13] Nothing could be done until the land dried, and quite simply, Lee was in no hurry to sink another profitless hole.

By mid-August the man had at least convinced one prospector to take on the West Columbia job. Frank Clemenger (a former associate now backed by Palacios, Texas, businessmen) had contracted to explore the field with a percentage of all oil produced reserved to Lee. The outfit was organized as the Palacios Oil Company and would test on the same 143 acres previously leased from Governor Hogg's estate, with a first well to go down near the last season's blowout. And as promised, a rig was up and ready to start drilling by the second week in September. This time there would be an additional incentive, as Markham Fuel Oil Company was also interested in drilling at West Columbia and had leased property adjacent to the Palacios site.[14]

At first it appeared that Palacios would have the field to itself, for by the end of the first week in October the company had a test down nearly 100 feet while Markham still had not broken ground. A common problem to both was obtaining enough wood to fire the boilers, and an unexpected shortage forced both outfits to experiment with crude-powered rigs. Yet by late October each company had a rig in operation while Palacios teased with reports of "good showings at shallow depths."[15]

Therefore, it was somewhat of a surprise when, on the morning of 7 December, one of Markham's two rigs was the first to strike oil, the well gushing in at between 200 and 400 barrels a day. Although by the end of the month the hole was producing merely 20 barrels of mixed water and crude, Palacios had to abandon its first test in January after drilling more than 1,200 feet. Unfortunately the rigs were not capable of boring deeper into the dome. Organizers of both outfits, however, pressed on with their explorations on the chance that pools of crude had seeped up to the shallower depths. Markham had a third derrick in place by late January, but it was not until spring that Palacios was able to put a second test on line. By summer this hole was also abandoned in rock and a third site had to be located.[16]

While prospects at the West Columbia field remained in doubt, Lee jostled between his East Columbia residence and the apartment maintained in Houston awaiting the unlikely news of a strike. This was a restless time of little activity. Worse, what did get accomplished usually managed to be destroyed: in 1909 a July hurricane slammed into Velasco and blew north up the Brazos River. East Columbia was still digging out from the debris one month later, with no one giving much attention to prospecting across the river. Not until Christmas, while Lee and Selina vacationed with Frank Bullock and his sister Emily at the Brazoria County ranch, was there any encouraging news. A test on the Palacios tract finally hit near the 500-foot sands, pumping 50 to 60 barrels of oil a day. More important, pressure at the wellhead was sufficiently strong so that crude might flow into the tanks for months. Yet the test was still not of the size that either Lee or Bullock had anticipated.[17]

The next eighteen months were spent coaxing the roustabouts to make the one big strike. However, with dry holes on the fourth and fifth wells, even Lee began to abandon hope and relinquish many of his rights to still another drilling association organized by Clemenger. The following months were passed either at the Houston apartment, where he dabbled in minor real estate transactions, or at the Bullock ranch on holiday visits, or even taking the mineral baths at Hot Springs, Arkansas. Not since his wife died had he occupied himself in so many nonproductive ways. Consequently, when his daughter graduated from St. Agnes Academy in May 1911, he virtually jumped at the first opportunity that promised to take him out of the doldrums.[18]

In Beaumont on 13 June, Lee, in association with Adriance Moor and J. B. "Bunny" Moore (both of Houston) organized the Ab-Moor Oil Company. With the venture capitalized at $3,000, the three proposed to drill into Spindletop, a field already renowned as the birthplace of the Texas oil industry.[19]

Beaumont and its neighboring communities were familiar territory; here, years before, Lee had run barges of lumber south across the shallow waters of Sabine Lake and had contributed to the opening at the pass on the Gulf. However, since his last visits Beaumont had mushroomed into a community of nearly thirty thousand residents with several six-storied buildings now fronting on the city's main street. The new wealth was a direct consequence of the turn-of-the-century gusher brought in by Captain A. F. Lucas on the domed rise called Spindletop, located about four miles southwest of the city. That boom had long since played out, but Lee was just as confident that undiscovered deposits still lay hidden in the shallower sands. By the end of June, a derrick marked the first test on a track known locally as the Trembly lease, with an Ab-Moor crew ready to hoist pipe and bore into the dome.[20]

Almost incidentally, on 18 July, Lee, Frank Bullock, Bullock's sister Emily, and E. B. Baldwin arrived at Columbia in order to dissolve the West Columbia Oil Company charter. The matter was handled in short order, and six days later Lee returned to Beaumont, where he became engrossed in his latest scheme. Earlier that month both he and Adriance Moor had each contributed $750 toward raising the first derrick on the lease. Although $1,500 was adequate capital to start the venture, a mid-August tornado threatened to close them out by leveling several of the ten rigs on the dome. Strangely, Ab-Moor's one derrick was spared, and by week's end a fifty-barrel pumper had been strained from the shallow depths. Soon after, Lee had the purely personal duty of announcing Selina's marriage to a Brazoria County rancher, James Price Phillips.[21]

Lee used his spare time to organize yet another outfit, and on 18 December he, Moor, and Erastus Hill (a Beaumont native) chartered the Nineteen Oil Company. The sole purpose of the new association was to explore Block Nineteen at Spindletop. This lease had been previously worked by Gladys City Oil, Gas, and Manufacturing Company without success; as important to Lee was the acquisition of new equipment. It first appeared, however, that the deal would turn sour, for during the preceding weeks all tests on the Hill had come up dry. Even on the day Lee was putting his pen to the new lease, a major operator in the field, Guffey Oil Company, had struck a gasser not far from Block Nineteen. Yet a derrick still went up and work began immediately. Lee also chose this time to move from his Houston apartment to a boardinghouse on Tevis Street in downtown Beaumont.[22]

As was probably expected, the first well came in dry, but Lee ordered his roustabouts to a second location at the far northeast corner of the lease. Although it took weeks of patient labor, by mid-April a sixty-barrel producer was finally drained from the sands. It was now thought that the first test could also be salvaged "if [likewise] finished properly." Lee's success immediately caught the attention of his fellow prospectors. Spindletop had been averaging less than 2,000 barrels of oil per day . . . ," and Lee's recent strikes indicated that field production might be turned around. As one prospector observed, "Spindle Top is again coming into the limelight. . . ."[23] Typically, the Wisconsin Yankee was at the vanguard.

Nineteen Oil added still another producer to its logs when at the end of June 1912 a third well came in flowing 15 barrels a day. This offset the disappointments of the worked-over No. 1 test and a fourth well having to be abandoned as dry holes. Lee was considerably more successful when he again concentrated on the Ab-Moor tract. There, both a second and a third well came in at 65 and 75 barrels, respectively; and within days production on a No. 3 test was increased to nearly 300 barrels a day. Ab-Moor counted still other successes in October and November when a worked-over No. 1 was put on the beam pumping 350 mixed barrels of water and crude; a fourth hole, 65 barrels; while a fifth, 8 barrels. Nineteen Oil held up its end with a producer brought in during late December averaging 10 barrels of crude. The year closed as a fifth derrick was raised for yet another test on Block Nineteen.[24]

Each success had been premised on methodical technique. When pipe was lost, Lee had the crew immediately stop drilling in order to fish the missing length to the surface; and when water seeped into the shaft, first a plug and then packing were set. Thus in October, when Ab-Moore's No. 1 well tested only 10 barrels, "the company doctored the hole, and it . . . [went] on the beam [pumping] about 350 barrels of fluid, 60 barrels of which [were] oil. . . ." Using similar methods, a total of nine wells had been brought into production in only twelve months, a feat that did not go unnoticed. One Beaumont daily even referred to Spindletop as a "new oil field," an acknowledgment that must have gratified the seventy-one-year-old Lee.[25]

While together in Beaumont on 31 March 1913, the junior partner of the venture, Bunny Moore, also resolved an outstanding commitment to Ab-Moor's charter. However, instead of money, items transferred onto the company's asset sheets included two derricks, a combination oil rig and boiler, and one fuel tank. These were in addition to the contributed labor of Moore's roustabouts. Each was no slight addition to the business, as the cost of drilling a single well had increased substantially over the years. Wages alone demanded that roustabouts be paid $75 a month, and rotary drillers, $150.[26]

The transfer of equipment and services also came at a propitious time; by March, production on the Hill had declined by as much as 20 percent. Even two Ab-Moor tests had faltered, and one—an eighth hole—had to be abandoned. The disappointment detracted from Nineteen Oil's fifth test, which during January came in at 50 mixed barrels of crude and water and a sixth Ab-Moor well that in February was put on the beam pumping 35 barrels. It was perhaps of some consolation that during these same weeks only one other Spindletop company brought anything into production. Lee, therefore, chose now to explore the deeper sands, and Moore's transfer of equipment and labor helped considerably; in fact, they saved the expense of outfitting a new operation.[27] As important, Moore also transferred the right to drill on another dormant lease.[28]

Although the concessions were Lee's reasons to expand, deep tests (then considered anything below 2,000 feet) apparently did not suit his methods. Beginning in April 1913 and throughout that summer, each attempt failed with a hole usually washed out by salt water.[29] But while attention focused on these deeper explorations, by summer's end other crews had brought into production two shallow wells on Nineteen Oil's lease. These were completed, although a storm on the night of 4 September destroyed nearly ninety derricks, eight of which belonged to Lee. However, lack of success with deep tests and destruction of derricks were only temporary setbacks, for at the time Lee was busy planning a further expansion of his investment. In fact, in August he acquired another of Moore's properties, the Twenty-Five Oil Company.[30]

Therefore, Lee's two principal enterprises now controlled four prime tracts at the top of America's foremost salt dome. At this pace and with thirteen successes to his credit, the man might have contemplated an early retirement from the trade while cushioned by royalties from past and future explorations. Yet even Lee failed to consider the clear warnings of Spindletop's dwindling potential.

The year 1914 began quietly enough. Lee met his first grandchild—Jack, Jr.—in March, when Selina and the baby arrived at Beaumont for a month's visit. He reciprocated by traveling to East Columbia in July. What he found was that Selina had settled comfortably into marriage, with her husband's new Phillips Lumber Company a testament to their prosperity. His only personal claim to a similar change in lifestyle was the move from his Tevis Street boardinghouse to the New Neches Hotel. In business matters he could only point to the recent eight-barrel well brought in on Block Nineteen. It was not a banner year. Yet, curiously, interest in an "old friend"—West Columbia—renewed as 1914 ended. A new outfit to the field, Producers Oil (Texaco), had taken up the challenge, and although drilling was screened from most spectators, a sudden rush for leases near the site seemed to indicate that a few still saw potential in the dome. The difference between this and Lee's earlier attempts was that improved technology now allowed crews to drill below the 2,000-foot depth.[31]

Therefore, it came as no surprise when in June 1915 Lee and Emily Bullock, co-owners of a two-acre West Columbia tract, negotiated for a test on their lease. The terms called for a one-eighth royalty on all oil produced and a similar agreement if gas was discovered. The deal came at an appropriate time, for Spindletop had nearly bottomed out. Field production was down to a mere 1,000 barrels of crude a day, and it had been weeks since anyone attempted new exploration. Lee's only contracts during these same months were the grant of right-of-way for a telephone and telegraph line over a strip of Beaumont property, and another to Harris County for the right to build a public road across one corner of Houston realty. Then, only days after the signing of the Producers Oil lease, Lee also sold Ab-Moor's interest in Block Forty-Two to Guffey Petroleum for $3,000.[32] As with other endeavors, sentiment did not keep the man from dispensing with unproductive assets.

It was also in Lee's character to push ahead with those matters that experience had taught him might prove successful, and again in August he reinvested at West Columbia by purchasing a one-eighth interest in a tract owned by Frank Bullock. This was done although Producers had abandoned its first well, shut down another, and had serious problems on a third. Yet each had gone below 2,000 feet, where ". . . gas pressure . . . [was] so strong that difficulty . . . [was] experienced in getting through. . . ." Lee himself had hit the same pocket near the 1,000-foot mark, and as one bystander noted, this would seem to indicate that "certainly there must be a great field at West Columbia. . . ."[33] But the question remained—how deep must exploration go before tapping the larger pool?

No one knew the answer. Instead, Lee tolerated still other disappointments, which at Spindletop included the almost complete destruction of the field in August when a hurricane swept across Beaumont. First estimates put the damage in excess of one million dollars.[34] During the months that followed and into the summer of 1916, Lee himself explored only one site, a worked-over ninth well on Nineteen Oil's lease.[35] Indeed, a reflection of Spindletop's diminished capacity was July's posted price of seventy cents for one barrel of crude.[36] Therefore, not surprisingly, Lee continued to look elsewhere for brighter prospects, with the most attractive still being at the unproven West Columbia field.

On 27 June and again on 7 October, in association with Emily Bullock in one instance and with S. W. Pipkin and F. E. Carroll in another, Lee leased still additional acres to Producers Oil. Not that the new outfit was any more successful than Lee's earlier attempts, for the company again had to abandon another well. But all knew that prospecting was a gamble in which a single strike might recoup all past disappointments. Lee and his coinvestors must have so reasoned, for in December they extended the Producers contracts into the next year.[37]

Lee welcomed 1917 from the familiar Beaumont surroundings of Mary Mennell's boardinghouse on Tevis Street. By that date he had also acquired part interest in another Spindletop investment, the tract owned by the Thomson-Moor Oil Company, and he immediately ordered a crew to begin drilling. Perhaps to Lee's surprise, by the end of February his roustabouts had brought a small fifteen- to twenty-barrel well into production from a shallow 550-foot depth. Consequently, Lee exchanged his over 3,200 shares in the company for the right to continue drilling. The agreement came only days after Ab-Moor reported no earnings during the first quarter of 1917, while Nineteen Oil posted slightly over $1,500 on the approximate 1,500 barrels produced. Even less encouraging was the report that another West Columbia test had gone off tract near the 2,000-foot mark.[38]

The new Thomson-Moor lease proved to be only moderately successful. Although a first attempt had to be abandoned, by August a second hole came in at between 50 and 60 barrels a day. It at least demonstrated that oil might still be drained from the shallow sands. Nevertheless, what little interest remained at Spindletop now principally centered on deeper explorations. Reports from West Columbia were as discouraging: two additional wells on the Producers lease had come up dry. Talk of a roustabout strike during early fall—and their subsequent walkout—merely added to the difficulty. Therefore, not unexpectedly, the quarter ending 31 December showed both Ab-Moor and Nineteen Oil pumping a total of only 650 barrels of crude.[39]

For months Lee patiently waited at his East Texas residence for success on any of his several investments. But nothing happened; only moderate increases were posted in quarterly incomes from previously drilled wells. Ironically, although he was now recognized as ". . . the first who developed the shallow sand at Spindletop, after the big [1901] boom died out . . . ," his rigs were the ones idled while others took successfully to the field.[40]

The visit to Beaumont in late spring 1918 of Selina and her family perhaps distracted him from the monotony of recent failures. It would have also called his attention to activity in Brazoria County, where the majors now ". . . [played] West Columbia for a field." Nothing definite, but even Houston had geared itself to the expected boom—not only at West Columbia but elsewhere—with Sinclair Oil building the town's first refinery on the city's ship channel. Yet Lee was still tied to East Texas, where by the end of the third quarter, only Nineteen Oil reported revenues on a mere 1,000 barrels produced.[41]

Unrelated to the problem but certainly an event that warranted Lee's attention, on Tuesday morning, 3 December 1918, the drill stem of Humble Oil's (Exxon) No. 1 Giraud test at West Columbia passed the 3,039-foot mark on its unobstructed path into the Brazos sands. As the bit inched deeper a telltale roar developed from the wellhead, and within seconds a geyser shot upward, spraying warm, black crude high above the derrick. This first Humble test on the West Columbia dome flowed with an estimated 4,000 to 5,000 barrels of oil a day, but, more important, its sustained volume confirmed speculation that a primary pool had been tapped. The field had finally been unlocked in the 3,000-foot sands.[42]

Within days a literal forest of derricks stood scattered at the top of the dome, with each hoping to tap its share of the bonanza. By then Humble Oil had a crew in the field, as did Texaco, with orders to survey a route for a new pipeline. Lee must have been one of the many who watched with amazement, for on 6 January 1919 he and five others (F. E. Carroll, F. N. Bullock, C. L. Nash, S. W. Pipkin, and Emily Bullock) signed with H. C. Weiss a lease of West Columbia property. In exchange for Humble's right to prospect on thirty lots near the dome, $10,710 was paid in addition to the promise of a one-sixth royalty on all minerals produced. Lee's excitement can only be imagined when two days later Texaco brought in a well at 20,000 barrels a day on the nearby Arnold lease.[43]

Apparently Lee could not restrain his curiosity, for during April he arrived at his daughter's East Columbia home to view the new field firsthand. On learning of his visit, a local reporter heralded him as one who "ten or twelve years ago . . . had faith enough in our field to drill here . . . ," but noted that "the only trouble was that they could not go deep enough at that time."[44] Certainly no one regretted that circumstance more than Lee, particularly when he considered the startling transformation taking place on the west side of the Brazos River.

At East Columbia proper, several new buildings had been raised, including a much-needed hotel. But at West Columbia, where once existed only the suggestion of a town, there now stood a booming community of banks, service shops, and professional offices in addition to the many tents and other temporary living quarters used by the roustabouts. Towering above it all were wooden derricks, seventeen of which had been built during the week of Lee's visit alone.[45] Indeed, West Columbia's sudden glut of oil was its most apparent problem.

Although Humble's and Texaco's two wells had been deliberately chocked off, other producers had pumped an additional 29,000 barrels into the inadequate earthen pits and steel tanks located haphazardly about the field. Even Humble's proposed 255,000-barrel tank would not be capable of handling the constant flow of crude now being pumped from the several wells in operation. The only hope was that the majors would shortly complete pipelines to area refineries. Yet Humble was still surveying a route to Goose Creek, while Texaco, although it had pipe on hand, merely promised to begin construction soon. The momentary solution was either to freight the oil out in tankers pulled along the outmoded rails of the Columbia Tap or to barge through the Velasco jetties and up the coast to Port Arthur refineries.[46]

The overview must have amazed the man who probably took in the sights from the comfort of his son-in-law's new automobile. Jack and Selina were themselves a testament to the area's prosperity, as their lumber business could barely keep pace with demand. It all made the 832 barrels produced by Nineteen Oil during the preceding quarter look paltry by comparison.[47]

Lee, however, grappled to turn West Columbia's boom to his own advantage, and he found an answer by negotiating his own deals with Humble—one contracted in Houston on 18 April for five lots of Harris County property, and the other in Beaumont one day later for yet another tract at West Columbia. His faith was not misplaced, for in July West Columbia surpassed all Texas fields in the production of oil.[48]

Meanwhile, the prospector had not given up on his East Texas investments; with some optimism in July he and three others organized the Newton County Oil Company, a trust capitalized at $50,000. The venture was the latest innovation of the trade, and the four obligated themselves to prospect under its terms on a four-hundred-acre site near Deweyville, a community located just north of Orange (see Map 7). The necessary leases, however, were not arranged until two weeks later, and inexplicably a first test on the site was not ready until fall. This perhaps suited Lee, for the value of Spindletop crude ($1.25 a barrel) was considerably below that of other fields. To drill now and even make a strike would probably have resulted in additional losses. Possibly for this reason and also to divest himself of another unprofitable asset, on 27 December Lee dissolved Ab-Moor's charter.[49] Apparently two schemes were all he believed necessary to continue his exploration of what few minerals remained locked in Beaumont's shallower depths.

Lee spent most of the week ending 17 January 1920 at his daughter's remodeled East Columbia home, where there was another new member of the family—a granddaughter, Lina Lee. The days spent with Selina also permitted Lee to lapse into conversation with his son-in-law and J. G. Phillips, Sr., of bygone cattle days. But attention was probably never far from current interests, and assuredly some time was given to discussing the latest developments at the West Columbia dome. Indeed, perhaps a reason for Lee's mid-winter visit was that, a week before, Humble Oil had brought a fifty-barrel well into production on a lease jointly owned by Lee and others. The strike certainly was not of the size anticipated, and Lee probably encouraged a deepening of the test. One of the more fortunate of West Columbia's investors was Lee's friend Bullock, who held a royalty in Texaco's No. 1 Abrams well, which came in during July at 26,000 barrels a day. The significance of the strike was that production held constant, and within a month over one million barrels had been pumped from the hole. In 1907 Lee held a similar option on the Abrams tract, but equipment had prevented him from tapping the same oil-rich sands.[50]

He thus had set his sights on less spectacular results, and again on 1 October 1920, Nineteen Oil contracted with Gladys City Oil, Gas, and Manufacturing Company to reopen Block Forty-Four in Beaumont. A similar arrangement was made the following month with yet another outfit near Block Forty-Two. A crew did not have the necessary equipment in place, however, until late December. The hoped-for deep tests in Newton County never materialized, as shortly after locating a first site one of four trustees resigned. A consequence was the forced division and sale of the trust, with Lee and his associates retaining a royalty interest should oil ever be discovered.[51] This, perhaps, was considered unlikely; besides, Lee now had a far more interesting prospect to occupy his attention.

At West Columbia the major companies in the field had one eye open to a recent Humble extension—a thirty-acre lease at the northeast corner of the dome located approximately 2,200 feet southwest of Texaco's No. 1 Abrams well. The new test was the first of a Pipkin-Lee series, and by Tuesday, 18 January, the well was 3,000 feet into the ground and still going deeper. At about the 3,225-foot mark the crew was rigged to put down yet another length of pipe when a dull rumble began to sound from deep within the earth. In that instant ". . . another monster well . . . flowing at the rate of 25,000 barrels a day . . ." began to spew high-grade crude above the derrick with the promise of "immense fortunes to [the] owners"—who were Lee, Emily Bullock, S. W. Pipkin, F. W. Carroll, and C. L. Nash. Lee also held another percentage in partnership with Nash. There was momentary excitement when the well sanded up in the first twenty-four hours, but a crew easily cleared the hole so that 10,000 barrels a day were able to flow into nearby tanks.[52]

The strike immediately set others scrambling to relocate their rigs, and outrageous deals were offered, including $5,000 bonuses and one-sixth overriding interest for the lease of a few lots near the extension. However, most found that the large outfits already had the site surrounded with derricks. Meanwhile, the Pipkin-Lee had leveled off to a constant flow of 3,100 barrels a day.[53]

What the eighty-year-old Lee made of all the excitement can only be imagined. Certainly, he welcomed the substantial profits about to come his way; however, the strike made his five-barrel producer brought in that same week on a Nineteen Oil lease look ridiculous by comparison.[54] Still, he could boast of his accomplishments, and Spindletop was yet important to the oil trade, in part due to his decade of explorations. One wonders, though, if Lee also thought back on West Columbia and the consequence to himself if only his earlier tests had been able to drill the additional depth—a mere 2,000 feet.

Epilogue

A second well on the Pipkin-Lee tract came in during April and was flowing 500 barrels a day. However, a third test, located only yards away, "blew a gasser, caught fire, and caused considerable damage," destroying both holes with an estimated loss of between $25,000 and $30,000. Three additional attempts were each abandoned as dry tests. But a seventh, an eighth, and a worked-over fifth well came in without much difficulty, pumping 100 barrels, 500 barrels, and another 500 barrels, respectively. The successes were representative of West Columbia's performance as a whole; of the 244 wells drilled from January 1919 through July 1921, 162 were brought in as producers.[1] It was not the same elsewhere.

By mid-April 1921, Spindletop's production was down to 975 barrels a day, with only two rigs in operation, one by Lee. And when a Nineteen Oil crew finally hit the producing sands in May, the new well flowed at the rate of only 8 barrels a day. No wonder, then, that when the last quarterly statement of Lee's remaining company showed revenues of only $102, on 29 December Nineteen Oil's charter was dissolved. Within months of the decision, Lee also moved back to a comfortable suite of rooms at Houston's Brazos Hotel, apparently satisfied with the prospect of royalties still to be drained from the West Columbia dome.[2]

The times now belonged to younger men, and Lee perhaps considered himself fortunate just to have survived those his own age. Most everyone he had done business with over the years was gone. Most recently, in February, a fellow organizer of the Brazos River Channel and Dock Company, George Angle, had died; and in March, Albert Reynolds, then eighty-one years old, had succumbed, after which he was eulogized as one of Colorado's "empire builders." However, Lee was still active, and on 8 November 1923, he married the attractive, forty-three-year-old Leila Schumacher, an Arkansas-born drama instructor.[3]

The two had spent barely one year together when on 1 January 1925 Lee collapsed in Houston from a chronic kidney ailment. He was now only a weak image of his former self, with a white goatee, a "small bay window" paunch, the need for spectacles, and merely the suggestion of a hairline. Eighty-three years had left their mark. Five days later, at 2:45 A.M. on Tuesday, 6 January, Lee died.[4]

The body was laid to rest at Leavenworth's Mount Muncie Cemetery on a cold Saturday morning, 10 January, with his sister Lillian and wife Leila at graveside.[5] The two women then departed this middle country of the American continent, one bound for Wisconsin and the other for Texas. Later, a simple memorial would be etched on the same marble headstone that already marked that of another wife and son.

A mere thirty-five miles southwest was Lawrence, Kansas, and the intersection of Massachusetts and Fourth streets where, over fifty-five years before, an ambitious young man had stridden impatiently toward a red brick building and an uncertain future. That adventure had ended. But Lee was adept at discovering new and profitable enterprises, and on his death certificate was recorded the new occupation of "real estate dealer."[6] Incredibly the man had accepted still another challenge, and in his ninth decade Houston was to be the next frontier.

Notes

Introduction

1. *Badger State*, 14 Nov. 1856, 10 June 1854; *Portage City Record*, 6 May 1857; undated issue of *Waukesha Republican*, cited in *Record*, 5 Aug. 1857; *An Early History of Columbia County, Wisconsin*, p. 970.

2. *An Early History of Columbia County, Wisconsin*, p. 970; "Family Register," copied from Perry Lee's Bible enclosed with the letter of Ruth Sutton-Doland to DFS, 20 Apr. 1977. Lee's date of birth was obtained from a Lee relative since deceased, in correspondence to Joseph H. Smith, a former Hereford, Texas, resident who during the early 1960s did selective research into Lee's life. Joseph H. Smith to DFS, 13 Jan. 1977.

3. *An Early History of Columbia County, Wisconsin*, p. 970.

4. *Badger State*, 14 Nov. 1856, 10 June 1845, 5 Dec. 1856.

5. See "Rules and Regulations of the Schools of Portage City," *Portage City Record*, 21 Sept. 1856.

6. The brother of W. M. D. Lee's son-in-law described Lee as "a tall man— 6 feet, four or five inches, had a high forehead, blue-eyes. . . ." J. G. Phillips, Jr., to DFS, 11 Apr. 1977.

7. *An Early History of Columbia County, Wisconsin*, p. 970; *Badger State*, 3 Oct., 31 Oct., 14 Nov. 1856, 17 Apr. 1857.

8. *Badger State*, 5 Feb. 1858, 16 Apr. 1859; *Portage City Record*, 27 Jan. 1858, 22 Dec., 23 Dec. 1857, 28 Dec. 1859.

9. Perry Lee's "Family Register," Ruth Sutton-Doland to DFS, 20 Apr. 1977; *An Early History of Columbia County, Wisconsin*, p. 970. For letters appearing in the Columbia County press that referred to the gold rush in New Mexico and might have caught the attention of Perry Lee, see *Badger State*, 15 July 1859.

10. See U.S. Department of Commerce, Bureau of the Census, *Seventh Census of the United States, 1850*: Population, Wisconsin, Columbia County, Hampden Township; Perry Lee's "Family Register," Ruth Sutton-Doland to DFS, 20 Apr. 1977; *Columbus Republican*, 2 June 1869, which refers to Perry Lee's family living at Hampden; *Wisconsin State Register*, 3 May 1862.

11. Obituary of W. M. D. Lee, *Houston Daily Post*, 7 Jan. 1925; obituary of J. B. Fargo, *Columbus Republican*, 1 Feb. 1896.

12. *Oil Trade Journal* 16 (Feb. 1925): 77; Col. A. D. Nelson to Col. Louis Merrill, Judge Advocate, Fort Leavenworth, Kansas, 22 Jan. 1870, Military Records Division, Navy and Old Army Branch, Records of the U.S. Army Continental Commands, 1821–1890, Letters Sent from Camp Supply, Oklahoma, 1868–1890, Record Group 393, National Archives, Washington, D.C. Unless otherwise specified, all documents of the U.S. Army Continental Commands will be cited as RG 393.

13. *Wisconsin State Register*, 20 July 1861, 20 Sept. 1862, 19 Nov. 1864, 8 Sept. 1866, 1 Aug. 1868, 31 July 1869; *Columbus Republican*, 2 June 1869.

1. Buffalo Robes

1. Letter of W. M. D. Lee, 1 Apr. 1870, Letters Received by the Office of Indian Affairs, 1824–1881, Letters Received from the Upper Arkansas Agency, 1869–1874, Record Group 75, Records of the Bureau of Indian Affairs, National Archives, Washington, D.C. Unless otherwise specified, all document of the Bureau of Indian Affairs will be cited as RG 75. Col. A. Nelson to Assistant Adjutant General, Department of the Missouri, 23 Apr. 1870, RG 75; License to Trade issued W. M. D. Lee by Brinton Darlington, 24 Sept. 1869, Agent's Letterbook 5 Aug. 1869 to 5 June 1876, pp. 174–175, Cheyenne and Arapaho Papers, Agent and Agency File, Division of Archives and Manuscripts, Oklahoma Historical Society, Oklahoma City, Oklahoma. Unless otherwise specified, all documents of this division of the Oklahoma Historical Society will be cited as Arch., OHS.

2. Alvin H. Sanders, *A History of Hereford Cattle*, pp. 1062, 1064. Also see Register of the Appointment of Sutlers Made by the Secretary of War, Register 1, p. 182, and Register 3, pp. 120–121, Records of the Office of the U.S. Army Adjutant General, Record Group 94, National Archives, Washington, D.C. (Unless otherwise specified, all documents of the Office of the Adjutant General will be cited as AG Records, RG 94); Wilbur Fisk Stone, *History of Colorado*, vol. 3, p. 544; testimony of A. E. Reynolds before House Committee on the Expenditures in the War Department, 19 Apr. 1876, *The Management of the War Department*, H. Rpt. 799, 44th Cong., 1st sess., 1876, p. 347; Col. A. Nelson to AAG, Dept. Mo., 12 Aug. 1870, Ltrs Sent/C. Supply, RG 393. For new material pertinent to the Lee and Reynolds partnership, see the Albert E. Reynolds Collection, Colorado Historical Society, Denver.

3. License issued to W. M. D. Lee by B. Darlington, 24 Sept. 1869, Agt's Ltrbook 5 Aug. 1869 to 5 June 1876, pp. 174–175, Chey. & Arap. Papers, Agt. & Ag. File, Arch., OHS; Ltr of W. M. D. Lee, 1 Apr. 1870, Ltrs Rec'd/Upper Ark. Ag., RG 75.

4. See Henry E. Fritz, "The Making of Grant's 'Peace Policy,'" *Chronicles of Oklahoma* 37 (Winter 1959–1960): 411–432.

5. Ltr of W. M. D. Lee, 1 Apr. 1870, and E. Hoag to E. S. Parker, CIA, 14 Jan. 1870, Ltrs Rec'd/Upper Ark. Ag., RG 75.

6. Medical History of Fort [Camp] Supply, Ind. Terr., vol. 116, pp. 2–3, AG Records, RG 94; LTC John R. Brooke to AAG, Mil. Div. Mo., 21 Oct. 1873, Ltrs Sent/C. Supply, RG 393; LTC [Brevet Maj. Gen.] G. A. Custer to MG P. H. Sheridan, Cmdg, Dept. Mo., 28 Nov. 1868, *New York Times*, 9 Dec. 1868; Col. A. Nelson to AG, U.S. Army, 4 Oct. 1870, Ltrs Sent/C. Supply, RG 393; Rpt. of the AG, *Rpt. of Sec. War*, H. Ex. Doc. 1, 41st Cong., 2d sess., 1869, vol. 1, pt. 2, p. 40; *Harper's Weekly* 22 (27 Feb. 1869): 140; Ltr of MG P. H. Sheridan, 8 Dec. 1868, *New York Times*, 20 Dec. 1868; John Murphy, "Reminiscenses of the Washita Campaign and of the Darlington Indian Agency," *Chronicles of Oklahoma* 1 (June 1923): 262.

7. B. Darlington to E. Hoag, 6 Sept. 1869, *Rpt. of Sec. Int.*, H. Ex. Doc. 1, 41st Cong., 3d sess., 1870, vol. 1, pt. 3, p. 824; *New York Times*, 14 Oct., 27 Nov. 1868; B. Darlington to [E. Hoag], 27 Aug. 1869, Ltrs Rec'd/Upper Ark. Ag., RG 75; E. Hoag to E. S. Parker, 22 Sept. 1869, *Rpt. of Sec. Int.*, H. Ex. Doc. 1, 41st Cong., 2d sess., 1869, vol. 1, pt. 3, p. 804; E. Hoag to E. S. Parker, 8 Oct. 1870, *Rpt. of Sec. Int.*, H. Ex. Doc. 1, 41st Cong., 3d sess., 1870, vol. 1, pt. 4, p. 717.

8. See MG W. B. Hazen to Gen. W. T. Sherman, 30 June 1869, *Rpt. of Sec. Int.*, H. Ex. Doc. 1, 41st Cong., 2d sess., 1869, vol. 1, pt. 3, p. 838; Cpt. Seth Bonney to Maj. W. A. Elderin, 8 Sept. 1869, C. Supply Ltrbook, 1869, p. 47, C. Supply Papers, Western History Collection, Univ. of Oklahoma, Norman, Oklahoma; 2/Lt Silas Pepoon to Bn. AG, C. Supply, 22 July 1869, Ltrs Rec'd/ Upper Ark. Ag., RG 75; Chief Medicine Arrow to B. Darlington, 2 Sept. 1869, and B. Darlington to E. Hoag, 17 Sept. 1869, Ltrs Rec'd/Upper Ark. Ag., RG 75.

9. E. Hoag to B. Darlington, 15 Oct. 1869; Ltr of W. M. D. Lee, 1 Apr. 1870; Col. A. Nelson to AAG, Dept. Mo., 23 Apr. 1870; and B. Darlington to Col. A. Nelson, 28 Mar. 1870, Ltrs Rec'd/Upper Ark. Ag., RG 75.

10. Ltr of W. M. D. Lee, 1 Apr. 1870, Ltrs Rec'd/Upper Ark. Ag., RG 75.

11. W. M. D. Lee to B. Darlington, 15 Jan. 1870, Chey. & Arap. Papers, Traders File, Arch., OHS; E. Hoag to E. S. Parker, 24 Jan. 1870; B. Darlington to E. Hoag, 29 Mar. 1870; Ltr of W. M. D. Lee, 1 Apr. 1870; and Col. A. Nelson to AAG, Dept. Mo., 23 Apr. 1870, Ltrs Rec'd/Upper Ark. Ag., RG 75; Col. A. Nelson to AAG, Dept. Mo., 22, 28 Jan. 1870, and Col. A. Nelson to MG J. M. Schofield, Dept. Mo., 3 Feb. 1870, Ltrs Sent/C. Supply, RG 393; AAG, Dept. Mo. to Col. A. Nelson, 11 Feb. 1870, Ltrs Rec'd/Ft. Supply, Okla., 1868–1895, RG 393.

12. Col. A. Nelson to AAG, Dept. Mo., 12 Aug. 1870, Ltrs Sent/C. Supply, RG 393; Sutlers Register, Reg. 3, pp. 120–121, AG Records, RG 94; testimony of A. E. Reynolds before House Committee on the Expenditures in the War Department, 19 Apr. 1876, *The Management of the War Department*, H. Rpt. 799, 44th Cong., 1st sess., 1876, pp. 242–245; "List of Post Traders Appointed Under the Act of July 15, 1870," *The Management of the War Department*, H. Rpt. 799, 44th Cong., 1st sess., 1876, p. 272.

13. Testimony of J. M. Hedrick, 21 Apr. 1876, *The Management of the War Department*, H. Rpt. 799, 44th Cong., 1st sess., 1876, pp. 215, 228; Sutlers Register, Reg. 2, p. 44, Reg. 3, pp. 120–121, AG Records, RG 94; Donald F.

Schofield, "W. M. D. Lee, Indian Trader," *Panhandle-Plains Historical Review* 54 (1981): 110–111. Hereafter, the *Panhandle-Plains Historical Review* will be cited as *P-PHR*.

14. B. Darlington to E. Hoag, 1 Sept. 1870, *Rpt. of Sec. Int.*, H. Ex. Doc. 1, 41st Cong., 3d sess., 1870, vol. 1, pt. 4, pp. 730–731.

15. See MG John Pope to AAG, Mil. Div. Mo., 31 Oct. 1870, *Rpt. of Sec. War*, H. Ex. Doc. 1, 41st Cong., 3d sess., 1870, vol. 1, pt. 2, p. 6; MG John Pope to AAG, Mil. Div. Mo., 2 Oct. 1871, *Rpt. of Sec. War*, H. Ex. Doc. 1, 42d Cong., 2d sess., 1871, vol. 1, pt. 2, p. 44; MG John Pope to AAG, Mil. Div. Mo., 28 Sept. 1872, *Rpt. of Sec. War*, H. Ex. Doc. 1, 42d Cong., 3d sess., 1872, vol. 1, pt. 2, pp. 46–47.

16. Col. A. Nelson to AAG, Dept. Mo., 23 Apr., 2 Nov. 1870; Col. A. Nelson to MG John Pope, 28 May, 2 Sept. 1870; and LTC J. W. Davidson to AAG, Dept. Mo., 31 Jan. 1872 [two ltrs], Ltrs Sent/Ft. Supply, RG 393; Col. A. Nelson to AAG, Dept. Mo., 23 Sept. 1870, Ltrs Rec'd/Upper Ark. Ag., RG 75; H. R. Clum, Acting CIA to E. Hoag, 30 Dec. 1872, Chey. & Arap. Papers, Arms & Ammunition File, Arch., OHS; John D. Miles to J. Richards, 31 Dec. 1873, Kiowa Papers, Foreign Relations File, Arch., OHS; C. Beede, Chief Clerk, Cen. Sup. to E. S. Parker, 7 Dec. 1870, Ltrs Rec'd/Upper Ark. Ag., RG 75; B. Darlington to E. Hoag, 16 Aug. 1871, *Rpt. of Sec. Int.*, H. Ex. Doc. 1, 42d Cong., 2d sess., 1871, vol. 1, pt. 5, p. 541; E. Hoag to J. Miles, 3 Jan. 1873, Ltrs Rec'd/Upper Ark. Ag., RG 75.

17. Medical History of Ft. Supply, Indian Territory, 30 May 1870, vol. 166, p. 8, AG Records, RG 94; Col. A. Nelson to AAG, Dept. Mo., 4 June 1870, Ltrs Sent/C. Supply, RG 393; license issued to W. M. D. Lee and A. E. Reynolds by B. Darlington, 3 July 1870, Agt's Ltrbook 5 Aug. 1869 to 5 June 1876, pp. 180–181, Chey. & Arap. Papers, Agt. & Ag. File, Arch., OHS.

18. O. P. Randall, C. Supply, to U.S. Agt., Chey. & Arap. Ag., 7 June 1870, Chey. & Arap. Papers, Depredations File, Arch., OHS; W. N. Hubbell to B. Darlington, 22 July 1870, Chey. & Arap. Papers, Traders File, Arch., OHS; Col. A. Nelson to AAG, Dept. Mo., 29 May 1870, Ltrs Rec'd/Upper Ark. Ag., RG 75; O. P. Randall, C. Supply, to Agt., Chey. & Arap. Ag., 7 June 1870, and Col. A. Nelson to E. Hoag, 18 June 1870, Chey. & Arap. Papers, Depredations File, Arch., OHS; Cpt. Kirk, Qtrmaster, C. Supply to [Brig.] Gen. Penrose, Ft. Lyon, Colo., 4 June 1870, *Weekly Colorado Chieftain*, 16 June 1870; E. Hoag to E. S. Parker, CIA, 8 Oct. 1870, *Rpt. of Sec. Int.*, H. Ex. Doc. 1, 41st Cong., 3d sess., 1870, vol. 1, pt. 4, p. 718; Col. A. Nelson to AAG, Dept. Mo., 7 May 1870, Ltrs Sent/Ft. Supply, RG 393.

19. License issued to W. M. D. Lee and A. E. Reynolds by B. Darlington, 3 July 1870, Agt's Ltrbook 5 Aug. 1869 to 5 June 1876, pp. 180–181, Chey. & Arap. Papers, Agt. & Ag. File, Arch., OHS; obituary of Col. William Bent, *Weekly Colorado Chieftain*, 27 May 1869; Lt. Gen. W. T. Sherman to AAG, Washington, D.C., 28 Jan. 1869, Ltrs Rec'd/Upper Ark. Ag., RG 75.

20. See interview of J. Wright Mooar with J. Evetts Haley, 12 Apr. 1936, W. S. Campbell Papers, Box 79, Western History Collection, Univ. of Oklahoma; interview of John G. Lang with L. F. Sheffy, 13 Oct. 1936; interview of Jesse Wynne with L. F. Sheffy, June 1934, Dr. L. F. Sheffy Memorial Collec-

tion, Cornette Library, WTSU; interview of J. E. McAllister with J. Evetts Haley, 1 July 1926, J. Evetts Haley Papers, Interview Files, P-PHM; Dennis Collins, *The Indians' Last Fight or the Dull Knife Raid*, pp. 17, 19.

21. Ltrbook of Agency Funds and Expenditures 31 Dec. 1869 to 31 Mar. 1872, pp. 50–51, 103, Chey. & Arap. Papers, Upright Files, Arch., OHS; receipt issued by B. Darlington to James C. Wilkinson, 21 July 1870, Chey. & Arap. Papers, Building File, Arch., OHS; Lee and Reynolds to Lt. W. S. Mackay, Post AG, C. Supply, 18 July 1870, Ltrs Rec'd/Ft. Supply, RG 393. Also see Col. A. Nelson to MG John Pope, Dept. Mo., 2 Sept. 1870, Ltrs Rec'd/Ft. Supply, RG 393; Col. A. Nelson to AAG, Dept. Mo., 29 May 1870, Ltrs Rec'd/ Upper Ark. Ag., RG 75; B. Darlington to E. Hoag, 1 Sept. 1870, *Rpt. of Sec. Int.*, H. Ex. Doc. 1, 41st Cong., 3d sess., 1870, vol. 1, pt. 4, p. 730; O. P. Randall to U.S. Agt., Chey. & Arap. Ag., 7 June 1870, and Col. A. Nelson to E. Hoag, 18 June 1870, Chey. & Arap. Papers, Depredations File, Arch., OHS; Medical Hist. of Ft. Supply, 30 May 1870, vol. 166, p. 8, AG Records, RG 94.

22. "Invoice of Indian Goods bought by Lee & Reynolds, 1872" and "Invoices, Lee & Reynolds Indian Traders 1873," Chey. & Arap. Papers, Traders File, Arch., OHS.

23. B. Darlington to E. Hoag, 2 Sept., 18 Oct. 1871, Ltrs Rec'd/Upper Ark. Ag., RG 75.

24. Ibid.; receipt issued to Lee and Reynolds by W. N. Hubbell, 11 Apr. 1871, Chey. & Arap. Papers, Freight & Transportation File, Arch., OHS; Ltrbook of Ag. Funds & Expenditures, 31 Dec. 1869 to 31 Mar. 1873, pp. 102–103, Chey. & Arap. Papers, Upright Files, Arch., OHS.

25. Cpt. W. B. Kennedy to AAG, Dept. Mo., 2 Mar. 1871, Ltrs Rec'd/Cen. Sup., RG 75.

26. LTC J. W. Davidson, Cmdg, C. Supply to AAG, Dept. Mo., 7 Apr., 20 Sept. 1871, Ltrs Sent/Ft. Supply, RG 393; for an account of the visits to New York City and Boston, see U.S., Cong., House, *Rpt. of Sec. Int.*, H. Ex. Doc. 1, 42d Cong., 2d sess., 1871, vol. 1, pt. 5, pp. 446–456.

27. Cpt. Edward Moale, Cmdg, Ft. Dodge to AAG, Dept. Mo., 28 Dec. 1872, Ltrs Sent/Ft. Dodge, RG 393; Robert M. Wright, *Dodge City: The Cowboy Capital*, pp. 160–161; for a contemporary description of Dodge City, see *Leavenworth Times*, 7 Nov. 1872.

28. For accounts of the Jordan family incident, see LTC J. W. Davidson to AAG, Dept. Mo., 29 Oct., 2 Nov. 1872, Ltrs Sent/Ft. Supply, RG 393.

29. Cpt. E. Moale, Cmdg, Ft. Dodge to AAG, Dept. Mo., 28 Dec. 1872, Ltrs Sent/Ft. Dodge, RG 393; Wright, *Dodge City*, 160–161.

30. LTC J. W. Davidson to AAG, Dept. Mo., 20 Oct. 1872, Ltrs Sent/C. Supply, RG 393.

31. Philip McCusker to "My Dear Genl. [probably MG P. H. Sheridan]," 1 May 1872, Ltrs Rec'd/Cen. Sup., RG 75; J. D. Miles to J. Richards, 31 Dec. 1873, Kiowa Papers, Foreign Relations File, Arch., OHS. For reports of other hunts from 1870 to 1874, see B. Darlington to E. Hoag, 26 Aug. 1871, *Rpt. of Sec. Int.*, H. Ex. Doc. 1, 42d Cong., 2d sess., 1871, vol. 1, pt. 5, p. 885; J. D. Miles to E. Hoag, 28 Aug. 1872, *Rpt. of Sec. Int.*, H. Ex. Doc. 1, 42d Cong., 3d sess., 1872, vol. 1, pt. 5, p. 633; J. F. Williams to E. Hoag, 22 Mar. 1873, Ltrs

Rec'd/Cen. Sup., RG 75; J. D. Miles to E. P. Smith, 30 Sept. 1874, *Rpt. of Sec. Int.,* H. Ex. Doc. 1, 43d Cong., 2d sess., 1874, vol. 1, pt. 5, p. 541; P. McCusker to E. P. Smith, 19 Jan. 1874, Ltrs Rec'd from Kiowa Agency, 1864–1880, RG 75; W. N. Hubbell, Lee, and Reynolds to J. D. Miles, 24 Mar. 1877, Ltrs Rec'd/ Chey. & Arap. Ag., RG 75.

32. Col. A. Nelson to MG John Pope, Dept. Mo., 28 May 1870, Ltrs Rec'd/ Upper Ark. Ag., RG 75.

33. See J. Huckleberry, U.S. Atty, U.S. Court of Western Dist. Ark., Ft. Smith to E. C. Barfield, Solicitor of the Treasury, 18 Oct. 1871, Ltrs Rec'd/ Cen. Sup., RG 75; Logan Roots, U.S. Marshal, Western Dist. Ark. to George Williams, U.S. Atty Gen., 1 Apr. 1872, Ltrs Rec'd/Cen. Sup., RG 75; LTC John R. Brooke to AAG, Dept. Mo., 16 July 1873, Ltrs Sent/C. Supply, RG 393; Rpt. of Henry E. Alvord, Oct., 1872, Ltrs Rec'd/Cen. Sup., RG 75; license issued to W. M. D. Lee and A. E. Reynolds by E. Hoag, 11 May 1872, Agt's Ltrbook 5 Aug. 1869 to 5 June 1876, pp. 144–145, Chey. & Arap. Papers, Agt. & Ag. File, Arch., OHS. For an account of Indian agent J. D. Miles's attempt to raid the ranches located along the road from Camp Supply to Ft. Dodge, see J. D. Miles to E. Hoag, 28 Jan. 1873, Ltrs Rec'd/Upper Ark. Ag., RG 75; for a general description of the ranches located along the Chisholm Trail, see Rpt. of H. E. Alvord, Oct. 1872, Ltrs Rec'd/Cen. Sup., RG 75.

34. P. McCusker to "My Dear Genl.," 1 May 1872, Ltrs Rec'd/Cen. Sup., RG 75; J. D. Miles to E. Hoag, 28 Aug. 1872, *Rpt. of Sec. Int.,* H. Ex. Doc. 1, 42d Cong., 3d sess., 1872, vol. 1, pt. 5, p. 633; J. D. Miles to E. Hoag, 4 June 1872, Ltrs Rec'd/Upper Ark. Ag., RG 75; Cpt. Orlando Moore to AAG, Dept. Mo., 17 May 1872, Kiowa Papers, Depredations File, Arch., OHS. Miles did not take official control of the agency until 1 June 1872.

35. E. Hoag to Lawrie Tatum, 2 June 1872, Kiowa Papers, Depredations File, Arch., OHS.

36. J. D. Miles to E. Hoag, 17 June 1872, Ltrs Rec'd/Upper Ark. Ag., RG 75.

37. Black Beaver to "Agent Miles," 7 Jan. 1873; J. D. Miles's "Monthly Reports for 1st and 2nd months, 1873"; Lee and Reynolds to LTC J. W. Davidson, 7 Jan. 1873; and Lee and Reynolds to J. D. Miles, 10 Jan. 1873, Ltrs Rec'd/ Upper Ark. Ag., RG 75.

38. J. D. Miles's "Monthly Reports for 1st and 2nd months, 1873," ibid.

39. Lee and Reynolds to J. D. Miles, 10 Jan. 1873, Ltrs Rec'd/Cen. Sup., RG 75.

40. Lee and Reynolds to J. D. Miles, 27 Oct. 1873, Ltrs Rec'd/Upper Ark. Ag., RG 75.

41. For Lee and Reynolds's competitors between 1870 and 1874, see Licenses to Trade, Agt's Ltrbook 5 Aug. 1869 to 5 June 1876, pp. 141, 148, 182–185, and licenses issued to W. M. D. Lee and A. E. Reynolds, pp. 144–145, 147, 149, Chey. & Arap. Papers, Agt. & Ag. File, Arch., OHS; also see E. Hoag to B. Darlington, 7 Sept. 1872, Chey. & Arap. Papers, Traders File, Arch., OHS.

42. D. H. Budlong, Collector, IRS, to John B. Jones, Indian Agt., 2 Sept. 1874, Ltrs Rec'd/Cen. Sup., RG 75; J. D. Miles to CIA, 5 Aug. 1879, Chey. & Arap. Ltrbook, 29 Nov. 1878 to 18 Nov. 1879, pp. 520–524, Edna May

Arnold Papers, Carnegie Library, El Reno, Oklahoma; LTC J. W. Davidson to Sec. War., 23 Feb. 1872, and Post AG, C. Supply, to Sgt. Alfred von Wilke, Co. D., 3d Inf., 23 Feb. 1873, Ltrs Sent/C. Supply, RG 393.

43. John F. Williams to E. Hoag, 22 Mar. 1873, Ltrs Rec'd/Cen. Sup., RG 75.

44. Lee and Reynolds to B. Darlington, 15 Aug. 1871; F. A. Walker, CIA, to E. Hoag, 1 Apr. 1872; and E. Hoag to B. Darlington, 5 Apr. 1872, Chey. & Arap. Papers, Arms & Ammunition File, Arch., OHS; J. M. Haworth to E. P. Parker, CIA, 15 May 1874, Ltrs Rec'd/Kiowa Ag., RG 75.

45. J. S. Evans & Co. to J. M. Haworth, 27 Apr. 1874, Ltrs Rec'd/Kiowa Ag., RG 75; George Fox to LTC J. W. Davidson, 2 Apr. 1874, Kiowa Papers, Depredations File, Arch., OHS.

46. New York Tribune, 16 Feb. 1872; LTC J. W. Davidson to AG, U.S. Army, 10 Mar. 1872, Ltrs Sent/Ft. Supply, RG 393; testimony of A. E. Reynolds before House Committee on the Expenditures in the War Department, 19 Apr. 1876, The Management of the War Dept., H. Rpt. 799, 44th Cong., 1st sess., 1876, p. 244.

47. A. E. Reynolds to Agt. Miles, 29 Dec. 1873, Chey. & Arap. Papers, Vices File, Arch., OHS.

2. Guns & Ammunition

1. LTC J. R. Brooke to AAG, Dept. Mo., 1 Mar. 1874, Ltrs Rec'd/Ft. Supply, RG 393; P. McCusker to [Edward] P. Smith, 11 June 1874, Ltrs Rec'd/ Cen. Sup., RG 75; Maj. C. L. Chipman to AAG, Dept. Mo., 18 Mar. 1874, Kiowa Papers, Depredations File, Arch., OHS; J. M. Haworth to E. P. Smith, 28 Jan. 1874, Ltrs Rec'd/Kiowa Ag., RG 75.

2. Interview of J. Wright Mooar with J. Evetts Haley, 25 Nov. 1927, J. Evetts Haley Papers, Interview Files, P-PHM; speech of J. Wright Mooar, n.d., John L. McCarty Papers, J. Wright Mooar File, Amarillo Public Library; Dodge City Messenger, 26 Feb. 1874.

3. J. D. Miles to E. Hoag, 28 Mar., 16 Apr. 1874, and E. C. Lefebere to J. D. Miles, 5 May 1874, Ltrs Rec'd/Upper Ark. Ag., RG 75.

4. Maj. C. E. Compton, Ft. Dodge, to AAG, Dept. Mo., 16 July 1874, Ltrs Rec'd/Cen. Sup., RG 75; J. D. Miles to E. Hoag, 16 Apr. 1874, Ltrs Rec'd/ Upper Ark. Ag., RG 75. Cpt. Tupper was also in command of the detachment that escorted Lee, Wright, and Spotted Wolf to the safety of Dodge City in December 1872.

5. J. D. Miles to E. Hoag, 16 Apr., 12 May 1874, Ltrs Rec'd/Upper Ark. Ag., RG 75.

6. Maj. C. L. Chipman to AAG, Dept. Mo., 18 Mar. 1874, Kiowa Papers, Depredations File, Arch., OHS; G. Bent to J. D. Miles, 6 May 1874; E. C. Lefebere to J. D. Miles, 5 May 1874; and J. D. Miles to E. Hoag, 7 May 1874, Ltrs Rec'd/Upper Ark. Ag., RG 75.

7. J. D. Miles to E. Hoag, 19 May 1874, and J. D. Miles to E. P. Smith, 18 June 1874, Ltrs Rec'd/Upper Ark. Ag., RG 75.

8. J. D. Miles to E. P. Smith, 30 Sept. 1874, Rpt. of Sec. Int., H. Ex. Doc. 1,

43d Cong., 2d sess., 1874, vol. 1, pt. 5, p. 541; J. D. Miles to E. P. Smith, 18 June 1874, Ltrs Rec'd/Upper Ark. Ag., RG 75; "Horse-Thieves and Whisky Traders among the Indians," *New York Times*, 15 May 1874; also see J. D. Miles to Cmdg Officer, C. Supply, 25 Apr. 1874, and J. D. Miles to E. Hoag, 12 May 1874, Ltrs Rec'd/Upper Ark. Ag., RG 75.

9. See Schofield, "W. M. D. Lee, Indian Trader," *P-PHR* 54 (1981): 113.

10. J. M. Haworth to E. P. Smith, CIA, 15 May 1874, Ltrs Rec'd/Kiowa Ag., RG 75.

11. Each robe was valued at $5.00.

12. See Schofield, "W. M. D. Lee, Indian Trader," *P-PHR* 54 (1981): 113.

13. J. D. Miles to J. M. Haworth, 8 May 1874, Kiowa Papers, Arms & Ammunition File, Arch., OHS. Although the letter predates Haworth's complaint, Miles was addressing a similar charge of 20 Apr. 1874. See J. M. Haworth to E. Hoag, 20 Apr. 1874, Ltrs Rec'd/Kiowa Ag., RG 75.

14. License issued to Lee and Reynolds by J. D. Miles, 14 May 1874, Agt's Ltrbook, 5 Aug. 1869 to 5 June 1876, p. 149, Chey. & Arap. Papers, Agt. & Ag. File, Arch., OHS; J. D. Miles to J. M. Haworth, 8 May 1874, Kiowa Papers, Arms & Ammunition File, Arch., OHS.

15. MG J. Pope to AG, Mil. Div. Mo., 7 Sept. 1874, *Rpt. of Sec. War*, H. Ex. Doc. 1, 43d Cong., 2d sess., 1874, vol. 1, pt. 2, p. 30.

16. Interview of J. Wright Mooar with J. Evetts Haley, 25 Nov. 1927, and interview of J. E. McAllister with J. Evetts Haley, 1 July 1926, J. Evetts Haley Papers, Interview Files, P-PHM. Also see *Dodge City Messenger*, 25 June 1874.

17. Interview of J. E. McAllister with J. Evetts Haley, 1 July 1926, J. Evetts Haley Papers, Interview Files, P-PHM; also see interview of J. Wright Mooar with J. Evetts Haley, 12 Apr. 1936, W. S. Campbell Papers, Box 79, West. Hist. Collect., Univ. of Oklahoma; *Dodge City Messenger*, 25 June 1874.

18. J. M. Haworth to E. Hoag, 3 June, 6 June 1874, Ltrs Rec'd/Kiowa Ag., RG 75; Rpt. of F. H. and J. M. Smith, Cmrs to E. P. Smith, CIA, 26 Sept. 1874, Ltrs Rec'd/Cen. Sup., RG 75; LTC J. R. Brooke to AAG, Dept. Mo., 18 May 1874, Ltrs Sent/C. Supply, RG 393; J. M. Haworth to E. P. Smith, 30 Sept. 1874, *Rpt. of Sec. Int.*, H. Ex. Doc. 1, 43d Cong., 2d sess., 1874, vol. 1, pt. 5, p. 528. For other contemporary accounts of Isa-tai's prophesies, see P. McCusker to E. P. Smith, 11 June 1874, Ltrs Rec'd/Cen. Sup., RG 75; "The Comanches Instigated to War by a 'Prophet,'" *New York Times*, 8 Aug. 1874.

19. J. M. Haworth to E. Hoag, 22 June 1874, Ltrs Rec'd/Kiowa Ag., RG 75; P. McCusker to E. P. Smith, 11 June 1874, Ltrs Rec'd/Cen. Sup., RG 75; J. M. Haworth to E. P. Smith, 1 Sept. 1874, *Rpt. of Sec. Int.*, H. Ex. Doc. 1, 43d Cong., 2d sess., 1874, vol. 1, pt. 5, p. 528; Rpt. of Smith & Smith, 26 Sept. 1874, Ltrs Rec'd/Cen. Sup., RG 75.

20. Rpt. of Smith & Smith, 26 Sept. 1874, Ltrs Rec'd/Cen. Sup., RG 75; J. M. Haworth to E. P. Smith, 1 Sept. 1874, *Rpt. of Sec. Int.*, H. Ex. Doc. 1, 43d Cong., 2d sess., 1874, vol. 1, pt. 5, p. 528.

21. J. D. Miles to E. P. Smith, 30 Sept. 1874, *Rpt. of Sec. Int.*, H. Ex. Doc. 1, 43d Cong., 2d sess., 1874, vol. 1, pt. 5, p. 544.

22. J. D. Miles to E. Hoag, 7 Feb. 1874, and B. Williams to J. D. Miles, 6 Feb. 1874, Ltrs Rec'd/Cen. Sup., RG 75.

23. J. C. Leach, Lee & Reynolds Ranch, Red Fork of the Arkansas, Ind. Terr., to M. B. Loyd, 10 July 1874, *Fort Worth Daily Democrat*, 25 July 1874; J. D. Miles to E. P. Smith, 10 July 1874, Ltrs Rec'd/Upper Ark. Ag., RG 75. Also see Lee and Reynolds to J. D. Miles, 25 May 1874, Chey. & Arap. Papers, Traders File, Arch., OHS; J. D. Miles to E. P. Smith, 30 Sept. 1874, *Rpt. of Sec. Int.*, H. Ex. Doc. 1, 43d Cong., 2d sess., 1874, vol. 1, pt. 5, p. 543.

24. J. C. Leach to M. B. Loyd, 10 July 1874, *Fort Worth Daily Democrat*, 25 July 1874; B. Wetherell to E. Hoag, 4 July 1874, Kiowa Papers, Depredations File, Arch., OHS.

25. J. D. Miles to E. P. Smith, 10 July 1874, Ltrs Rec'd/Chey. & Arap. Ag., RG 75.

26. J. D. Miles to Dr. [William] Nicholson, Cen. Sup., 17 June 1876, Agt's Ltrbook, 12 Dec. 1875 to 6 Dec. 1876, pp. 466–470, Chey. & Arap. Papers, Agt. & Ag. File, Arch., OHS; J. D. Miles to E. P. Smith, 30 Sept. 1874, *Rpt. of Sec. Int.*, H. Ex. Doc. 1, 43d Cong., 2d sess., 1874, vol. 1, pt. 5, p. 541; Brevet Brig. Gen. Thomas H. Neill to AAG, Dept. Mo., 16 Mar. 1875, and J. D. Miles to E. P. Smith, 12 June, 10 July 1874, Ltrs Rec'd/Chey. & Arap. Ag., RG 75; J. C. Leach to M. D. Loyd, 10 July 1874, *Fort Worth Daily Democrat*, 25 July 1874.

27. J. D. Miles to E. P. Smith, 10 July 1874, Ltrs Rec'd/Upper Ark. Ag., RG 75; J. D. Miles to E. P. Smith, 30 Sept. 1874, *Rpt. of Sec. Int.*, H. Ex. Doc. 1, 43d Cong., 2d sess., 1874, vol. 1, pt. 5, p. 543; P. McCusker to [Agt. J. Richards], 4 July 1874, Kiowa Papers, Depredations File, Arch., OHS; telegram of J. D. Miles to E. P. Smith, 7 July 1874, *New York Times*, 8 July 1874; J. D. Miles to E. P. Smith, 10 July 1874, Ltrs Rec'd/Upper Ark. Ag., RG 75; J. C. Leach to M. B. Loyd, 10 July 1874, *Fort Worth Daily Democrat*, 25 July 1874.

28. J. D. Miles to E. P. Smith, 10 July 1874, Ltrs Rec'd/Upper Ark. Ag., RG 75; rpt. of Smith & Smith, 26 Sept. 1874, Ltrs Rec'd/Cen. Sup., RG 75; J. C. Leach to M. B. Loyd, 10 July 1874, *Fort Worth Daily Democrat*, 25 July 1874; telegram of J. D. Miles to E. P. Smith, 7 July 1874, *New York Times*, 8 July 1874.

29. For accounts of the raid, see Fred Leonard, Adobe Walls, to "Dear [A. C.] Myers," 1 July 1874, *New York Times*, 17 July 1874; J. Wright Mooar to "Sister," 7 July 1874, John Wesley Mooar Papers, Correspondence and Notes—1871–1917, Southwest Collect., Texas Tech Univ.; J. M. Haworth to E. P. Smith, 1 Sept. 1874, *Rpt. of Sec. Int.*, H. Ex. Doc. 1, 43d Cong., 2d sess., 1874, vol. 1, pt. 5, p. 528; Rpt. of Smith & Smith, 26 Sept. 1874, Ltrs Rec'd/ Cen. Sup., RG 75. For individual recollections of the event, see "The 'Adobe Walls'" [interview of Billy Dixon], *Dallas Morning News*, 13 Mar. 1888; interview of J. Wright Mooar, interviewer unidentified, 29 May 1938, J. Wright Mooar File, Southwest Collect., Texas Tech Univ; W. B. [Bat] Masterson to Frederick S. Barde, W. S. Campbell Papers, Box 79, West. Hist. Collect., Univ. of Oklahoma; "The Indians," New York Times, 25 July 1874.

30. Telegram of Charles Rath & Co., Myers & Leonard, Dodge City, to Gov. Thomas A. Osborne, 8 July 1874; telegram of MG J. Pope to Gov. T. Osborne, 8 June 1874; and telegram of T. Osborne to [Railroad] Agt., Dodge City, Kan., 9 July 1874, Gov. Osborne Papers, 1873–1877, Correspondence Rec'd, Box 2, Indians 1874, Kansas State Historical Society; LTC W. H.

Lewis to AAG, Dept. Mo., 10 July 1874, Ltrs Sent/C. Supply, RG 393.

31. J. Wright Mooar to "Sister," 7 July 1874, John Wesley Mooar Papers, Correspondence and Notes—1871–1917, Southwest Collect., Texas Tech Univ.; MG Nelson A. Miles to AAG, Dept. Mo., 25 Aug. 1874, Ltrs Rec'd/ Cen. Sup., RG 75; J. J. Long, "My Indian Recollections," n.d., J. J. Long Papers, Interview Files, P-PHM; interview of J. E. McAllister with J. Evetts Haley, 1 July 1926, J. Evetts Haley Papers, Interview Files, P-PHM; 1/Lt H. J. Farnsworth to Field AG, 8th Cav. Bn., 23 Sept. 1874, Ltrs Rec'd/Cen. Sup., RG 75.

32. Interview of Judge O. H. Nelson with J. Evetts Haley, 26 Feb. 1927, J. Evetts Haley Papers, Interview Files, P-PHM.

33. MG J. Pope to AAG, Mil Div. Mo., 7 Sept. 1874, *Rpt. of Sec. War*, H. Ex. Doc. 1, 43d Cong., 2d sess., 1874, vol. 1, pt. 2, p. 30.

34. Interview of J. Wright Mooar with J. Evetts Haley, 12 Apr. 1936, W. S. Campbell Papers, Box 79, West. Hist. Collect., Univ. of Oklahoma; J. D. Miles to E. P. Smith, 30 June 1874, Ltrs Rec'd/Upper Ark. Ag., RG 75.

35. J. D. Miles to E. P. Smith, 10 July, 18 July 1874, Ltrs Rec'd/Upper Ark. Ag., RG 75; *New York Times*, 8 July, 21 July 1874. However, in 1884 Miles was tried by the federal authorities at Leavenworth for abandoning the agency and for the alleged embezzlement of $40,000 from the Indians. He was acquitted on both counts. See "The Fighting Quaker Vindicated," *Leavenworth Times*, 22 Oct. 1884.

36. Sec. War W. Belknap to Gen. of Army, 20 July 1874, *New York Times*, 22 July 1874.

37. J. D. Miles to E. P. Smith, 22 July, 8 Aug., 14 Aug. 1874, Ltrs Rec'd/Upper Ark. Ag., RG 75; J. D. Miles to E. P. Smith, 30 Sept. 1874, *Rpt. of Sec. Int.*, H. Ex. Doc. 1, 43d Cong., 2d sess., 1874, vol. 1, pt. 5, p. 542; J. D. Miles to E. P. Smith, 20 Jan. 1875, and Brig. Gen. T. H. Neill to AAG, Dept. Mo., 18 Jan. 1875, Ltrs Rec'd/Chey. & Arap. Ag., RG 75; J. D. Miles to E. P. Smith, 30 Sept. 1875, *Rpt. of Sec. Int.*, H. Ex. Doc. 1, 44th Cong., 1st sess., 1875, vol. 1, pt. 5, pp. 770–771; J. D. Miles to E. P. Smith, 30 Sept. 1874, *Rpt. of Sec. Int.*, H. Ex. Doc. 1, 43d Cong., 2d sess., 1874, vol. 1, pt. 5, p. 544.

38. MG N. A. Miles to AAG, Dept. Mo., 15 Aug., 25 Aug. 1874, 4 Mar. 1875, Ltrs Rec'd/Cen. Sup., RG 75; Rpt. of AG, *Rpt. of Sec. War*, H. Ex. Doc. 1, 43d Cong., 2d sess., 1874, vol. 1, pt. 2, pp. 70–71; LTC W. H. Lewis, Cmdg, C. Supply, to AAG, Dept. Mo., 15 Sept. 1874, Ltrs Sent/C. Supply, RG 393.

39. John H. Talley, Special Dpty U.S. Marshal, to W. S. Tough, U.S. Marshal, Dist. Kan., 1 Oct. 1874, Ltrs Rec'd/Cen. Sup., RG 75; J. [Wright] Mooar to "Mother," 31 Oct. 1874, John Wesley Mooar Papers, Correspondence and Notes—1871–1917, Southwest Collect., Texas Tech Univ.

40. MG N. A. Miles to AAG, Dept. Mo., 25 Aug. 1874, Ltrs Rec'd/Cen. Sup., RG 75; LTC W. H. Lewis to Lee and Reynolds, 16 Sept. 1874; and LTC W. H. Lewis to AAG, Dept. Mo., 12 Sept. 1874, Ltrs Sent/C. Supply, RG 393; Med. Hist. of Ft. Supply, 12 Sept., 14 Sept. 1874, vol. 166, p. 29, AG Records, RG 94.

41. LTC W. H. Lewis to AAG, Dept. Mo., 31 Aug., 25 Oct., 4 Nov., 11 Nov., 12 Nov., 24 Dec., 30 Dec. 1874, 4 Jan. [two ltrs], 15 Jan., 17 Jan., 23 Jan., 30 Jan., 31 Jan. 1875; and LTC W. H. Lewis to MG N. A. Miles, 25 Oct. 1874, Ltrs Sent, C. Supply, RG 393.

42. Articles of Agreement between J. D. Miles, Lee and Reynolds, 27 Mar. 1875, Chey. & Arap. Papers, Traders File, Arch., OHS; Lee and Reynolds to J. D. Miles, 29 Mar. 1875, Ltrs Rec'd/Chey. & Arap. Ag., RG 75; Sutlers Register, Reg. 3, pp. 120–121, AG Records, RG 94; Edward C. Kemble, U.S. Ind. Inspector, to E. P. Parker, CIA, 18 Jan. 1875, Ltrs Rec'd/Kiowa Ag., RG 75; J. D. Miles to E. P. Smith, CIA, 1 Mar. 1875, and J. D. Miles to E. P. Smith, 1 Mar. 1875, Ltrs Rec'd/Chey. & Arap. Ag., RG 75. For two accounts of the Battle of Sand Hill, see Brig. Gen. T. H. Neill to AAG, Dept. Mo., 7 Apr. 1875, Ltrs Rec'd/Chey. & Arap. Ag., RG 75; J. D. Miles to E. P. Smith, 30 Sept. 1875, *Rpt. of Sec. Int.*, H. Ex. Doc. 1, 44th Cong., 1st sess., 1875, vol. 1, pt. 5, p. 771; also see J. A. Covington to E. P. Smith, 7 Apr. 1875, *New York Times*, 15 Apr. 1875.

43. *Columbus Democrat*, 8 May 1875; Ruth Sutton-Doland to DFS, 27 Mar. 1977.

44. Interview of R. "Dick" Bussell with J. Evetts Haley, 19 July 1926, J. Evetts Haley Papers, Interview Files, P-PHM.

3. Buffalo Hides

1. Rpt. of AG, *Rpt. of Sec. War*, H. Ex. Doc. 1, 44th Cong., 1st sess., 1875, vol. 1, pt. 2, pp. 142–143; John R. Cook, *The Border and the Buffalo*, p. 150.

2. Cook, *The Border and the Buffalo*, pp. 150–151; interview of George A. Simpson with L. F. Sheffy, 30 Nov. 1929, L. F. Sheffy Papers, Interview Files, P-PHM; J. M. Haworth to E. P. Smith, 20 Sept. 1875, *Rpt. of Sec. Int.*, H. Ex. Doc. 1, 44th Cong., 1st sess., 1875, vol. 1, pt. 5, p. 776; Emanuel Dubbs, et al., *Pioneer Days in the Southwest*, p. 91.

3. Interview of R. "Dick" Bussell with J. Evetts Haley, 19 July 1926, J. Evetts Haley Papers, Interview Files, P-PHM.

4. B. Williams to J. D. Miles, 22 Oct. 1875, Ltrs Rec'd/Chey. & Arap. Ag., RG 75; J. D. Miles to W. Nicholson, 31 Aug. 1876, *Rpt. of Sec. Int.*, H. Ex. Doc. 1, 44th Cong., 2d sess., 1876, vol. 1, pt. 5, p. 450; J. D. Miles to E. Hoag, 8 Dec. 1875, and camp trade permits issued by J. D. Miles, 1 Dec. 1875, Ltrs Rec'd/Chey. & Arap. Ag., RG 75; license issued to W. N. Hubbell by J. D. Miles, 12 May 1875, and licenses issued to W. N. Hubbell, Lee and Reynolds, 11 June 1875, Agt's Ltrbook, 5 Aug. 1869 to 5 June 1876, pp. 152–155, Chey. & Arap. Ag. File, Arch., OHS.

5. B. Williams to J. D. Miles, 22 Oct. 1875; J. D. Miles to E. Hoag, 13 Nov., 24 Nov., 30 Nov., 31 Dec. 1875; and ammunition permits issued by J. D. Miles, 24 Nov. 1875, Ltrs Rec'd/Chey. & Arap. Ag., RG 75; J. D. Miles to W. Nicholson, 31 Aug. 1876, *Rpt. of Sec. Int.*, H. Ex. Doc. 1, 44th Cong., 2d sess., 1876, vol. 1, pt. 5, p. 451; MG J. Pope to E. Hoag, 20 Nov. 1875, Ltrs Rec'd/Chey. & Arap. Ag., RG 75.

6. U.S., Cong., Senate, Proceedings of the Senate Sitting for the Trial of William W. Belknap, 44th Cong., 1st sess., 1876, *Congressional Record*, vol. 4, pt. 7, p. 1. For the specific committee reports on the affairs of the War Department, see Reports of the Majority and Minority, *The Management of the War Department*, H. Rpt. 799, 44th Cong., 1st sess., 1876. For Belknap's letter of resignation, see *Washington Evening Star*, 2 Mar. 1876.

7. Undated letter of MG W. B. Hazen, *New York Tribune*, 16 Feb. 1872; for congressional use of the letter, see Proceedings of the Senate Sitting for the Trial of William W. Belknap, 44th Cong., 1st sess., 1876, *Cong. Record*, vol. 4, pt. 7, pp. 177–178. See also Testimony of A. E. Reynolds before House Committee on the Expenditures in the War Dept., 19 Apr. 1876, *The Management of the War Department*, H. Rpt. 799, 44th Cong., 1st sess., 1876, pp. 244, 246; *Columbus Democrat*, 18 Mar. 1876; undated issue of *St. Louis Republican*, cited in "The Belknap Case," *Washington Evening Star*, 4 Mar. 1876; Maj. C. E. Goodwin to AG, U.S. Army, 29 Mar. 1876, Ltrs Sent/C. Supply, RG 393.

8. See Proceedings of the Senate Sitting for the Trial of William W. Belknap, 44th Cong., 1st sess., 1876, *Cong. Record*, vol. 4, pt. 7, esp. p. 210.

9. W. M. D. Lee to Sec. War, 28 Apr. 1876, Sutlers Register, Reg. 2, p. 106, and Reg. 3, p. 159, AG Records, ACP, Index No. 2445, RG 94; license issued to William M. D. Lee and Albert Reynolds by J. D. Miles, 19 May 1876, and license issued to W. N. Hubbell by J. D. Miles, 12 May 1876, Agt's Ltrbook, 5 Aug. 1869 to 5 June 1876, pp. 158–159, 163–164, Chey. & Arap. Papers, Agt. & Ag. File, Arch., OHS; J. D. Miles to W. Nicholson, 15 May 1876, and W. Nicholson to J. G. Smith, CIA, 12 July 1876, Ltrs Rec'd/Chey. & Arap. Ag., RG 75; J. D. Miles to W. Nicholson, 31 Aug. 1876, *Rpt. of Sec. Int.*, H. Ex. Doc. 1, 44th Cong., 2d sess., 1876, vol. 1, pt. 5, p. 451.

10. LTC Rufus Saxton, Quartermaster, Dept. Mo., to QM, U.S. Army, 18 Apr. 1876, Consolidated Quartermaster Correspondence Files, Index No. 4772, RG 92; 2/Lt W. M. Williams, Assistant Army Quartermaster, Ft. Elliott, to A. E. Reynolds, 2 May 1876; 2/Lt W. M. Williams to Chief QM, Ft. Leavenworth, 12 May 1876, and 2/Lt W. M. Williams to Chief QM, Dept. Mo., 27 May, 31 Aug. 1876, Ltrs Sent/Ft. Elliott Quartermaster, RG 393; Texas, Wheeler County, County Clerk, Deed Records, Texas Land Company to W. M. D. Lee and A. E. Reynolds, 27 Mar. 1876, vol. 1A, pp. 418–420; LTC R. Saxton, QM, Dept. Mo., to QM General, U.S. Army, 18 Apr. 1876, Consol. QM Corresp. Files, Index No. 4772, RG 92; testimony of Lt. Frank L. Shoemaker before the House Committee on the Expenditures in the War Dept., 11 Apr. 1876, *The Management of the War Department*, H. Rpt. 799, 44th Cong., 1st sess., 1876, pp. 214–215.

11. Cpt. P. H. Remington to AG, U.S. Army, 12 Aug. 1876, Ltrs Sent/C. Supply, RG 393; Alvin H. Sanders, *A History of Hereford Cattle*, p. 1064. For the pre-hunt notoriety, see the newspaper accounts recorded by the *Fort Worth Democrat*, 18 Aug., 19 Aug., 14 Sept., 22 Sept. 1876. See also *Columbus Republican*, 30 Sept. 1876; *Columbus Democrat*, 30 Sept., 18 Nov. 1876; Sutlers Register, Reg. 2, p. 44, and Reg. 3, p. 159, AG Records, RG 94.

12. License issued to William M. D. Lee and Albert Reynolds by J. D. Miles, 19 May 1876, Agt's Ltrbook, 5 Aug. 1869 to 5 June 1876, pp. 163–174, Chey. & Arap. Papers, Agt. & Ag. File, Arch., OHS; G. Bent to B. H. Miles, 16 Oct. 1876, Chey. & Arap. Papers, George Bent File, Arch., OHS; B. H. Miles to W. Nicholson, 12 Oct. 1876, Agt's Ltrbook, 12 Dec. 1875 to 6 Dec. 1876, pp. 805–806, Chey. & Arap. Papers, Agt. & Ag. File, Arch., OHS; G. Bent to J. D. Miles, 4 Nov. 1876, Chey. & Arap. Papers, George Bent File, Arch., OHS.

13. G. Bent to J. D. Miles, 10 Nov., 15 Nov. 1876, Chey. & Arap. Papers, George Bent File, Arch., OHS.

14. J. D. Miles to W. Nicholson, 31 Aug. 1877, *Rpt. of Sec. Int.*, H. Ex. Doc. 1, 45th Cong., 2d sess., 1877, vol. 1, pt. 5, p. 478; G. Bent to J. D. Miles, 26 Nov. 1876, Chey. & Arap. Papers, George Bent File, Arch., OHS; J. D. Miles to Frank Maltby, Acting Agt., Kiowa & Comanche Ag., 19 Dec. 1876, Chey. & Arap. Papers, Miscellaneous Traders File, Arch., OHS; W. N. Hubbell, Lee and Reynolds to J. D. Miles, 24 Mar. 1877, Ltrs Rec'd/Chey. & Arap. Ag., RG 75.

15. Rex Strickland, ed., "The Recollections of W. S. Glenn, Buffalo Hunter," *P-PHR* 22 (1949): 50; also see undated letter of Frank Collinson to Jack McCarty, John L. McCarty Papers, Frank Collinson File, Am. Pub. Lib.; interview of R. "Dick" Bussell with J. Evetts Haley, 19 July 1926, J. Evetts Haley Papers, Interview Files, P-PHM.

16. Strickland, ed., "Recollections of W. S. Glenn," *P-PHR* 22 (1949): 45, 50; also see interview of J. Wright Mooar with Frank P. Hill, J. B. Slaughter, Jr., and Jim Weatherford, 15 May 1936, J. Wright Mooar Papers, Interview Files, P-PHM. It is common to refer to Reynolds City as Rath City. However, the hunters knew the community as Reynolds City, a probable reference to A. E. Reynolds. See deposition of L. N. York, 28 Apr. 1903, and deposition of William Benson, 24 Aug. 1912, *W. S. Glenn vs. U.S.*, Nos. 1892–1893 Court of Claims J73187, pp. 4, 120; interview of S. P. Merry with J. Evetts Haley, 21 Aug. 1926, J. Evetts Haley Papers, Interview Files, P-PHM; undated letter of F. Collinson to J. McCarty, John L. McCarty Papers, Frank Collinson File, Am. Pub. Lib.

17. *Fort Worth Daily Democrat*, 9 Sept., 14 Sept. 1876; depositions of T. Hickey, 8 Aug. 1899, A. G. Brook, 17 Feb. 1900, and L. N. York, 28 Apr. 1903, *W. S. Glenn vs. U.S.*, Nos. 1892–1893 Court of Claims J73187, pp. 97–99, 147; *Fort Worth* [weekly] *Democrat*, 17 Sept. 1876; interview of J. Wright Mooar with Frank P. Hill, J. B. Slaughter, Jr., Jim Weatherford, 15 May 1936, J. Wright Mooar Papers, Interview Files, P-PHM.

18. Interview of S. P. Merry with J. Evetts Haley, 21 Aug. 1926, J. Evetts Haley Papers, Interview Files, P-PHM; deposition of A. G. Brook, 17 Feb. 1900, *W. S. Glenn vs. U.S.*, Nos. 1892–1893 Court of Claims J73187, p. 97; deposition of William Benson, 24 Aug. 1912, *W. S. Glenn vs. U.S. Court of Claims*, Nos. 1892–1893 Court of Claims 61311, pp. 9–10; J. D. Miles to W. Nicholson, 31 Aug. 1877, *Rpt. of Sec. Int.*, H. Ex. Doc. 1, 45th Cong., 2d sess., 1877, vol. 1, pt. 5, p. 478. For a brief account of Lee and Reynolds's distribution of hides once arrived at the Cheyenne and Arapaho Agency, see "Hollister: The Ride from Fort Sill to Leavenworth," *Leavenworth Times*, 4 July 1878.

19. J. D. Miles to W. Nicholson, 18 Mar. 1877, Ltrs Rec'd/Chey. & Arap. Ag., RG 75; deposition of William Benson, 24 Aug. 1923, and testimony of W. S. Glenn, *W. S. Glenn vs. U.S.*, Nos. 1892–1893 Court of Claims 61311, pp. 4–5, 45–46. Garrett believed that he was at Reynolds City during the fall of 1877 rather than the fall of 1876; see deposition of Pat Garrett, 2 Sept. 1899, *W. S. Glenn vs. U.S.*, Nos. 1892–1893 Court of Claims J74287, pp. 252–257. For an account of the first raid, see *Dodge City Times*, 2 June

1877; for a personal recollection of the raid and the subsequent skirmishes, see Strickland, ed., "Recollections of W. S. Glenn," *P-PHR* 22 (1949): 42–53.

20. J. D. Miles to W. Nicholson, 31 Aug. 1877, *Rpt. of Sec. Int.*, H. Ex. Doc. 1, 45th Cong., 2d sess., 1877, vol. 1, pt. 5, p. 478; P. McCusker to A. C. Williams, Ind. Agt. for Wichita & Affiliated Bands, 29 May 1877, Ltrs Rec'd/ Chey. & Arap. Ag., RG 75.

21. *Dodge City Times*, 14 July, 28 July 1877. See the explanation of J. D. Miles to W. Nicholson, 27 Mar. 1877, Ltrs Rec'd/Chey. & Arap. Ag., RG 75; also see Lee and Reynolds to J. D. Miles, 15 Mar. 1877, Ltrs Rec'd/Chey. & Arap. Ag., RG 75.

22. For an account of one teamster's freight hauls during 1877, see the account book of John Wesley Mooar, 1877, John Wesley Mooar Papers, bound vols. 1876–1890, Southwest Collect., Texas Tech Univ.

23. *Dodge City Times*, 28 July 1877.

24. The probable date for the opening of the two outlets was the summer of 1877 as the season marked the peak of the Texas hunt. If the partners had waited until 1878, the Texas kill would have been near its end. The information about two robe outlets in New York and Chicago is based on an undated business card of Lee and Reynolds and S. J. Arnold, Joseph Smith Papers, Miscellaneous Papers, Southwest Collect., Texas Tech Univ.

25. Lee and Reynolds to LTC W. H. Lewis, Cmdg, Ft. Dodge, 1 Aug. 1877, Consol. QM Corresp. Files, Ft. Dodge, Box 260, RG 92. The expansion was approved by the secretary of war on 25 Aug. 1877. See Letter Order of Sec. War issued by John Tweedle, Acting Chief Clerk, 25 Aug. 1877, Consol. QM Corresp. Files, Ft. Dodge, Box 260, RG 92; J. D. Miles to W. Nicholson, 12 July 1877, Ltrs Rec'd/Chey. & Arap. Ag., RG 75.

26. *Columbus Republican*, 22 Sept., 22 Dec. 1877; *Columbus Democrat*, 12 May, 22 Dec. 1877; *Dodge City Times*, 8 Sept., 29 Sept. 1877; 1/Lt Thomas M. Wenie, AAQM, Ft. Elliott, to Chief QM, Dept. Mo., 13 Aug., 14 Sept., 23 Dec. 1877, Ltrs Sent/Ft. Elliott QM, RG 393.

27. J. D. Miles to Hayt, CIA, 31 Aug. 1878, *Rpt. of Sec. Int.*, H. Ex. Doc. 1, 45th Cong., 3d sess., 1878, vol. 1, pt. 5, p. 550; J. D. Miles to E. A. Hayt, CIA, 29 Oct., 20 Dec., 1877, Ltrs Rec'd/Chey. & Arap. Ag., RG 75; J. D. Miles to E. A. Hayt, 31 Aug. 1878, *Rpt. of Sec. Int.*, H. Ex. Doc. 1, 45th Cong., 3d sess., 1878, vol. 1, pt. 5, p. 550. Also see Cpt. G. Gunther to Post AG, Ft. Reno, 4 Dec. 1877, Ltrs Rec'd/Chey. & Arap. Ag., RG 75; Col. John P. Hatch to U.S. Ind. Agt., 8 Dec. 1877, Chey. & Arap. Ag., RG 75; also see 2/Lt J. W. Martin to Post AG, Ft. Elliott, 11 Dec. 1877, and Col. J. P. Hatch to AAG, Dept. Mo., 19 Dec. 1877, Ltrs Rec'd/Cen. Sup., RG 75.

28. Cpt. G. Gunther to Post AG, Ft. Reno, 4 Dec. 1877; Col. J. P. Hatch, Cmdg, Ft. Elliott to AAG, Dept. Mo., 12 Dec. 1877; and J. D. Miles to Lee and Reynolds, 13 Dec. 1877, Ltrs Rec'd/Chey. & Arap. Ag., RG 75; Maj. H. A. Hambright to Cmdg Officer, Camp Supply, 21 Dec. 1877, Ltrs Sent/C. Supply, RG 393.

29. Maj. H. A. Hambright to Cmdg Officer, Camp Supply, 21 Dec. 1877, Ltrs Sent/C. Supply, RG 393; Lee and Reynolds to J. D. Miles, 27 Dec. 1877; J. D. Miles to E. A. Hayt, CIA, 12 Mar. 1878; C. Schurz, Sec. Int., to CIA,

29 June 1878; and J. A. Covington to J. D. Miles, 1 July 1878, Ltrs Rec'd/ Chey. & Arap. Ag., RG 75.

30. Contract between LTC R. Saxton and W. M. D. Lee, 22 Dec. 1877, Consol. QM Corresp. Files, Box 555, RG 92; J. A. Covington to J. D. Miles, 7 Jan. 1878, and Cpt. W. J. Lyster to AAG, Dept. Mo., 28 Nov. 1878, Ltrs Rec'd/ Chey. & Arap. Ag., RG 75.

31. J. D. Miles to CIA, 31 Aug. 1878, *Rpt. of Sec. Int.*, H. Ex. Doc. 1, 45th Cong., 3d sess., 1878, vol. 1, pt. 5, p. 551; undated deposition of J. V. Cousey, *W. S. Glenn vs. U.S.*, Nos. 1892–1893 Court of Claims 61311, p. 223; J. D. Miles to E. A. Hayt, 2 May 1878, Ltrs Rec'd/Chey. & Arap. Ag., RG 75; J. D. Miles to Thomas P. Fenlon, 17 Feb. 1879, pp. 76–77, Chey. & Arap. Ag. Ltrbook, 29 Nov. 1878 to 28 Nov. 1879, Edna May Arnold Papers, Carnegie Library; Maj. H. A. Hambright to AAG, Dept. Mo., 6 Jan. 1878, Ltrs Sent/C. Supply, RG 393; Lee and Reynolds to J. D. Miles; A. E. Reynolds to E. A. Hayt, 9 Mar. 1878; A. E. Reynolds to "Mr. Leeds," Chief Clerk, Indian Office, 18 June 1878; and C. Schurz, Sec. Int., to CIA, 29 June 1878, Ltrs Rec'd/Chey. & Arap. Ag., RG 75. (For new material pertinent to the Lee and Reynolds partnership, see the Albert E. Reynolds Collection, Colorado Historical Society, Denver.)

32. J. D. Miles to CIA, 31 Aug. 1879, *Rpt. of Sec. Int.*, H. Ex. Doc. 1, 46th Cong., 2d sess., 1879, vol. 1, pt. 5, p. 167; also see the criticism of Lee and Reynolds's methods made by LTC Richard I. Dodge, Cmdg, New Cantonment, to AAG, Dept. Mo., 4 Mar. 1880, Ltrs Rec'd/Chey. & Arap. Ag., RG 75. Spec. Agt. J. M. Crowell to David B. Parker, Postmaster, 17 Sept. 1879, U.S., Cong., House, *Inquiry into the Postal Star Service*, H. Misc. Doc. 31, 46th Cong., 2d sess., 1880, p. 310.

33. P. McCusker to E. A. Hayt, 3 Mar. 1878, Ltrs Rec'd/Chey. & Arap. Ag., RG 75.

34. Maj. J. K. Mizner, Cmdg, Ft. Reno, to AAG, Dept. Mo., 18 Sept. 1878, *Rpt. of Sec. War*, H. Ex. Doc. 1, 45th Cong., 3d sess., 1878, vol. 1, pt. 2, p. 44; J. D. Miles to CIA, 31 Aug. 1878, *Rpt. of Sec. Int.*, H. Ex. Doc. 1, 45th Cong., 3d sess., 1878, vol. 1, pt. 5, p. 164; *Leavenworth Times*, 26 Sept. 1878; Cpt. W. J. Lyster to AAG, Dept. Mo., 18 Nov. 1878, Ltrs Sent/C. Supply, RG 393; LTC J. P. Hatch to AAG, Dept. Mo., 28 Nov. 1878, and Cpt. E. H. Liscum to Post AG, Ft. Elliott, 9 Dec. 1878, Ltrs Rec'd/Chey. & Arap. Ag., RG 75.

35. *Dodge City Times*, 10 Aug. 1878; J. D. Miles to E. A. Hayt, 12 Oct. 1878, Ltrs Rec'd/Chey. & Arap. Ag., RG 75.

36. W. N. Hubbell to E. B. French, Second Auditor, Dept. Int., 10 Dec. 1878, Ltrs Rec'd/Chey. & Arap. Ag., RG 75.

37. Ibid.

38. Compare this incident with Lee's methods during a similar crisis at the Cheyenne and Arapaho Agency in the spring of 1871, discussed in Chapter 1.

39. P. McCusker to E. A. Hayt, 3 Mar. 1878, Ltrs Rec'd/Chey. & Arap. Ag., RG 75; *Dodge City Times*, 15 Nov. 1879; Post AG, Ft. Supply, to Lee and Reynolds, Agt. for Volz & Keeling, 19 July 1879, and Minutes of Proceedings Relative to a Malicious Trespass . . . held at Fort Supply, I. T., 7 May 1879,

Ltrs Rec'd/Ft. Supply, RG 393; *Ford County Globe,* 19 Aug. 1879.

40. Contract between LTC R. Saxton, QM, Dept. Mo., and W. M. D. Lee, 7 Mar. 1878, Consol. QM Corresp. Files, Box 555, RG 92.

41. For the Camp Supply contract, see contract between LTC R. Saxton and W. M. D. Lee, 22 May 1878; for the Fort Elliott contract, see contract between LTC R. Saxton and W. M. D. Lee, 22 May 1878, and contract between LTC R. Saxton and W. M. D. Lee, 10 May 1878, Consol. QM Corresp. Files, Box 555, RG 92.

42. Contract between LTC R. Saxton and W. M. D. Lee, 2 June 1879, Consol. QM Corresp. Files, Box 555, RG 92. The particular contract for hay deliveries is lost; however, two area newspapers refer to Lee and Reynolds's "extensive contract for hay." *Dodge City Times,* 17 Aug. 1878; *Ford County Globe,* 4 Aug. 1878. See also *Dodge City Times,* 5 July 1879; *Leavenworth Times,* 17 July 1879; Cpt. George K. Beavy, Cmdg, Ft. Supply, to Cmdg Officer, Cantonment North Fork of the Canadian River, 29 Aug. 1879, Ltrs Sent./Ft. Supply, RG 393.

43. Lee and Reynolds to Post AG, C. Supply, 4 Apr. 1879, Ltrs Rec'd/Ft. Supply, RG 393; *Fort Griffin Echo,* 12 Apr. 1879; *Ford County Globe,* 19 Feb. 1878, 29 June 1879.

44. LTC J. W. Davidson to AAG, Dept. Mo., 14 June 1879, Ltrs Sent/Ft. Elliott, RG 393.

45. G. W. Arrington to [Texas] AG John B. Jones, 18 June 1879, *Galveston Daily News,* 6 July 1879; LTC J. W. Davidson to AAG, Dept. Mo., 15 June 1879, Ltrs Sent/Ft. Elliott, RG 393.

46. G. W. Arrington to [Texas] AG J. B. Jones, 18 June 1879, *Galveston Daily News,* 6 July 1879; LTC J. W. Davidson to AAG, Dept. Mo., 15 June 1879, Ltrs Sent/Ft. Elliott, RG 393.

47. *Ford County Globe,* 25 June 1879.

48. Affidavit of Emanuel [Dubbs], County Judge, Wheeler County, ca. 21 June 1879, *Galveston Daily News,* 6 July 1879; see Donnelly's explanation at Affidavit of John Donnelly, 18 June 1879, *Galveston Daily News,* 6 July 1879.

49. See G. W. Arrington to [Texas] AG J. B. Jones, 18 June and 21 June 1879; G. W. Arrington to LTC J. W. Davidson, 18 June 1879, *Galveston Daily News,* 6 July 1879; one of the petitioners, J. W. Huselby, later repudiated his signature: J. W. Huselby to AG, State of Texas, 24 June 1879, *Galveston Daily News,* 6 July 1879.

50. G. W. Arrington to [Texas] AG J. B. Jones, 21 June 1879, *Galveston Daily News,* 6 July 1879.

51. Petition of Benjamin Williams, John [Donnelly], J. W. Huselby, Commissioners of Wheeler County, to O. M. Roberts, Gov. Texas, ca. 27 June 1879, ibid.

52. *Dodge City Times,* 7 Jan., 22 Mar. 1879; *Ford County Globe,* 19 Aug., 26 Aug. 1879.

53. LTC R. I. Dodge to AAG, Dept. Mo., 4 Mar. 1880, and Lt. J. H. Pardee, Post AG, Cantonment North Fork of Canadian River, to J. E. McAllister, 25 Apr. 1879, Ltrs Rec'd/Chey. & Arap. Ag., RG 75.

NOTES TO PAGES 49–53   **157**

54. LTC R. I. Dodge to AAG, Dept. Mo., 4 Mar. 1880, Ltrs Rec'd/Chey. & Arap. Ag., RG 75.

55. Charles E. Campbell to E. A. Hayt, 9 Oct., 11 Oct. 1879; J. D. Miles to E. A. Hayt, 19 Jan. 1880; and Affidavit of Mah-min-nick [Cheyenne Indian] with George Bent, 16 Dec. 1879, Ltrs Rec'd/Chey. & Arap. Ag., RG 75.

56. J. Q. Smith, CIA, to W. Nicholson, 14 June 1878; P. McCusker to A. C. Williams, U.S. Agt. for Wichita Bands, 29 May 1877; and Charles Rath to Cmdg Officer, Ft. Supply, 24 July 1879, Ltrs Rec'd/Ft. Supply, RG 393; *Ford County Globe*, 14 Oct. 1879; Special Agt. J. M. Crowell to David B. Parker, Postmaster, 17 Sept. 1879, U.S., Cong., House, *Inquiry into the Postal Star System*, H. Misc. Doc. 31, 46th Cong., 2d sess., 1880, p. 310.

57. H. P. N. Gammel, *The Laws of Texas, 1822–1892*, vol. 8, pp. 188–191, 1078.

58. Interview of Ellen O'Loughlin with J. Evetts Haley, 17 July 1926, J. Evetts Haley Papers, Interview Files, P-PHM; *Dodge City Times*, 1 June 1878; *Ford County Globe*, 15 Oct. 1878; *Fort Griffin Echo*, 12 Apr. 1879; *Lee & Reynolds vs. Henry Flemming*, Texas, Court of Civil Appeals (1881), White & Willson, vol. 1, pp. 638–639.

59. *Ford County Globe*, 15 July 1879.

60. Texas, Clay County, County Clerk, Minutes of the Commissioners' Court, 13 Mar. 1879, vol. 1, pp. 223–225.

61. *Ford County Globe*, 15 July 1879.

62. Ibid., 10 June 1879; *Dodge City Times*, 26 Apr. 1879; Texas, Wheeler County, County Clerk, Minutes of the Commissioners' Court, 5 June 1879, vol. 1, pp. 42–45.

63. George W. Arrington to [Texas] AG J. B. Jones, 18 June 1879, *Galveston Daily News*, 6 July 1879; *Dodge City Times*, 30 Aug. 1879.

64. Texas, Wheeler County, County Clerk, Deed Records, Gunter and Munson to Lee and Reynolds, 17 Dec. 1879, vol. 1A, pp. 104–106; E. D. Townsend, AG, U.S. Army, to Cmdg Officer, Ft. Supply, 16 Jan. 1880, Ltrs Rec'd/Ft. Supply, RG 393. For McKinney's past employment, see *Ford County Globe*, 19 Feb. 1878.

4. Three Brands

1. *Ford County Globe*, 10 May, 10 Aug. 1880; *Dodge City Times*, 1 May, 15 May 1880; Sanders, *A History of Hereford Cattle*, p. 1065; *Cheyenne Transporter*, 10 Sept. 1880.

2. John Arnot, "Tascosa Recollections," unpub. ms. dated Sept., 1934, and interview of James East with J. Evetts Haley, 27 Sept. 1927, Dr. L. F. Sheffy Memorial Collect., Cornette Lib., WTSU; interview of Harry Ingerton with J. Evetts Haley, 13 Apr. 1927, J. Evetts Haley Papers, Interview Files, P-PHM; *Dodge City Times*, 18 Oct. 1879.

3. For a description of the early cattle operations centered at Tascosa, see *Ford County Globe*, 2 Sept. 1879, 28 Dec. 1880; Texas, Oldham County, County Clerk, Brand Records, vol. 1, p. 20; interview of Harry Ingerton with J. Evetts Haley, 13 Apr. 1927, J. Evetts Haley Papers, and [W. B. Munson] to

Laura V. Hamner, 29 June 1921, Laura V. Hamner Papers, Interview Files, P-PHM; interview of James East with J. Evetts Haley, 27 Sept. 1927, Dr. L. F. Sheffy Memorial Collect., Cornette Lib., WTSU.

4. For contemporary recollections of Billy the Kid's raids into the Panhandle, see interview of James East with J. Evetts Haley, 27 Sept. 1927, Dr. L. F. Sheffy Memorial Collect., Cornette Lib., WTSU; interview of Judge O. H. Nelson with J. Evetts Haley, 27 Feb. 1927, J. Evetts Haley Papers, Interview Files, P-PHM; John W. Poe, *Billy the Kid*, p. 8. John G. Lang, a Panhandle contemporary of Billy the Kid, said, "He [Billy] worked for Lew Cramer and he had a ranch just over the line in [New] Mexico." Interview of John G. Lang with L. F. Sheffy, 13 Oct. 1936, Dr. L. F. Sheffy Memorial Collect., Cornette Lib., WTSU.

5. The earliest reference to McAllister as an LE foreman is in a 27 June 1880 issue of *Ford County Globe*.

6. Texas, Wheeler County, County Clerk, Deed Records, James Campbell and E. Goodwin-Austen to W. M. D. Lee and A. E. Reynolds, 22 May 1880, vol. 1A, pp. 228–230; interview of James East with J. Evetts Haley, 27 Sept. 1927, Dr. L. F. Sheffy Memorial Collect., Cornette Lib., WTSU.

7. Sanders, *A History of Hereford Cattle*, p. 1066.

8. *New York Times*, 8 May 1881.

9. *Dodge City Times*, 15 May, 25 Dec. 1880, 29 Jan. 1881; *Ford County Globe*, 10 Aug., 28 Dec. 1880.

10. *Ford County Globe*, 15 Mar. 1881; *Fort Griffin Echo*, 19 Feb. 1881. See above notes on the yearly purchases of LE cattle; also see *Cheyenne Transporter*, 10 June 1881; *New York Times*, 8 May 1881.

11. *Dodge City Times*, 24 Feb. 1881; also see Sanders, *A History of Hereford Cattle*, p. 1065; *Ford County Globe*, 21 June 1881; *Breeder's Gazette* 11 (17 Feb. 1887): 257; 12 (1 Sept. 1887): 317.

12. *New York Times*, 8 May 1881. For details of past Scott endorsements, see Chapters 1 and 3.

13. Texas, Oldham County, County Clerk, Deed Records, Jot Gunter to Lucien Scott, 3 Dec. 1880, vol. 1, pp. 33–35.

14. *New York Times*, 8 May 1881.

15. Poe, *Billy the Kid*, p. 7.

16. Ibid., pp. 7–8. For a short contemporary account of Garrett's apprehension of Billy at Portales, see *Ford County Globe*, 4 June 1881.

17. Minutes of a Proceeding Relative to a Malicious Trespass . . . held at Ft. Supply, I. T., 7 May 1880; Col. Granville O. Haller to AAG, Dept. Mo., 6 May 1880; and Col. Haller to AG, U.S. Army, 12 May 1880, Ltrs Rec'd/Ft. Supply, RG 393; *Kansas City Times*, 23 Dec. 1880, cited in *Wichita Weekly Beacon*, 29 Dec. 1880; *Fort Griffin Echo*, 7 Aug. 1880; *Ford County Globe*, 28 Dec. 1880. For a discussion of the trail issue and the effect of "Texas fever," see U.S., Cong., House, *Letter from the Secretary of the Treasury . . . in Regard to the Range and Ranch Cattle Traffic in the Western States and Territories*, H. Ex. Doc. 267, 48th Cong., 2d sess., 1885.

18. Texas, Wheeler County, County Clerk, Minutes of the Commissioners' Court, 8 Nov. 1880, vol. 1, p. 60; *Ford County Globe*, 28 Dec. 1880; *Lee and*

Reynolds vs. Henry Flemming, Texas Court of Civil Appeals, 18 May 1881, *White & Willson*, vol. 1, p. 639; Stone, *History of Colorado*, vol. 3, p. 547; interview of James East with J. Evetts Haley, 27 Sept. 1927, Dr. L. F. Sheffy Memorial Collect., Cornette Lib., WTSU.

19. Louisa Ward Arps [confidant of Albert Reynolds's daughter] to DFS, 12 June 1976; interview of an unidentified cowboy cited in Dulcie Sullivan, *The LS Brand*, p. 32. For new material pertinent to the Lee and Reynolds partnership, see the Albert E. Reynolds Collection, Colorado Historical Society, Denver.

20. J. D. Miles to CIA, 22 Sept. 1881, Chey. & Arap. Ag., Ltrbook, 2 Sept. 1881 to 2 Feb. 1882, pp. 68–70, Chey. & Arap. Papers, Arch., OHS; *Cheyenne Transporter*, 13 Oct. 1883; *Dodge City Times*, 28 July 1881; Texas, Oldham County, County Clerk, Brand Records, vol. 1, p. 20; Texas, Oldham County, County Clerk, Deed Records, Agreement between W. M. D. Lee and A. E. Reynolds, 15 Apr. 1882, vol. 2, pp. 12–17; W. M. D. Lee to Cmdg Officer, Ft. Elliott, 25 Feb. 1880, and D. W. Van Horn to Cmdg Officer, Ft. Elliott, 27 Feb. 1880, AG Records, ACP, Index No. 1475, RG 94; Sutlers Register, Reg. 3, p. 159, AG Records, RG 94; contracts between Col. J. D. Bingham, QM, Dept. Mo., and W. M. D. Lee, 16 June, 23 June 1881, Consol. QM Corresp. Files, Box 555, RG 92. It was not until June 1882 that the government recognized Lee as Fort Supply's sole trader. See Sutlers Register, Reg. 4, p. 24, AG Records, RG 94; A. Reynolds to Cmdg Officer, Ft. Supply, 31 May 1882, and W. M. D. Lee to Cmdg Officer, Ft. Supply, 31 May 1882, Ltrs Rec'd/Ft. Supply, RG 393; George Leigh to *Texas Livestock Journal*, 16 Aug. 1881, cited in *Caldwell Post*, 8 Sept. 1881.

21. For contemporary reference to the building of the drift fence, see *Dallas Morning News*, 12 Feb. 1886; interview of Judge O. H. Nelson with J. Evetts Haley, 13 July 1926, Dr. L. F. Sheffy Memorial Collect., Cornette Lib., WTSU; interview of Vas Stickley with J. Evetts Haley, n.d., J. Evetts Haley Papers, Interview Files, P-PHM; interview of Charles Bennett with Mrs. Larry W. Cook, n.d., Charles Bennett Papers, Interview Files, P-PHM; W. B. Munson to Laura V. Hamner, 29 June 1921, Laura V. Hamner Papers, Interview Files, P-PHM.

22. *Dodge City Times*, 24 Aug. 1882.

23. The cattle sales are recorded in *Ford County Globe*, 4 Oct., 1 Nov., 8 Nov. 1881.

24. *Ford County Globe*, 18 Jan. 1882; *Caldwell Post*, 16 Mar. 1882; Texas, Wheeler County, County Clerk, Brand Records, vol. 1, p. 101.

25. Texas, Oldham County, County Clerk, Deed Records, W. M. D. Lee to A. E. Reynolds, 15 Apr. 1882, vol. 2, pp. 7–11; Texas, Oldham County, County Clerk, Deed Records, Mortgage of A. E. Reynolds to W. M. D. Lee, 15 Apr. 1882, vol. 2, pp. 17–24; Texas, Oldham County, County Clerk, Deed Records, Agreement between W. M. D. Lee and A. E. Reynolds, 15 Apr. 1882, vol. 2, pp. 12–17.

26. Obituary of Lucien Scott, *Leavenworth Times*, 1 June 1893.

27. Texas, Oldham County, County Clerk, Deed Records, O. M. Roberts, Gov., State of Texas, to W. M. D. Lee, 1 Mar. 1881, vol. 1, pp. 44–45, 47–48,

vol. 2, pp. 61, 357–360, 362. Fifty thousand acres were purchased; however, Lee sold approximately twenty-five thousand acres to two Wheeler County speculators. See ibid., W. M. D. Lee to Lawrence P. Brown and Francisco A. Manzanares, 18 Mar. 1881, vol. 1, pp. 49–54.

28. Scott's acquisitions in Oldham and Hartley counties and Lee's retention of a one-half interest in all LE lands are discussed earlier in this chapter.

29. Interview of James East with J. Evetts Haley, 27 Sept. 1927, and interview of John G. Lang with L. F. Sheffy, 13 Oct. 1936, Dr. L. F. Sheffy Memorial Collect., Cornette Lib., WTSU; Texas, Oldham County, County Clerk, Deed Records, O. M. Roberts, Gov., State of Texas, to W. M. D. Lee, 2 Nov. 1882, vol. 7, p. 88, 3 Nov. 1882, vol. 7, p. 89, vol. 19, pp. 290, 406, 408, vol. 24, pp. 83–84, vol. 29, p. 456, 4 Nov. 1882, vol. 29, p. 455; J. N. Browning, "Abstract of Warranty Deed on LS Ranch Holdings," 20 May 1905, Colden Whitman Papers, Interview Files, P-PHM; *Ford County Globe*, 19 Dec. 1882; *Dodge City Times*, 7 Dec. 1882.

30. *New York Times*, 8 May 1881; Texas, Oldham County, District Clerk, Civil Docket, Memorandum of Agreement between L. A. Mosty and the Lee-Scott Cattle Co., Case No. 26; *Ford County Globe*, 28 Nov., 19 Dec. 1882; Sanders, *A History of Hereford Cattle*, p. 769; *Breeder's Gazette* 1 (25 Mar. 1882): 671.

31. See Texas, Wheeler County, District Clerk, Civil Docket, Memorandum of Agreement between L. A. Mosty and the Lee-Scott Cattle Co., 26 Feb. 1881, Case No. 26; *Fort Griffin Echo*, 5 Nov., 3 Dec., 10 Dec. 1881; Texas, Wheeler County, District Clerk, Civil Docket, *R. E. McAnulty vs. W. M. D. Lee et al.*, 23 Aug. 1882, Case Nos. 30 and 31; *Dodge City Times*, 31 Aug. 1882.

32. Texas, Oldham County, County Clerk, Minutes of the Commissioners' Court, 8 May 1882, vol. 1, p. 20, 14 Feb. 1883, vol. 1, p. 28.

33. *Texas Livestock Journal*, 24 Nov. 1882. For the direction of the fence as finally constructed and for the many outfits involved, see interview of Judge O. H. Nelson with J. Evetts Haley, 26 Feb. 1927, J. Evetts Haley Papers, Interview Files, P-PHM; interview of Newt Bowers with L. F. Sheffy, 13 Feb. 1927, Dr. L. F. Sheffy Memorial Collect., Cornette Lib., WTSU.

34. Interview of J. E. McAllister with J. Evetts Haley, 1 July 1926, J. Evetts Haley Papers, Interview Files, P-PHM.

35. *Dodge City Times*, 29 June 1882.

36. *Ford County Globe*, 20 Mar. 1883; interview of Garrett H. "Kid" Dobbs with John McCarty and Mel Armstrong, 12 Sept. 1942, John L. McCarty Papers, Kid Dobbs Interview File, Am. Pub. Lib.; interview of John G. Lang with L. F. Sheffy, 13 Oct. 1936, Dr. L. F. Sheffy Memorial Collect., Cornette Lib., WTSU.

37. For recollections of the 1883 cowboy strike, see interview of A. H. Webster with J. Evetts Haley, 9 Apr. 1927, interview of G. N. Jowell with J. Evetts Haley, 17 Jan. 1927, interview of Harry Ingerton with J. Evetts Haley, 13 Apr. 1927, and interview of Vas Stickley with J. Evetts Haley, n.d., J. Evetts Haley Papers, Interview Files, P-PHM; interview of Garrett H. "Kid" Dobbs with John McCarty and Mel Armstrong, 12 Sept. 1942, John L. McCarty Pa-

pers, Kid Dobbs Interview File, Am. Pub. Lib.; "Terms of Settlement, Cow Boy Association," Mar. 1883, Cowboy Association Papers, Interview Files, P-PHM; also see speech of R. E. Baird before a history class, WTSU, as transcribed by A. P. Bralley, 22 Aug. 1933, R. E. Baird Papers, Interview Files, P-PHM; L. Gough, "Reminiscenses," unpub. ms., n.d., L. Gough Papers, Interview Files, P-PHM.

38. *Fort Worth Daily Democrat*, 16 Mar. 1883, put the figure of striking cowboys at 160; also see interview of James East with J. Evetts Haley, 27 Sept. 1927, Dr. L. F. Sheffy Memorial Collect., Cornette Lib., WTSU; *Fort Worth Daily Democrat*, 25 Mar. 1883; interview of Garrett H. "Kid" Dobbs with John McCarty and Mel Armstrong, 12 Sept. 1942, John L. McCarty Papers, Kid Dobbs Interview File, Am. Pub. Lib.

39. *Fort Worth Daily Democrat*, 16 Mar. 1883; interview of Garrett H. "Kid" Dobbs with John McCarty and Mel Armstrong, 12 Sept. 1942, John L. McCarty Papers, Kid Dobbs Interview File, Am. Pub. Lib.

40. See the dates specified for settlement of Reynolds's mortgage in Texas, Oldham County, County Clerk, Deed Records, Mortgage of A. E. Reynolds to W. M. D. Lee, 15 Apr. 1881, vol. 2, pp. 17–24.

41. Interview of Garrett H. "Kid" Dobbs with John McCarty, 12 Sept. 1942 and 20 Oct. 1942, John L. McCarty Papers, Kid Dobbs Interview File, Am. Pub. Lib.

42. Undated issue of *Kansas City Indicator*, cited in *Caldwell Post*, 29 Mar. 1883; L. Gough, "Reminiscences," unpub. ms., n.d., L. Gough Papers, Interview Files, P-PHM; interview of Garrett H. "Kid" Dobbs with John McCarty and Mel Armstrong, 12 Sept. 1942, John L. McCarty Papers, Kid Dobbs Interview File, Am. Pub. Lib.

43. Interview of Garrett H. "Kid" Dobbs with John McCarty and Mel Armstrong, 12 Sept. 1942, John L. McCarty Papers, Kid Dobbs Interview File, Am. Pub. Lib.

44. Ibid.; interview of R. E. Baird before a WTSU history class as transcribed by A. P. Bralley, 22 Aug. 1933, R. E. Baird Papers, Interview Files, P-PHM.

45. Interview of Harry Ingerton with J. Evetts Haley, 13 Apr. 1927, J. Evetts Haley Papers, Interview Files, P-PHM; interview of Jesse Jenkins with Laura V. Hamner and Winnie D. Hall, 11 Sept. 1936, Jesse Jenkins Papers, Interview Files, P-PHM; interview of James East with J. Evetts Haley, 27 Sept. 1927, Dr. L. F. Sheffy Memorial Collect., Cornette Lib., WTSU; interview of Garrett H. "Kid" Dobbs with John McCarty and Mel Armstrong, 12 Sept. and 13 Sept. 1942, John L. McCarty Papers, Kid Dobbs Interview File, Am. Pub. Lib.; interview of Judge O. H. Nelson with J. Evetts Haley, 26 Feb. 1927, J. Evetts Haley Papers, Interview Files, P-PHM.

46. Kansas, Leavenworth County, County Clerk, Deed Records, Joseph H. and Ellen Ferrell to William M. D. Lee, 9 June 1883, vol. 86, p. 205.

47. Texas, Oldham County, County Clerk, Deed Records, Lucien Scott to Lee Scott Cattle Co., 21 June 1883, and W. M. D. Lee to Lee Scott Cattle Co., 21 June 1883, vol. 2, pp. 117–122, 126–128, 183–184.

48. Interview of James East with J. Evetts Haley, 27 Sept. 1927, Dr. L. F.

Sheffy Memorial Collect., Cornette Lib., WTSU; Texas, Oldham County, County Clerk, Minutes of the Commissioners' Court, 18 June 1883, vol. 1, p. 35; U.S., Cong., House, *Letter from the Secretary of the Interior . . . in Regard to the Range and Ranch Cattle Traffic in the Western States and Territories*, H. Ex. Doc. 267, 48th Cong., 2d sess., 1885, pp. 29–32; *Ford County Globe*, 8 Apr. 1884; interview of Judge O. H. Nelson with J. Evetts Haley, 26 Feb. 1927, J. Evetts Haley Papers, Interview Files, P-PHM; Richard L. Spader, Asst. Dir. Pub. Rel., American Angus Association, St. Joseph, Mo., to DFS, 27 Jan. 1977.

49. See statement of George M. Maverick, *Las Vegas Stock Grower*, 8 Dec. 1888; interview of Judge O. H. Nelson with J. Evetts Haley, 26 Feb. 1927, J. Evetts Haley Papers, Interview Files, P-PHM; interview of Garrett H. "Kid" Dobbs with John McCarty and Mel Armstrong, 12 Sept. 1942, John L. McCarty Papers, Kid Dobbs Interview File, Am. Pub. Lib.

50. Texas, City of Houston, Office of the Registrar, Bureau of Vital Statistics, Death Certificate of Lucien W. Lee, 1905, No. 6412.

51. *Leavenworth Times*, 21 Dec., 27 Dec. 1883, 4 Jan., 27 Feb. 1884; *Breeder's Gazette* 4 (27 Dec. 1883): 890; undated issue of *Denver Live-Stock Journal*, cited in *Breeder's Gazette* 7 (23 Apr. 1885): 632; *Breeder's Gazette* 7 (9 Apr. 1885): 543. For a contemporary debate by one organization of the cattle trail issue, see *Ford County Globe*, 29 Jan., 8 Apr. 1884.

52. Interview of Garrett H. "Kid" Dobbs with John McCarty and Mel Armstrong, 12 Sept. 1942, John L. McCarty Papers, Kid Dobbs Interview File, Am. Pub. Lib.

53. Interview of Harry Ingerton with J. Evetts Haley, 13 Apr. 1927, J. Evetts Haley Papers, Interview Files, P-PHM; interview of Garrett H. "Kid" Dobbs with John McCarty and Mel Armstrong, 12 Sept. 1942, John L. McCarty Papers, Kid Dobbs Interview File, Am. Pub. Lib.

54. Interview of Garrett H. "Kid" Dobbs with John McCarty and Mel Armstrong, 12 Sept. 1942, John L. McCarty Papers, Kid Dobbs Interview File, Am. Pub. Lib.

55. Pat T. Garrett to Gov. John Ireland, 28 Apr. 1884, Gov. John Ireland Papers, Folders 22–24, June to Dec. 1884, Texas State Archives.

56. Interview of Garrett H. "Kid" Dobbs with John McCarty and Mel Armstrong, 12 Sept. 1942, John L. McCarty Papers, Kid Dobbs Interview File, Am. Pub. Lib.; Pat T. Garrett to W. H. King [Texas AG], 19 May 1884, Gov. John Ireland Papers, Folders 22–24, Jan. to Dec. 1884, Tx. St. Arch.; interview of James East with J. Evetts Haley, 27 Sept. 1927, Dr. L. F. Sheffy Memorial Collect., Cornette Lib., WTSU.

57. *Austin Daily Statesman*, 18 Apr. 1884. Also see interview of Garrett H. "Kid" Dobbs with John McCarty and Mel Armstrong, 12 Sept. 1942, John L. McCarty Papers, Kid Dobbs Interview File, Am. Pub. Lib.; speech of R. E. Baird before a WTSU history class as transcribed by J. B. Lewis, 22 Aug. 1933, R. E. Baird Papers, Interview Files, P-PHM.

58. Interview of Garrett H. "Kid" Dobbs with John McCarty and Mel Armstrong, 12 Sept. 1942, John L. McCarty Papers, Kid Dobbs Interview File, Am. Pub. Lib.; John Arnot, "Tascosa Recollections," unpub. ms., n.d.,

Dr. L. F. Sheffy Memorial Collect., Cornette Lib., WTSU; Pat T. Garrett to
W. H. King, 19 May 1884, Gov. John Ireland Papers, Folders 22–24, Jan. to
Dec. 1884, Tx. St. Arch.; *Cheyenne Democratic Leader*, 14 May 1884; undated issue of *Northwest Live-Stock Journal*, cited in *Breeder's Gazette* 5
(22 May 1884): 797; *Ford County Globe*, 13 May 1884.

59. Interview of Garrett H. "Kid" Dobbs with John McCarty and Mel
Armstrong, 12 Sept. 1942, John L. McCarty Papers, Kid Dobbs Interview
File, Am. Pub. Lib.; interview of James East with J. Evetts Haley, 27 Sept.
1927, Dr. L. F. Sheffy Memorial Collect., Cornette Lib., WTSU; John Arnot,
"Tascosa Recollections," unpub. ms., n.d., Dr. L. F. Sheffy Memorial Col-
lect., Cornette Lib., WTSU.

60. *Dodge City Globe Live-Stock Journal*, 26 Aug. 1884, 25 Nov. 1884
(5 cattle cars); *Kansas Cowboy*, 23 Sept. (32 cattle cars), 11 Oct. (25 cattle
cars), 12 Oct. (16 cattle cars), 28 Oct. (30 cattle cars) 1884.

61. Interview of Garrett H. "Kid" Dobbs with John McCarty and Mel
Armstrong, 12 Sept. 1942, John L. McCarty Papers, Kid Dobbs Interview
File, Am. Pub. Lib.; interview of James East with J. Evetts Haley, 27 Sept.
1927, Dr. L. F. Sheffy Memorial Collect., Cornette Lib., WTSU; New Mexico, San Miguel County, Deed Records, John Donnelly to Lee Scott Cattle
Co., 8 July 1884, vol. 26, p. 149; Duncan L. Cage to Lee Scott Cattle Co.,
6 Aug. 1884, vol. 126, p. 380; Pleas Sanders to Lee Scott Cattle Co., 19 Aug.
1884, vol. 126, p. 381.

62. W. B. Munson to W. M. D. Lee, 19 Sept. 1884, Ltrbook of 10 Jan. 1883 to
16 Feb. 1885, p. 426, W. B. Munson Papers, P-PHM; *Globe Live-Stock Journal*, 6 Jan. 1885.

5. Showdowns

1. R. C. Drum, AG, U.S. Army, to W. M. D. Lee, 14 Jan. 1885, AG Records,
ACP, Index No. 832, RG 94; Sutlers Register, Reg. 4, p. 24, AG Records, RG
94; Col. J. H. Potter, Cmdg, Ft. Supply, to AAG, U.S. Army, 2 Feb. 1885,
AG Records, ACP, Index No. 832, RG 94; Cullis, Lynch, and Edge, *Leavenworth City Directory and Business Mirror*, 1872: 90, 1873: 101, 1878: 67,
1879–1880: 65, 1880–1881: 83, 1882: 83; *Leavenworth Times*, 22 Feb.
1885; State of Kansas Census, Leavenworth County, City of Leavenworth,
1885, p. 325, Watson Lib., Univ. of Kansas.

2. Interview of James East with J. Evetts Haley, 27 Sept. 1927, Dr. L. F.
Sheffy Memorial Collect., Cornette Lib., WTSU; interview of Garrett H.
"Kid" Dobbs with John McCarty and Mel Armstrong, 12 Sept. 1942, John
McCarty Papers, Kid Dobbs Interview File, Am. Pub. Lib. James East's mar-
riage is from *Kansas Cowboy*, 13 Dec. 1884; for another incident involving
Wade (Waddy) Woods, see Chapter 4.

3. Interview of Garrett H. "Kid" Dobbs with John McCarty and Mel
Armstrong, 12 Sept. 1942, John L. McCarty Papers, Kid Dobbs Interview
File, Am. Pub. Lib.

4. Ibid.; interview of James East with J. Evetts Haley, 27 Sept. 1927, Dr.
L. F. Sheffy Memorial Collect., Cornette Lib., WTSU.

5. Interview of Garrett H. "Kid" Dobbs with John McCarty and Mel Armstrong, 12 Sept. 1942, John L. McCarty Papers, Kid Dobbs Interview File, Am. Pub. Lib.

6. Interview of James East with J. Evetts Haley, 27 Sept. 1927, Dr. L. F. Sheffy Memorial Collect., Cornette Lib., WTSU.

7. Ibid.; interview of Garrett H. "Kid" Dobbs with John McCarty and Mel Armstrong, 12 Sept. 1942, John L. McCarty Papers, Kid Dobbs Interview File, Am. Pub. Lib.

8. *Yellowstone Journal*, 10 Jan., 28 Mar. 1885. For Leavenworth reports of the severe Montana winter, see *Leavenworth Times*, 2 Jan. 1885.

9. Interview of John G. Lang with L. F. Sheffy, 13 Oct. 1936, Dr. L. F. Sheffy Memorial Collect., Cornette Lib., WTSU; Texas, Oldham County, County Clerk, Minutes of the Commissioners' Court, 29 June 1885, vol. 1, pp. 79–80; undated issue of *Denver Live-Stock Journal*, cited in *Breeder's Gazette* 7 (23 Apr. 1885): 632.

10. Undated issue of *Mobeetie Panhandle*, cited in *Globe Live-Stock Journal*, 31 Mar., 7 Apr. 1885; undated issue of *Mobeetie Panhandle*, cited in *Breeder's Gazette* 7 (9 Apr. 1885): 543. The conflict was soon called the Winchester Quarantine. Interview of Judge O. H. Nelson with J. Evetts Haley, 26 Feb. 1927, J. Evetts Haley Papers, Interview Files, P-PHM.

11. Undated issue of *Kansas City Indicator*, cited in *Globe Live-Stock Journal*, 28 Apr. 1885; *Kansas Cowboy*, 25 Apr. 1885.

12. *Globe Live-Stock Journal*, 31 Mar. 1885.

13. Ibid. Also see interview of Judge O. H. Nelson with J. Evetts Haley, 26 Feb. 1927, J. Evetts Haley Papers, Interview Files, P-PHM; *Breeder's Gazette* 8 (11 June 1885): 893; interview of J. E. McAllister with J. Evetts Haley, 1 July 1926, J. Evetts Haley Papers, Interview Files, P-PHM; undated issue of *Cheyenne Live-Stock Journal*, cited in *Breeder's Gazette* 7 (28 May 1885): 819–820; undated issue of *Mobeetie Panhandle*, cited in *Breeder's Gazette* 8 (2 June 1885): 13.

14. *Leavenworth Times*, 11 July 1885; undated issue of *Medicine Lodge Cresset*, cited in *Breeder's Gazette* 8 (9 July 1885): 48.

15. *Leavenworth Times*, 11 July 1885.

16. *Yellowstone Journal*, 6 Oct. 1885; undated issue of *Chicago Times*, cited in *Kansas Cowboy*, 26 Sept. 1885; Report of W. T. Gass, State Agt., to Gov. John Ireland and Members of the State Land Board, 26 Nov. 1885, cited in *Dallas Morning News*, 29 Nov. 1885; A. Taylor to A. E. Reynolds, 12 Dec. 1885, and A. E. Reynolds to Abner Taylor, 9 Dec. 1885, XIT Ranch Papers, Ltrs Rec'd / B. H. Campbell, 1885–1887, P-PHM; also see statement of Judge O. H. Nelson, cited in *Dallas Morning News*, 12 Feb. 1886; W. Maud [XIT foreman] to Col. A. Taylor, 9 Apr. 1886, XIT Ranch Papers, Miscellaneous Correspondence to B. H. Campbell from Various Persons, 1886, P-PHM.

17. *Caldwell Journal*, 14 Jan. 1886; *Dallas Morning News*, 12 Feb. 1886; *Dodge City Democrat*, 4 Jan. 1886; interview of Vas Stickley with J. Evetts Haley, n.d., J. Evetts Haley Papers, Interview Files, P-PHM; W. Maud to [B. H. Campbell], 15 Jan. 1886, XIT Ranch Papers, Corresp. to B. H. Campbell, 1886, P-PHM; interview of Harry Ingerton with J. Evetts Haley, 13 Apr.

1927, J. Evetts Haley Papers, Interview Files, P-PHM; interview of Newt Bowers with L. F. Sheffy, 13 Feb. 1927, Dr. L. F. Sheffy Memorial Collect., Cornette Lib., WTSU.

18. Interview of Garrett H. "Kid" Dobbs with John McCarty and Mel Armstrong, 12 Sept. 1942, John L. McCarty Papers, Kid Dobbs Interview File, Am. Pub. Lib.; interview of James East with J. Evetts Haley, 27 Sept. 1927, Dr. L. F. Sheffy Memorial Collect., Cornette Lib., WTSU.

19. Texas, Oldham County, County Clerk, Minutes of the Commissioners' Court, 17 Mar. 1886, vol. 1, pp. 96–97; Fort Worth Gazette, 23 Mar. 1886.

20. J. V. Farwell to J. J. Stuart & Co., 25 Mar. 1886, XIT Ranch Papers, Letters of Abner Taylor, 27 Jan. 1886 to 1 Feb. 1887, P-PHM; W. Maud to [B. H. Campbell], 27 Feb. 1886, XIT Ranch Papers, Misc. Corresp. to B. H. Campbell, 1886, P-PHM.

21. Leavenworth Times, 24 Jan., 21 Mar. 1886.

22. Texas, Oldham County, County Clerk, Criminal Docket, Ex Parte Emory, 1886, Case No. 192; also see Stock Growers Journal, 10 Apr. 1886; interview of Harry Ingerton with J. Evetts Haley, 13 Apr. 1927, J. Evetts Haley Papers, Interview Files, P-PHM.

23. Stock Growers Journal, 20 Mar. 1886.

24. Ibid., 10 Apr. 1886; interview of John G. Lang with L. F. Sheffy, 13 Oct. 1936, Dr. L. F. Sheffy Memorial Collect., Cornette Lib., WTSU.

25. Interview of John G. Lang with L. F. Sheffy, 13 Oct. 1936, Dr. L. F. Sheffy Memorial Collect., Cornette Lib., WTSU; Fort Worth Gazette, 30 Mar. 1886.

26. Fort Worth Gazette, 30 Mar. 1886, from which the dialogue is taken; interview of John G. Lang with L. F. Sheffy, 13 Oct. 1936, Dr. L. F. Sheffy Memorial Collect., Cornette Lib., WTSU.

27. Interview of John G. Lang with L. F. Sheffy, 13 Oct. 1936, Dr. L. F. Sheffy Memorial Collect., Cornette Lib., WTSU, from which the dialogue is taken; Fort Worth Gazette, 30 Mar. 1886; Stock Growers Journal, 10 Apr. 1886.

28. Fort Worth Gazette, 30 Mar. 1886; interview of Garrett H. "Kid" Dobbs with John McCarty and Mel Armstrong, 12 Sept. 1942, John L. McCarty Papers, Kid Dobbs Interview File, Am. Pub. Lib.; interview of John G. Lang with L. F. Sheffy, 13 Oct. 1936, Dr. L. F. Sheffy Memorial Collect., Cornette Lib., WTSU.

29. Stock Growers Journal, 10 Apr. 1886; interview of E. C. G. Austen with J. Evetts Haley, 4 Aug. 1925, J. Evetts Haley Papers, Interview Files, P-PHM; Fort Worth Gazette, 26 Mar., 30 Mar. 1886; interview of John G. Lang with L. F. Sheffy, 13 Oct. 1936, Dr. L. F. Sheffy Memorial Collect., Cornette Lib., WTSU; interview of Garrett H. "Kid" Dobbs with Mel Armstrong, 13 Sept. 1942, John L. McCarty Papers, Kid Dobbs Interview File, Am. Pub. Lib.; "Opinion of Judge Frank Willis," cited in Texas, Oldham County, County Clerk, Criminal Docket, Ex Parte Emory, 1886, Case No. 192.

30. Interview of Garrett H. "Kid" Dobbs with John McCarty and Mel

Armstrong, 12 Sept. 1942, John L. McCarty Papers, Kid Dobbs Interview File, Am. Pub. Lib.

31. Ibid.; interview of E. C. G. Austen with J. Evetts Haley, 4 Aug. 1925, J. Evetts Haley Papers, Interview Files, P-PHM; *Fort Worth Gazette*, 30 Mar. 1886; *Stock Growers Journal*, 10 Apr. 1886.

32. *Leavenworth Evening Standard*, 31 Mar. 1886; interview of Garrett H. "Kid" Dobbs with John McCarty and Mel Armstrong, 12 Sept. 1942, John L. McCarty Papers, Kid Dobbs Interview File, Am. Pub. Lib.

33. Texas, Oldham County, County Clerk, Deed Records, Realty Agreement between Lee Scott Cattle Co. and Abner Taylor, 5 Apr. 1886, vol. 3, pp. 412–415; J. N. Browning, Abstract of Warranty Deed on LS Ranch Holdings, 20 May 1905, p. 61, Colden Whitman Papers, Interview Files, P-PHM; A. Taylor to A. E. Reynolds, 8 Apr. 1886, and [A. Taylor] to W. Maud, 26 Apr. 1886, Ltrbook of A. Taylor, 27 Jan. 1886 to 1 Feb. 1887, pp. 157–158, 225–227, XIT Ranch Papers, P-PHM; Texas, Oldham County, County Clerk, Minutes of the Commissioners' Court, 12 May 1886, vol. 1, pp. 98–100; A. B. Taylor to B. H. Campbell, 21 May 1886, Ltrs of A. Taylor to B. H. Campbell, 1886, XIT Ranch Papers, P-PHM; *Tascosa Pioneer*, 14 Aug. 1886.

34. Texas, Oldham County, County Clerk, Minutes of the Commissioners' Court, 10 May 1886, vol. 1, pp. 98–100.

35. Ibid., 9 Aug., 31 Aug. 1886, vol. 1, pp. 11, 113.

36. A. Taylor to W. M. D. Lee, 24 Aug. 1886, Ltrbook of A. Taylor, 27 Jan. 1886 to 1 Feb. 1887, p. 385, XIT Ranch Papers, P-PHM.

37. *Globe Live-Stock Journal*, 27 Apr. 1886; *Tascosa Pioneer*, 29 Sept., 3 Nov. 1886; *Yellowstone Journal*, 27 Aug., 28 Aug. 1886.

38. See A. Taylor to W. M. D. Lee, 16 June 1886, Ltrbook of A. Taylor, 27 Jan. 1886 to 1 Feb. 1887, p. 385, XIT Ranch Papers, P-PHM; New Mexico, San Miguel County, County Clerk, Deed Records, J. E. McAllister to Luana M. McAllister, 13 Mar. 1886; interview of Garrett H. "Kid" Dobbs with John McCarty and Mel Armstrong, 12 Sept. 1942, John L. McCarty Papers, Kid Dobbs Interview File, Am. Pub. Lib.; *Tascosa Pioneer*, 29 Sept. 1886.

39. See *Breeder's Gazette* 11 (17 Feb. 1887): 257; also see Chapter 4.

40. *St. Joseph Herald*, 31 Aug., 1 Sept. 1886; *Leavenworth Times*, 31 Aug. 1886; *Breeder's Gazette* 10 (9 Sept. 1886): 368.

41. *St. Joseph Herald*, 1 Sept. 1886.

42. *Breeder's Gazette* 10 (16 Sept. 1886): 408–410; for documentation pertaining to His Highness VI, see *Breeder's Gazette* 11 (17 Feb. 1887): 257.

43. *Kansas City Star*, 13 Sept., 14 Sept. 1886.

44. *Breeder's Gazette* 10 (23 Sept. 1886): 449–454.

45. Ibid. 10 (4 Nov. 1886): 676–677; ibid. 10 (18 Nov. 1886): 748; *Chicago Tribune*, 17 Nov. 1886.

46. *Field and Farm* 2 (20 Nov. 1886): 8; undated issue of *Southwest Stockman*, cited in *Stock Grower*, 22 Oct. 1886; *Fort Worth Gazette*, 23 Apr. 1886; A. Taylor to W. M. D. Lee, 8 Dec. 1886, Ltrbook of A. Taylor, 11 Sept. 1886 to 30 Nov. 1887, XIT Ranch Papers, P-PHM.

47. *Tascosa Pioneer*, 3 Nov. 1886.

48. Interview of Garrett H. "Kid" Dobbs with John McCarty and Mel

Armstrong, 12 Sept. 1942, John L. McCarty Papers, Kid Dobbs Interview File, Am. Pub. Lib.; Texas, Oldham County, County Clerk, Minutes of the Commissioners' Court, 30 Oct. 1886, vol. 1, pp. 116–119.

49. *Leavenworth Times*, 10 Jan., 19 Dec. 1886; obituary of Lucien Scott, *Leavenworth Times*, 1 June 1893.

50. Ibid., 9 Jan., 11 Jan. 1887; statement of W. M. D. Lee in an undated issue of *Field and Farm*, cited in *Dallas Morning News*, 27 Nov. 1887; also see interview of J. E. McAllister with J. Evetts Haley, 1 July 1926, J. Evetts Haley Papers, Interview Files, P-PHM.

51. See *Leavenworth Times*, 1 Jan., 15 Mar., 18 Mar., 26 Mar. 1887; *Breeder's Gazette* 11 (10 Feb. 1887): 214; 11 (17 Feb. 1887): 257; 11 (6 Jan. 1887): 6–7; for a May sale, see 11 (9 June 1887): 912; *Tascosa Pioneer*, 19 Jan., 14 May 1887; statement of W. M. D. Lee in an undated issue of *Field and Farm*, cited in *Dallas Morning News*, 9 June 1887. The roundup date is from *Tascosa Pioneer*, 30 Mar. 1887.

52. *Tascosa Pioneer*, 30 Apr. 1887.

53. Ibid., 9 Feb. 1887; Maj. Louis H. Carpenter, Cmdg, Ft. Supply, to AAG, Dept. Mo., 5 May 1887, Ltrs Sent/Ft. Supply, RG 393; *Caldwell Journal*, 5 May 1887.

54. *Field and Farm* 4 (30 July 1887): 4.

55. Agreement between the American Pastoral Co., Lee Scott Cattle Co., Cap. Freehold Land and Inv. Co., Prairie Cattle Co., Reynolds Land and Cattle Co., Glidden and Sandborne, Hansford Land and Cattle Co., 3 May 1887, Ltrs Sent to R. N. Larrabee, 1887, XIT Ranch Papers, P-PHM.

56. Texas, Oldham County, County Clerk, Minutes of the Commissioners' Court, 9 May 1887, vol. 1, p. 131; *Tascosa Pioneer*, 14 May 1887.

57. *Leavenworth Times*, 9 June 1887; *Dallas Morning News*, 9 June 1887; *Tascosa Pioneer*, 28 May 1887; *Field and Farm* 4 (23 July 1887): 4.

58. Statement of W. M. D. Lee in an undated issue of *Field and Farm*, cited in *Dallas Morning News*, 9 June 1887; *Tascosa Pioneer*, 27 Aug. 1887; Texas, Oldham County, County Clerk, Deed Records, R. M. Hall, Cmsr., General Land Office, to W. M. D. Lee, 11 Aug. 1887, vol. 7, pp. 488–491.

59. *Field and Farm* 4 (6 Aug. 1887): 4; 4 (20 Aug. 1887): 4; *Fort Worth Gazette*, 26 Nov. 1887.

60. *Leavenworth Times*, 29 June 1887.

61. Ibid., 7 Sept. 1887; undated issue of *Tascosa Pioneer*, cited in *Stock Grower*, 10 Sept. 1887; *Tascosa Pioneer*, 17 Sept. 1887. For accounts of the Iowa State Fair, see *Breeder's Gazette* 11 (15 Sept. 1887): 427, 429; of the Nebraska State Fair, see *Lincoln Daily News*, 14 Sept. 1887; *Daily Nebraska State Journal*, 14 Sept. 1887; *Breeder's Gazette* 11 (22 Sept. 1887): 467–469; of the Kansas State Fair, see *Topeka Daily Optic*, 23 Sept. 1887; *Breeder's Gazette* 11 (29 Sept. 1887): 511.

62. *Tascosa Pioneer*, 24 Sept. 1887; *Fort Worth Gazette*, 2 Oct. 1887; undated issue of *Mobeetie Panhandle*, cited in *Stock Grower*, 18 June 1887; AAQM, Ft. Elliott, to Chief QM, Dept. Mo., 29 Sept. 1887, Ltrs Sent/Ft. Elliott QM, RG 393.

63. *Tascosa Pioneer*, 17 Sept. 1887; *Fort Worth Gazette*, 20 Sept. 1887.

64. *Tascosa Pioneer,* 17 Sept. 1887.

65. *Fort Worth Gazette,* 2 Oct. 30 Oct. 1887; *Dallas Morning News,* 22 Nov. 1887. Amarillo was established in mid-summer 1887 as a staging town for cowboys working the central Panhandle ranches. *Tascosa Pioneer,* 16 July 1887.

66. *Tascosa Pioneer,* 19 Nov. 1887; *Fort Worth Gazette,* 25 Nov., 26 Nov. 1887; circular of Cheyenne, Texas, *Dallas Morning News,* 1 Dec. 1887.

67. *Fort Worth Gazette,* 14 Dec. 1887; circular of Cheyenne, Texas, *Dallas Morning News,* 1 Dec. 1887; *Tascosa Pioneer,* 17 Dec. 1887.

68. *Tascosa Pioneer,* 17 Dec. 1887; *Las Vegas Daily Optic,* 19 Jan. 1888; *Fort Worth Gazette,* 8 Jan. 1888.

69. *Leavenworth Times,* 25 Sept., 25 Oct., 28 Dec. 1887, 10 Jan. 1888; *Columbus Democrat,* 30 Sept. 1887.

70. J. N. Browning, Abstract of Warranty Deed on LS Ranch Holdings, pp. 75–80, Colden Whitman Papers, Interview Files, P-PHM; *Tascosa Pioneer,* 4 Feb., 11 Feb. 1888; *Fort Worth Gazette,* 6 Dec. 1887.

71. *Leavenworth Times,* 8 Feb. 1888; *Fort Worth Gazette,* 28 Oct. 1887.

72. *Fort Worth Gazette,* 13 Oct. 1887; *Field and Farm* 4 (15 Oct. 1887): 5.

73. *Leavenworth Times,* 15 Feb. 1888.

6. Three-Masted Schooners

1. *Austin Daily Statesman,* 17 Feb. 1888.

2. Charter of the Brazos River Channel and Dock Company, 16 Feb. 1888, U.S., Cong., Senate, *Improvements at the Mouth of the Brazos River, Texas,* S. Doc. 138, 54th Cong., 2d sess., 1897, pp. 40–41.

3. Ibid. The six original members of the board of directors were Ira Evans of Austin; Jot Gunter of Dallas; George W. Angle of San Antonio; Lee, Ferguson, and A. J. Tullock, all of Leavenworth.

4. Testimony of Guy M. Bryan, Jr., and J. L. Hudgins before the special hearing of the U.S. Army Corps of Engineers, 11 Jan. 1897, ibid., pp. 56–57.

5. Maj. O. H. Earnst to Chief Eng., U.S. Army, 6 Sept. 1887, U.S., Cong., House, *Brazos River, Texas,* H. Ex. Doc. 109, 50th Cong., 1st sess., 1888, pp. 2–8.

6. *Houston Daily Post,* 15 Feb. 1889; undated issue of *Houston Daily Post,* cited in *Galveston Daily News,* 15 Jan. 1890. Also see George Y. Wisner, "The Brazos River Harbor Improvement," *Transactions of the American Society of Civil Engineers* 25 (July–Dec. 1891): 519–562.

7. See Wisner, "The Brazos River Harbor Improvement," *Transactions of the American Society of Civil Engineers* 25 (July–Dec. 1891): 519–562; U.S., Cong., Senate, *Improvements at the Mouth of the Brazos River, Texas,* S. Doc. 138, 54th Cong., 2d sess., 1897.

8. *Fort Worth Gazette,* 13 Sept. 1891; for another contemporary account of the Tap's capabilities, see *Galveston Daily News,* 12 June 1890.

9. R. B. Taylor to Maj. C. J. Allen, 19 Feb. 1891, U.S., Cong., House, *Brazos River, Texas,* H. Ex. Doc. 63, 52d Cong., 1st sess., 1892, p. 4.

10. The description was written by an anonymous journalist while on

board the Brazos Company's *Alice Blair*. See *Galveston Daily News*, 20 Aug. 1891.

11. See interview of E. L. Cothrell, *Houston Daily Post*, 15 Feb. 1889; U.S., Cong., House, *Deep Harbor, Gulf of Mexico*, H. Ex. Doc. 56, 51st Cong., 1st sess., 1890, pp. 9–12, 17.

12. See statement of Thomas Hurley, *San Antonio Express*, 24 Jan. 1889, cited in *Fort Worth Gazette*, 30 Jan. 1889; *Austin Daily Statesman*, 23 Feb. 1888; Charter of the Brazos River Channel and Dock Company, U.S., Cong., Senate, *Improvements at the Mouth of the Brazos River, Texas*, S. Doc. 138, 54th Cong., 2d sess., 1897, p. 41.

13. *Houston Daily Post*, 21 Mar. 1888; Texas, Brazoria County, County Clerk, Deed Records, Option to Purchase given by Guy M. Bryan and M. A. Bryan to William M. D. Lee and John M. Ferguson, 7 Mar. 1888, vol. 1, p. 521 (for biographical sketch of Guy M. Bryan, Jr., see *Houston Chronicle*, 5 Sept. 1921); Texas, Brazoria County, County Clerk, Deed Records, Howell Stevens to William M. D. Lee and John M. Ferguson, 19 Mar. 1888; Frank W. Stevens to W. M. D. Lee and J. M. Ferguson, 19 Mar. 1888, vol. 1, pp. 170–174; statement of Thomas Hurley, *Fort Worth Gazette*, 4 Apr. 1889; testimony of Guy M. Bryan, Jr., before the special hearing of the U.S. Army Corps of Engineers, 11 Jan. 1897, U.S., Cong., Senate, *Improvements at the Mouth of the Brazos River, Texas*, S. Doc. 138, 54th Cong., 2d sess., 1897, p. 60; Charter of the Texas Land and Immigration Co., 16 Feb. 1888, U.S., Cong., Senate, *Improvements at the Mouth of the Brazos River, Texas*, S. Doc. 138, 54th Cong., 2d sess., 1897, p. 43.

14. *Leavenworth Times*, 29 Mar., 4 Apr. 1888; obituary of George W. Angle, *Angleton Times*, 4 Mar. 1921; interview of Richard Crain, 20 Nov. 1891, *Velasco Times* [weekly], 21 Nov. 1891.

15. U.S., Cong., House, Proceedings of 27 June 1888, 7 Aug. 1888, 50th Cong., 1st sess., *Cong. Record* 19, pt. 7, pp. 6945–6946, 7311; U.S., Cong., Senate, Proceedings of 1 May 1888, 1 Aug. 1888, 7 Aug. 1888, 50th Cong., 1st sess., *Cong. Record* 19, pt. 4, p. 3549, pt. 7, pp. 7107, 7293.

16. Undated issue of *New York World*, cited in *Fort Worth Gazette*, 27 May 1892; interview of ex-senator C. B. Farwell, *Houston Daily Post*, 23 Mar. 1891; U.S., Cong., House, Proceedings of 22 Aug. 1888, 50th Cong., 1st sess., *Cong. Record* 19, pt. 8, p. 7833.

17. *Fort Worth Gazette*, 3 Nov. 1888; Minutes of a Stockholders Meeting [of the Brazos River Channel and Dock Co.], 3 Nov. 1888, U.S., Cong., Senate, *Improvements at the Mouth of the Brazos River, Texas*, S. Doc. 138, 54th Cong., 2d sess., 1897, p. 41.

18. *Miles City, Stock Grower's Journal*, 28 July 1888; *Breeder's Gazette* 14 (8 Aug. 1888): 129; 14 (29 Aug. 1888): 202; 14 (19 Sept. 1888): 280; 14 (26 Sept. 1888): 308–309; 14 (21 Nov. 1888): 531–532; *Iowa State Register*, 13 Nov.–15 Nov. 1888.

19. Contract between Gustav Wilke and Brazos River Channel and Dock Co., 24 Dec. 1888, attached as an exhibit to U.S., Cong., Senate, *Improvements at the Mouth of the Brazos River, Texas*, S. Doc. 138, 54th Cong., 2d sess., 1897. For contemporary references to Wilke's construction of the

Texas capitol, see *Houston Daily Post,* 17 Jan. 1889; *Galveston Daily News,* 19 Jan. 1889.

20. *Galveston Daily News,* 10 Jan., 12 Jan. 1889; *Houston Daily Post,* 11 Jan. 1889.

21. *Houston Daily Post,* 17 Jan. 1889.

22. Ibid.

23. Ibid., 23 Jan. 1889.

24. The company officers were Lee, president; Ira H. Evans, vice-president; T. J. Hurley, secretary; J. M. Ferguson, treasurer. The board of directors consisted of John Winches, Brazoria; T. B. Yale, Brazoria; C. W. Ogden, San Antonio; G. W. Angle, San Antonio; Ira H. Evans, San Antonio; T. J. Hurley, Fort Worth; J. Otis Wetherbee, Boston; W. C. D. Gannis, Chicago; Abner Taylor, Chicago; Charles B. Farwell, Chicago; and Lee. See *Galveston Daily News,* 31 Mar. 1889; *Fort Worth Gazette,* 4 Apr. 1889; *Houston Daily Post,* 31 Mar. 1889.

25. *Galveston Daily News,* 27 Mar. 1889; undated issue of *Houston Daily Post,* cited in *Velasco Times* [daily], 22 Jan. 1892; also see Abner Taylor to Col. Henry M. Robert, Corps of Eng., 28 Dec. 1896, U.S., Cong., Senate, *Improvements at the Mouth of the Brazos River, Texas,* S. Doc. 138, 54th Cong., 2d sess., 1897, p. 14.

26. *Fort Worth Gazette,* 4 Apr. 1889.

27. *Houston Daily Post,* 16 Apr. 1890; *Galveston Daily News,* 27 Aug. 1890.

28. *Galveston Daily News,* 5 Apr. 1889; *Houston Daily Post,* 29 May 1889; *Galveston Daily News,* 4 Aug., 14 Sept. 1889.

29. Interview of T. Hurley, 31 May 1889, cited in *Fort Worth Gazette,* 4 Apr. 1889; *Galveston Daily News,* 18 Jan., 14 Mar., 14 May, 4 Aug. 1889.

30. *Galveston Daily News,* 20 Aug. 1889; also see *Houston Daily Post,* 29 May 1889. Angle is probably named after George Angle or a member of his family; the town later changed its name to Angleton, which became the county seat of Brazoria County.

31. A. Taylor to Walter Potter, 13 May 1889, Ltrbook of A. Taylor, 5 Feb. 1889 to 12 Apr. 1892, p. 58, XIT Ranch Papers, P-PHM.

32. A. Taylor to W. M. D. Lee, 22 Aug. 1889, Ltrbook of A. Taylor, 5 Feb. 1889 to 12 Apr. 1892, pp. 99–100, XIT Ranch Papers, P-PHM.

33. A. Taylor to Col. H. M. Robert, U.S. Army Corps of Eng., 28 Dec. 1896, U.S., Cong., Senate, *Improvements at the Mouth of the Brazos River, Texas,* S. Doc. 138, 54th Cong., 2d sess., 1897, p. 14; *Galveston Daily News,* 5 Dec., 18 Dec. 1889; *Houston Daily Post,* 10 Jan. 1890; contract between Gustav Wilke and the Brazos River Channel and Dock Co., 24 Dec. 1888, attached as an exhibit to U.S., Cong., Senate, *Improvements at the Mouth of the Brazos River, Texas,* S. Doc. 138, 54th Cong., 2d sess., 1897. E. L. Cothrell to Col. Henry M. Robert, 9 Jan. 1897, U.S., Cong., Senate, *Improvements at the Mouth of the Brazos River, Texas,* S. Doc. 138, 54th Cong., 2d sess., 1897, p. 26.

34. *Houston Daily Post,* 15 Jan. 1890; *Galveston Daily News,* 19 Jan. 1890.

35. *Houston Daily Post,* 12 Apr. 1890.

36. *Fort Worth Gazette,* 11 Apr. 1890; also see *Galveston Daily News,* 26 Mar. 1890; *Houston Daily Post,* 12 Apr. 1890.

37. *Houston Daily Post,* 20 May 1890; *Leavenworth Times,* 27 May, 8 June 1890.

38. *Leavenworth Times,* 13 Aug. 1890; *Galveston Daily News,* 26 Aug., 27 Aug. 1890; *Houston Daily Post,* 1 Sept. 1890.

39. *Fort Worth Gazette,* 30 Aug., 4 Sept. 1890; *Galveston Daily News,* 31 Aug. 1890.

40. *Galveston Daily News,* 4 Sept., 9 Sept. 1890; *Fort Worth Gazette,* 4 Sept., 11 Sept. 1890; A. Taylor to Col. Henry M. Robert, U.S. Army Corps of Eng., 28 Dec. 1896, U.S., Cong., Senate, *Improvements at the Mouth of the Brazos River, Texas,* S. Doc. 138, 54th Cong., 2d sess., 1897, p. 14.

41. *Boston Evening Transcript,* 15 Sept. 1890. The arrest was made on the charge of Charles Richardson of Philadelphia that Potter and Lovell had embezzled $450,000 from the Edgehill Furnace Company. However, the firm's mishandling of the Brazos bonds was an underlying issue.

42. Ibid., 5 Dec. 1890.

43. A. Taylor to Col. Henry M. Robert, U.S. Army Corps of Eng., 28 Dec. 1896, U.S., Cong., Senate, *Improvements at the Mouth of the Brazos River, Texas,* S. Doc. 138, 54th Cong., 2d sess., 1897, p. 16; Texas, Oldham County, County Clerk, Deed Records, W. M. D. Lee and Lina W. Lee to Lucien Scott, 29 Nov. 1890, vol. 3, pp. 224–242; Texas, Oldham County, County Clerk, Deed Records, Contract between Lucien Scott and W. M. D. Lee, 29 Nov. 1890, vol. F-1, p. 164.

44. *Houston Daily Post,* 27 Mar. 1891.

45. *Galveston Daily News,* 24 Apr. 1891.

46. Ibid., 8 Apr., 24 Apr. 1891.

47. Ibid., 15 June 1891; *Houston Daily Post,* 10 May, 18 June 1891.

48. *Galveston Daily News,* 15 June 1891.

49. Ibid.; W. M. D. Lee to W. B. Munson, 2 June [1891], W. B. Munson Papers, Ltrs Received by W. B. Munson, 1891, P-PHM; *Houston Daily Post,* 18 June 1891.

50. Letter of O. W. Crawford [advertising agent of the Brazos River Channel and Dock Co.], 12 Sept. 1891, in undated issue of *Kansas City Times,* cited in *Houston Daily Post,* 4 Oct. 1891; *Houston Daily Post,* 25 July, 2 Aug. 1891; *Galveston Daily News,* 13 July, 29 July 1891.

51. *Galveston Daily News,* 6 Aug. 1891; W. M. D. Lee to W. B. Munson, 10 Aug. 1891, and Ike [Munson], Velasco, to W. B. Munson, 16 Aug. 1891, W. B. Munson Papers, Ltrs Rec'd/W. B. Munson, 1891, P-PHM. Also see *Velasco Times* [weekly], 21 Jan. 1892, for Lee's contradiction of the jetty problem.

52. *Fort Worth Gazette,* 17 Nov. 1891; *Houston Daily Post,* 22 Aug., 6 Oct., 29 Nov. 1891.

53. Statement of O. W. Crawford, 1 Jan. 1892, *Houston Daily Post,* 11 May 1892; *Houston Daily Post,* 1 Nov., 6 Nov., 7 Nov. 1891; the other members of the board of directors were E. J. Wilson, Gustav Wilke, F. W. Vaughn, W. W.

Anderson, Frank Caldwell, and Larry Deger. Charter of the Velasco Terminal Railway Co., 27 July 1891, U.S., Cong., Senate, *Improvements at the Mouth of the Brazos River, Texas*, S. Doc. 138, 54th Cong., 2d sess., 1897, p. 44.

54. See *Houston Daily Post*, 24 Apr. 1891.

55. Ibid., 31 July, 29 Oct., 30 Oct., 6 Nov., 7 Nov. 1891; *Galveston Daily News*, 11 Nov. 1891; *Velasco Times* [weekly], 14 Nov. 1891.

56. *Houston Daily Post*, 13 Oct. 1891; *Velasco Times* [daily], 24 Dec. 1891.

57. *Fort Worth Gazette*, 18 Nov., 19 Nov. 1891; also see *Houston Daily Post*, 20 Nov. 1891.

58. *Fort Worth Gazette*, 18 Nov., 19 Nov. 1891; *Houston Daily Post*, 5 Nov. 1891.

59. *Velasco Times* [daily], 24 Dec. 1891; *Velasco Times* [weekly], 21 Nov. 1891; *Houston Daily Post*, 20 Nov. 1891.

60. *Denver Republican*, 19 Nov. 1891; *Houston Daily Post*, 16 Sept. 1891.

61. *Dallas Morning News*, 17 Dec. 1891; also see *Houston Daily Post*, 17 Dec., 18 Dec. 1891.

62. *Dallas Morning News*, 17 Dec. 1891; *Houston Daily Post*, 13 Dec. 1891.

63. *Dallas Morning News*, 17 Dec. 1891; *Fort Worth Gazette*, 18 Dec. 1891.

64. *Fort Worth Gazette*, 18 Dec. 1891; *Dallas Morning News*, 18 Dec. 1891; *Houston Daily Post*, 18 Dec. 1891.

65. Ibid.; *Richmond Climax*, 27 Dec. 1891, cited in *Velasco Times* [weekly], 21 Jan. 1892.

66. *Fort Worth Gazette*, 18 Dec. 1891; *Dallas Morning News*, 18 Dec. 1891; *Houston Daily Post*, 18 Dec. 1891.

67. *Velasco Times* [daily], 24 Dec. 1891; 2 Feb. 1892; *Velasco Times* [weekly], 2 Jan., 28 Jan. 1892; undated issue of *Houston Daily Post*, cited in *Velasco Times* [daily], 31 Dec. 1891; undated issue of *Houston Daily Post*, cited in *Velasco Times* [daily], 21 Jan. 1891; A. Taylor to Col. Henry M. Robert, U.S. Army Corps of Eng., 28 Dec. 1896, U.S., Cong., Senate, *Improvements at the Mouth of the Brazos River, Texas*, S. Doc. 138, 54th Cong., 2d sess., 1897, p. 17.

68. *Austin Daily Statesman*, 5 Feb. 1892.

7. Tugs & Barges

1. *Velasco Times* [weekly], 30 Mar. 1892.

2. Ibid., 25 Feb., 17 Mar. 1892; *Houston Daily Post*, 1 July 1892; undated issue of *Houston Daily Post*, cited in *Velasco Times* [weekly], 4 Feb. 1892; *Velasco Times* [weekly], 10 Mar., 24 Mar. 1892; *Fort Worth Gazette*, 3 Apr. 1892; undated issue of *Clay County Chieftain*, cited in *Velasco Times* [daily], 25 Feb. 1892.

3. *Houston Daily Post*, 27 Mar. 1892, cited in *Velasco Times* [weekly], 30 Mar. 1892; testimony of L. R. Bryan before the U.S. Army Corps of Eng., 11 Jan. 1897, U.S., Cong., Senate, *Improvements at the Mouth of the Brazos River, Texas*, S. Doc. 138, 54th Cong., 2d sess., 1897, p. 62.

4. *Fort Worth Gazette*, 7 Apr. 1892; U.S., Cong., House, Proceedings of 5 Apr. 1892, 52d Cong., 1st sess., *Cong. Record* 23, pt. 3, p. 2968; *Velasco Times* [weekly], 28 Apr. 1892.

5. *Houston Daily Post*, 1 July, 12 July 1892; also see *Velasco Times* [weekly], 7 July, 25 Aug. 1892.

6. Annual Report of the Velasco Terminal Railway Co., 30 June 1892, pp. 29, 31, 35, 61, 65, Texas Railroad Commission Annual Reports, Record Group 455, Texas State Archives; *Velasco Times* [weekly], 21 Apr., 13 May, 25 Aug. 1892; *Galveston Daily News*, 8 June 1892, 15 July 1893; Ike [Munson] to W. B. Munson, 17 May 1892, W. B. Munson Papers, Ltrs Rec'd/W. B. Munson, 1892, P-PHM; *Houston Daily Post*, 14 July 1892.

7. *Galveston Daily News*, 26 Nov. 1892; *Velasco Times* [weekly], 17 Feb. 1893.

8. *Fort Worth Gazette*, 3 Feb. 1893; *Velasco Times* [weekly], 17 Feb., 17 Mar. 1893; *Galveston Daily News*, 15 July 1893.

9. *Galveston Daily News*, 5 Apr. 1893; *Velasco Times* [weekly], 31 Mar. 1893.

10. *Galveston Daily News*, 15 July, 26 Aug., 27 Aug., 31 Aug. 1893; A. Taylor to Col. Henry M. Robert, U.S. Army Corps of Eng., 28 Dec. 1896, U.S., Cong., Senate, *Improvements at the Mouth of the Brazos River, Texas*, S. Doc. 138, 54th Cong., 2d sess., 1897, p. 18; Annual Report of the Velasco Terminal Railway Co., 30 June 1893, pp. 7, 18, 22, 31, 59, 61, 65, Texas Railroad Commission Annual Reports, RG 455, Texas State Arch.; *Houston Daily Post*, 28 Aug., 22 Oct. 1893.

11. A. Taylor to Col. Henry M. Robert, U.S. Army Corps of Eng., 28 Dec. 1896, U.S., Cong., Senate, *Improvements at the Mouth of the Brazos River, Texas*, S. Doc. 138, 54th Cong., 2d sess., 1897, p. 14; *Houston Daily Post*, 4 Aug. 1894.

12. *Houston Daily Post*, 11 Oct. 1894; also see *Galveston Daily News*, 11 Oct. 1894.

13. *Galveston Daily News*, 9 Dec., 19 Dec. 1894; *Houston Daily Post*, 21 Dec. 1894; undated issue of *Manufacturer's Record*, cited in *Houston Daily Post*, Jan. 1895; also see *Galveston Daily News*, 28 July 1894.

14. *Houston Daily Post*, 21 Dec. 1894; *Galveston Daily News*, 24 Dec. 1894.

15. *Austin Daily Statesman*, 9 Feb. 1895; Texas, Office of the Secretary of State, Charter of the Velasco Construction Co., 11 Feb. 1895, Division of Inactive Corporations. Lee's coinvestors were John Winches, J. A. Wilkins, and J. B. Shea. Telegram of G. W. Angle to A. M. Shannon, Galveston, 14 Jan. 1895, *Galveston Daily News*, 15 Jan. 1895. Also see A. Taylor to Col. Henry M. Robert, U.S. Army Corps of Eng., 28 Dec. 1896, U.S., Cong., Senate, *Improvements at the Mouth of the Brazos River, Texas*, S. Doc. 138, 54th Cong., 2d sess., 1897, p. 15; *Houston Daily Post*, 17 June 1895. For accounts of the barges owned by Lee, see *Galveston Daily News*, 13 Dec. 1893, 17 June 1894; also see 29 May, 27 June, 28 July, 7 Aug. 1895.

16. Maj. James Quinn, U.S. Army Corps of Eng. to U.S. Army Eng., 3 Feb. 1897, U.S., Cong., House, *Survey of Sabine Lake, Texas*, H. Doc. 299, 54th

Cong., 2d sess., 1897, p. 2; *Galveston Daily News*, 20 Oct., 30 Oct. 1894; *Houston Daily Post*, 30 Mar. 1895.

17. *Galveston Daily News*, 15 Sept., 2 Oct., 10 Oct., 15 Oct., 29 Oct., 14 Nov., 15 Nov., 21 Nov. 1895; *Leavenworth Times*, 11 Sept., 14 Sept. 1895; *Houston Daily Post*, 14 Oct., 21 Oct. 1895; A. Taylor to Col. Henry M. Robert, U.S. Army Corps of Eng., 28 Dec. 1896, U.S., Cong., Senate, *Improvements at the Mouth of the Brazos River, Texas*, S. Doc. 138, 54th Cong., 2d sess., 1897, p. 15; *Fort Worth Gazette*, 29 Nov. 1895.

18. Minutes of Stockholders Meeting of the Velasco Construction Co., 2 Dec. 1895, Texas Sec. State, Div. Inactive Corp.; Edward Perry to W. B. Munson, 19 Dec. 1895, W. B. Munson Papers, Ltrs Rec'd/W. B. Munson, 1895, P-PHM; *Fort Worth Gazette*, 6 Nov., 21 Nov. 1895.

19. Texas, Galveston County, County Clerk, Deed Records, Mortgage Release by Robert L. Pillow to Gulf Towing Co., 31 Aug. 1897, vol. 159, pp. 638–639; E. Perry to W. B. Munson, 19 Dec. 1895, W. B. Munson Papers, Ltrs Rec'd/W. B. Munson, 1895, P-PHM.

20. *Galveston Daily News*, 27 Dec., 28 Dec. 1895, 1 Jan., 2 Jan. 1896; *Fort Worth Gazette*, 2 Jan. 1896.

21. *Houston Daily Post*, 27 Dec. 1895.

22. *Lake Charles American*, 5 Feb. 1896; *Galveston Daily News*, 27 Feb., 28 Feb. 1896; E. Perry to J. T. Munson, 2 Apr. 1896, W. B. Munson Papers, Ltrs Rec'd/W. B. Munson, 1896, P-PHM.

23. *Galveston Daily News*, 10 Apr., 13 Apr. 1896; A. Taylor to Col. Henry M. Robert, U.S. Army Corps of Eng., 28 Dec. 1896, U.S., Cong., Senate, *Improvements at the Mouth of the Brazos River, Texas*, S. Doc. 138, 54th Cong., 2d sess., 1897, p. 15.

24. *Galveston Daily News*, 16 Mar., 13 Apr. 1896.

25. U.S., Cong., Senate, *Improvements at Mouth and Passes of Calcasieu River, Louisiana*, Annual Report of the Chief Eng., U.S. Army to Sec. War, H. Doc. 2, 54th Cong., 1st sess., 1895, pt. 3, 1896, p. 2; *Lake Charles American*, 15 Jan., 25 Mar., 8 Apr., 29 Apr. 1896; *New Orleans Picayune*, 28 Apr. 1896; *Galveston Daily News*, 27 Apr. 1896.

26. *Galveston Daily News*, 7 June 1896; U.S., Cong., House, *Preliminary Examination, Survey and Appropriations* [of Rivers and Harbors], H. Doc. 482, 55th Cong., 2d sess., 1898, p. 209; *Lake Charles American*, 19 Aug. 1896; *Beaumont Enterprise*, 25 Mar. 1914.

27. *Galveston Daily News*, 31 May, 4 July 1896; E. Perry to J. T. Munson, 2 Apr. 1896, W. B. Munson Papers, Ltrs Rec'd/W. B. Munson, 1896, P-PHM; *Dallas Morning News*, 21 Mar. 1896; *Houston Daily Post*, 31 Jan. 1897.

28. *Galveston Daily News*, 27 Apr., 14 May 1896, 22 July 1897; U.S., Cong., House, *Preliminary Examination, Survey and Appropriations*, H. Doc. 482, 55th Cong., 2d sess., 1898, p. 265.

29. *Leavenworth Evening Standard*, 30 Oct., 12 Nov. 1896; *Leavenworth Times*, 5 Nov. 1896; *Galveston Daily News*, 10 Oct., 24 Oct., 22 Nov., 28 Nov., 1 Dec. 1896; *Houston Daily Post*, 3 Dec. 1896; A. Taylor to Col. Henry M. Robert, U.S. Army Corps of Eng., 28 Dec. 1896, U.S., Cong., Sen-

NOTES TO PAGES 119-121   175

ate, *Improvements at the Mouth of the Brazos River, Texas,* S. Doc. 138, 54th Cong., 2d sess., 1897, p. 14.

30. *Dallas Morning News,* 8 Jan. 1897; *Galveston Daily News,* 9 May, 2 June, 13 Aug. 1897; *Houston Daily Post,* 15 May 1897.

31. *Galveston Daily News,* 18 Aug., 14 Sept., 15 Sept., 18 Sept., 21 Sept. 1897; *Dallas Morning News,* 15 Sept., 18 Sept. 1897; *Leavenworth Times,* 9 Oct. 1897.

32. Ruth Sutton-Doland to DFS, 28 Jan. 1977; Louisa Arps to DFS, 12 June 1976; Texas, Brazoria County, County Clerk, Death Certificate of Selina Phillips, vol. 20, p. 119A; *Leavenworth Times,* 14 Oct. 1897; J. G. Phillips, Jr., to DFS, 11 Apr. 1977. The precise date when Selina was adopted into the Lee family cannot be fixed. However, it must have been later than 1894, when Lina and her son still visited alone at Velasco; it also had to be some time before Lina's death in 1900, as the girl formed a very warm relationship with her adopted mother. The only discovered instance when the Lees were visited by a New York resident (the region of Selina's birth) was the October visit of a Mrs. Johnson.

33. *Beaumont Enterprise,* 9 Dec., 25 Dec. 1897, 15 Jan. 1898; U.S., Cong., House, *Dredge Boat for Use at Sabine Pass,* H. Rpt. 212, 55th Cong., 2d sess., 1898, n.p.; U.S., Cong., House, Proceedings of 16 June 1898, 55th Cong., 2d sess., *Cong. Record* 31, pt. 7, pp. 6040–6046; *Galveston Daily News,* 17 June 1898; *Leavenworth Times,* 24 Feb., 12 Apr. 1898, 23 Apr. 1899; *Galveston Daily News,* 4 June 1898, 12 Mar. 1899.

34. *Morrison and Fourmy's General Directory of the City of Houston,* 1899, pp. 44–45, 96, 178. Lee at first was listed only as general manager of the company, with Ferguson acting as secretary-treasurer; the founder, J. C. Baldwin, was still the nominal president.

35. *Las Vegas Daily Optic,* 1 Sept., 3 Sept. 1900; *Leavenworth Evening Standard,* 10 Dec., 11 Dec. 1900; *Leavenworth Times,* 29 Sept., 3 Oct., 12 Oct., 11 Dec. 1900; *Columbus Republican,* 22 Dec. 1900; Burial Certificate of Lina W. Lee, 1900, No. 7515, Mount Muncie Cemetery Assoc. of Leavenworth.

36. *Leavenworth Times,* 13 Dec., 14 Dec., 20 Dec. 1900; *Leavenworth Evening Standard,* 14 Dec. 1900; Burial Certificate of Lina W. Lee, 1900, No. 7515, Mount Muncie Cemetery Assoc. of Leavenworth.

37. *Leavenworth Times,* 12 May, 6 Aug. 1901; Burial Certificate of Lina W. Lee, 1900, No. 7515, Mount Muncie Cemetery Assoc. of Leavenworth.

38. *Leavenworth Times,* 4 Sept. 1901; Kansas, Leavenworth County, County Clerk, Deed Records, William M. D. Lee to Henry Jackson, 4 Sept. 1901, vol. 184, p. 417; *Columbus Republican,* 13 Sept. 1902; receipts of Lillian Lee given to E. A. Kelly, 17 Nov. 1903, 18 Mar., 19 Aug., 25 Oct. 1904, Kansas, Leavenworth County, County Clerk, Probate Court Papers, Guardianship of Lucien Lee, Pre-1935 Records.

39. Years later family members recollected Aunt Lillian with fondness. J. G. Phillips, Jr., to DFS, 11 Apr. 1977; interview of J. P. Phillips, Jr., with DFS, 27 Jan. 1978.

40. *Houston Daily Post,* 11 June 1905; *Houston Transfer Co. vs. Lee,* 97 *Southwestern Reporter* 842 (Texas Court of Civil Appeals, 7 Nov. 1906), rehearing denied, 5 Dec. 1906; *Leavenworth Times,* 14 Mar. 1906.

41. *Houston Daily Post,* 18 May, 11 June 1905; *Houston Chronicle,* 18 May, 10 June 1905; Texas, City of Houston, Office of the Registrar, Bureau of Vital Statistics, Death Certificate of Lucien W. Lee, 10 June 1905, Reg. No. 6412; *Leavenworth Times,* 11 June 1905; *Columbus Republican,* 10 June 1905.

42. Texas, City of Houston, Office of the Registrar, Bureau of Vital Statistics, Death Certificate of John M. Ferguson, 12 Mar. 1906; *Houston Chronicle,* 13 Mar. 1906; *Houston Daily Post,* 13 Mar. 1906.

43. *Houston Daily Post,* 29 July 1906; *Columbus Republican,* 11 Aug. 1906.

8. Salt Domes

1. *Houston Daily Post,* 1 Sept. 1906; *Columbus Republican,* 1 Sept. 1906; the hotel description is from *Houston Daily Post,* 11 Nov. 1906. Patricia Quinlan, Alumnae Director, St. Agnes Academy, Houston, to DFS, 26 Sept. 1977.

2. Texas, Sec. State, Charter of the West Columbia Oil Co., 27 Dec. 1906, No. 016735-0, Div. Inactive Corp.; Texas, Brazoria County, County Clerk, Deed Records, Will C. and Ima Hogg to C. W. Nelson and F. J. Clemenger, 27 Oct. 1906, vol. 73, pp. 486–488; W. F. and Kate Arnold to W. M. D. Lee, 2 Nov. 1906, vol. 70, pp. 421–422; Charles Brown et al. to F. J. Clemenger and Charles W. Nelson, 17 Dec. 1906, vol. 73, pp. 488–492; S. D. Gupton and Dora Sexton to Charles W. Nelson and F. J. Clemenger, 22 Dec. 1906, vol. 73, pp. 479–481.

3. *Oil Trade Journal* 9 (May 1918): 92; *Houston Daily Post,* 30 June 1918; *Oil and Gas Journal* 5 (5 June 1907): 12; 5 (18 Dec. 1906): 10; *Houston Chronicle,* 30 June 1918.

4. *Galveston Daily News,* 27 Jan. 1907.

5. *Oil and Gas Journal* 5 (19 Mar. 1907): 4; 5 (5 May 1907): 5; *Oil Trade Journal* 9 (May 1918): 92; *Houston Daily Post,* 12 May 1907; Texas, Brazoria County, County Clerk, Deed Records, Lease from T. L. Smith to West Columbia Oil Co., 10 Apr. 1907, vol. 73, pp. 477–478; Lease from H. Masterson to W. M. D. Lee, 18 Apr. 1907, vol. 73, pp. 475–477; Lease from J. G. Phillips and J. A. Bordages to West Columbia Oil Co., 27 Apr. 1907, vol. 73, pp. 482–484; Lease from W. H. Abrams to F. J. Clemenger, 30 Apr. 1907, vol. 73, pp. 484–486.

6. *Oil and Gas Journal* 5 (19 May 1907): 3; 5 (5 June 1907): 12; *Houston Daily Post,* 12 May 1907; *Oil Trade Journal* 9 (May 1918): 12; *Houston Chronicle,* 30 June 1918.

7. *Houston Daily Post,* 12 May 1907; *Oil and Gas Journal* 5 (19 May 1907): 3.

8. Texas, Sec. State, Charter Amendment of the West Columbia Oil Co., 21 May 1907, No. 016735-0, Div. Inactive Corp; *Houston Daily Post,* 12 May and 28 May 1907; *Oil Trade Journal* 9 (May 1918): 92–93; *Oil and Gas Jour-*

nal 5 (19 May 1907): 3; 5 (5 June 1907): 12, 17; *Galveston Daily News*, 21 May 1907.

9. Texas, Sec. State, Charter Amendment of the West Columbia Oil Co., 21 May 1907, No. 016735-0, Div. Inactive Corp; *Galveston Daily News*, 25 May, 11 June 1907; *Houston Daily Post*, 25 May, 31 May 1907; *Oil and Gas Journal* 5 (5 June 1907): 12.

10. *Angleton Times*, 7 June, 28 June, 26 July 1907; *Houston Daily Post*, 18 June, 21 June 1907; *Oil and Gas Journal* 5 (5 June 1907): 12; 6 (5 July 1907): 21 *Houston Chronicle*, 21 June 1907; *Galveston Daily News*, 18 June 1907; *Oil Trade Journal* 9 (May 1918): 93.

11. *Angleton Times*, 19 July, 6 Sept. 1907; *Houston Daily Post*, 6 June 1907; *Oil Trade Journal* 9 (May 1918): 93; *Oil and Gas Journal* 7 (6 Jan. 1909): 20. Also see Texas, Brazoria County, County Clerk, Deed Records, Lease from H. Masterson to W. M. D. Lee, 18 Apr. 1907, vol. 73, pp. 475–477; Lease from J. G. Phillips and J. A. Bordages to West Columbia Oil Co., 27 Apr. 1907, vol. 73, pp. 482–484.

12. *Angleton Times*, 14 Sept. 1900, 24 Apr. 1908; *Galveston Daily News*, 3 Apr. 1908; *Houston Daily Post*, 22 May 1901.

13. *Angleton Times*, 27 Mar., 17 Apr. 1908; *Galveston Daily News*, 11 June, 12 June 1908.

14. *Angleton Times*, 21 Aug., 11 Sept. 1908; *Oil and Gas Journal* 7 (6 Jan. 1909): 20; Texas, Sec. State, Charter of Palacios Oil Co., 22 Aug. 1908, No. 19353-0, Div. Inactive Corp.

15. *Angleton Times*, 2 Oct., 9 Oct., 30 Oct. 1908; *Oil and Gas Journal* 7 (6 Oct. 1908): 7; 7 (20 Oct. 1908): 19.

16. *Angleton Times*, 11 Dec. 1908, 29 Jan., 5 Mar., 14 May 1909; *Houston Chronicle*, 10 Dec. 1908; *Oil and Gas Journal* 7 (6 Jan. 1909): 20; 8 (20 July 1909): 9; *Oil Trade Journal* 9 (May 1918): 92–93.

17. For evidence that Lee still maintained an apartment in Houston in addition to his East Columbia cottage, see *Morrison and Fourmy's General Directory of the City of Houston*, 1908–1909, p. 261; 1910–1911, p. 381. *Houston Daily Post*, 23 July 1909; *Angleton Times*, 30 July, 13 Aug., 31 Dec. 1909; *Oil Trade Journal* 9 (May 1918): 93.

18. *Oil Trade Journal* 9 (May 1918): 93; *Oil and Gas Journal* 9 (27 Apr. 1911): 19; Texas, Harris County, County Clerk, Deed Records, W. M. D. Lee to Howard E. Figg, 23 Mar. 1910, vol. 244, pp. 558–559; *Galveston Daily News*, 8 Jan. 1911; *Houston Daily Post*, 2 Nov. 1910; *Angleton Times*, 9 June 1911; Patricia Quinlan, Alumnae Dir., St. Agnes Academy, Houston, to DFS, 26 Apr. 1977.

19. Texas, Sec. State, Charter of the Ab-Moor Oil Co., 13 June 1911, No. 023389-0, Div. Inactive Corp.

20. *Beaumont Journal*, 29 Sept. 1912; *Houston Daily Post*, 11 Jan., 12 Jan. 1901; *Oil and Gas Journal* 10 (20 July 1911): 25.

21. Texas, Sec. State, Dissolution of West Columbia Oil Co., 18 July 1911, No. 016735-0, Div. Inactive Corp.; *Beaumont Journal*, 24 July 1911; Texas, Sec. State, Charter of the Ab-Moor Oil Co., 13 June 1911, No. 023389-0, Div. Inactive Corp.; *Oil and Gas Journal* 10 (27 June 1911): 15; 10 (17 Aug. 1911):

16; *Beaumont Enterprise,* 12 Aug. 1911; *Houston Chronicle,* 19 Sept. 1911; Texas, Harris County, County Clerk, Marriage Certificate of James Price Phillips and Selina Harris Lee, 25 Sept. 1911, vol. 4, p. 370, No. 21975.

22. Texas, Jefferson County, County Clerk, Deed Records, Lease from W. G. and W. F. Taliaferro, L. J. Laughman, to W. M. D. Lee, Erastus Hill, J. A. Moor, 16 Dec. 1911, vol. 131, pp. 536–538; Lease from W. M. D. Lee, Erastus Hill, and J. A. Moor to Nineteen Oil Co., 16 Dec. 1911, vol. 132, pp. 284–286; Texas, Sec. State, Charter of the Nineteen Oil Co., 18 Dec. 1911, No. 92910-0, Div. Inactive Corp.; *Galveston Daily News,* 16 Dec., 20 Dec. 1911; Texas, Jefferson County, County Clerk, Deed Records, Lease from W. M. D. Lee, Erastus Hill, J. A. Moor to Nineteen Oil Co., 30 Dec. 1911, vol. 132, pp. 184–186; *Morrison and Fourmy's Directory Co., Inc.'s Directory of the City of Beaumont,* 1913, pp. 33, 166.

23. *Oil and Gas Journal* 10 (1 Feb. 1912): 20; 10 (8 Feb. 1912): 20; 10 (28 Mar. 1912): 23; 10 (18 Apr. 1912): 22; 10 (25 Apr. 1912): 20; 10 (2 May 1912): 21; *Houston Daily Post,* 29 Jan. 1912; *Beaumont Journal,* 7 Apr. 1912.

24. *Oil and Gas Journal* 11 (18 July 1912): 28; 11 (20 June 1912): 39; 11 (29 Aug. 1912): 15; 11 (29 Aug. 1912): 15; 11 (12 Sept. 1912): 17; 11 (21 Nov. 1912): 39; 11 (28 Nov. 1912): 14; 11 (19 Dec. 1912): 39; 11 (2 Jan. 1913): 19; *Beaumont Journal,* 8 Dec. 1912.

25. *Oil and Gas Journal* 11 (30 May 1912): 20; 11 (15 Aug. 1912): 16; 11 (10 Oct. 1912): 18–19; *Beaumont Journal,* 4 Jan. 1913.

26. Texas, Sec. State, Charter of the Ab-Moor Oil Co., No. 023389-0, Div. Inactive Corp.; *Oil and Gas Journal* 12 (23 Apr. 1914): 16.

27. *Galveston Daily News,* 21 Mar. 1913; *Oil and Gas Journal* 11 (2 Apr. 1913): 16; 11 (30 Jan. 1913): 17; 11 (17 Feb. 1913): 16; 11 (20 Feb. 1913): 39; 11 (20 Mar. 1913): 14; 11 (10 Apr. 1913): 18.

28. The agreement is deduced from drilling information provided in *Oil and Gas Journal* 11 (22 May 1913): 16; and Texas, Jefferson County, County Clerk, Deed Records, Ab-Moor Co. to J. M. Guffey Petroleum Co., 6 July 1915, vol. 150, pp. 399–402.

29. See the weekly issues of *Oil and Gas Journal* beginning 17 Apr. through 21 Aug. 1913, specifically each section detailing the drilling efforts at Spindletop.

30. *Oil and Gas Journal* 12 (28 Aug. 1913): 17; 12 (7 Aug. 1913): 21; 12 (18 Sept. 1913): 19; *Beaumont Enterprise,* 6 Sept. 1913; *Galveston Daily News,* 6 Sept. 1913; in 1912, Moore was listed as one of three incorporators of Twenty-Five Oil Company. *Dallas Morning News,* 19 Jan. 1912.

31. *Angleton Times,* 13 Apr., 10 Apr., 17 Apr., 24 July 1914; 22 Jan. 1915; *Morrison and Fourmy's Directory Co., Inc.'s Directory of the City of Beaumont,* 1914, pp. 136, 424; *Oil and Gas Journal* 13 (11 June 1914): 46; 13 (7 Jan. 1915): 21; 13 (14 Jan. 1915): 12.

32. Texas, Brazoria County, County Clerk, Deed Records, Lease from W. M. D. Lee and S. E. Bullock to Producers Oil Co., 22 June 1915, vol. 125, pp. 630–632; *Beaumont Enterprise,* 25 July 1915; Texas, Jefferson County, County Clerk, Deed Records, Right of Way of South Beaumont Water and Light Co., 2 Jan. 1915, vol. 134, pp. 172–178; Texas, Harris County, County

Clerk, Deed Records, W. M. D. Lee to Harris County, 27 May 1915, vol. 343, pp. 400–406; Texas, Jefferson County, County Clerk, Deed Records, Lease from the Ab-Moor Oil Co. to J. M. Guffey Petroleum Co., 6 July 1915, vol. 150, pp. 399–402.

33. *Oil and Gas Journal* 14 (7 Oct. 1915): 14; *Angleton Times*, 1 Oct. 1915.

34. *Oil and Gas Journal* 14 (25 Aug. 1915): 12.

35. See *Oil and Gas Journal* 15 (15 June 1916): 50, and subsequent weekly articles on Spindletop.

36. *Beaumont Enterprise*, 30 July 1916.

37. Texas, Brazoria County, County Clerk, Deed Records, Lease from W. M. D. Lee and S. E. Bullock to Producers Oil Co., 27 June 1916, vol. 134, pp. 100–102; Lease from S. W. Pipkin, F. E. Carroll, W. M. D. Lee, S. E. Bullock to Producers Oil Co., 7 Oct. 1916, vol. 134, pp. 317–319; *Houston Chronicle*, 24 Dec. 1916; Texas, Brazoria County, County Clerk, Deed Records, Lease from S. W. Pipkin, F. E. Carroll, W. M. D. Lee, S. E. Bullock to Producers Oil Co., 1 Dec. 1916, vol. 134, p. 392.

38. *Morrison and Fourmy's Directory Co., Inc.'s Directory of the City of Beaumont*, 1916, pp. 126, 270; Texas, Jefferson County, County Clerk, Deed Records, Lease from Thomson-Moor Oil Co. to W. M. D. Lee, 20 Apr. 1917, vol. 205, pp. 284–287; *Oil and Gas Journal* 15 (1 Mar. 1917): 14; 15 (19 Apr. 1917): 50; *Beaumont Journal*, 2 Mar. 1917; *Gulf Coast Oil News* 9 (2 June 1917): 27; *Houston Chronicle*, 1 Apr. 1917.

39. *Gulf Coast Oil News* 10 (7 July 1917): 12; 10 (8 Sept. 1917): 14; 12 (16 Feb. 1918): 18; *Beaumont Journal*, 20 Mar., 5 Aug., 1 Nov. 1917, 31 Jan. 1918; *Oil Trade Journal* 8 (Sept. 1917): 76; 8 (Oct. 1917): 90; 8 (Nov. 1917): 123; 8 (Dec. 1917): 84; *Houston Chronicle*, 2 June, 12 Aug., 23 Sept., 7 Oct. 1917; *Oil Trade Journal* 8 (Nov. 1917): 123; 8 (Dec. 1917): 84; *Beaumont Enterprise*, 2 Nov., 3 Nov. 1917.

40. *Gulf Coast Oil News* 13 (25 May 1918): 22; 14 (31 Aug. 1918): 20; *Galveston Daily News*, 7 Jan. 1915; *Oil Trade Journal* 9 (Aug. 1918): 94.

41. *Angleton Times*, 24 May, 14 June 1918; *Oil Trade Journal* 9 (May 1918): 92–94; *Houston Chronicle*, 7 Apr. 1918; *Oil Weekly* [formerly *Gulf Coast Oil News*] 15 (20 Nov. 1918): 20.

42. *Angleton Times*, 6 Dec. 1918; *Oil Weekly* 15 (7 Dec. 1918): 13.

43. *Oil Weekly* 15 (14 Dec. 1918): 12; *Angleton Times*, 13 Dec. 1918, 10 Jan. 1919; Texas, Brazoria County, County Clerk, Deed Records, Lease from S. W. Pipkin, F. E. Carroll, W. M. D. Lee, F. N. Bullock, C. L. Nash, S. E. Bullock to Humble Oil and Refining Co., 6 Jan. 1919, vol. 158, pp. 388–391.

44. *Angleton Times*, 11 Apr. 1919.

45. Ibid., 21 Mar., 4 Apr. 1919.

46. Ibid., 14 Mar., 21 Mar., 4 Apr. 1919; *Beaumont Enterprise* 9 Mar., 5 Apr. 1919.

47. Interview of J. P. Phillips, Jr., with DFS, 27 Jan. 1978; *Angleton Times*, 7 Mar., 14 Mar. 1919; *Oil Weekly* 13 (10 May 1919): 6.

48. Texas, Harris County, County Clerk, Deed Records, Lease from W. M. D. Lee to Humble Oil and Refining Co., 18 Apr. 1919, vol. 424, pp. 444–445; Texas, Brazoria County, Lease from S. W. Pipkin, F. E. Carroll, W. M. D. Lee,

F. N. Bullock, C. L. Nash, S. E. Bullock to Humble Oil and Refining Co., 19 Apr. 1919, pp. 388–391; *Angleton Times*, 4 July 1919.

49. Texas, Newton County, County Clerk, Deed Records, Trust of Newton County Oil Co., 26 July 1919, vol. 20, pp. 101–105; Lease from Daniel and James Gallup to D. G. Price, R. S. Livingston, R. C. Davis, and W. M. D. Lee, 6 Aug. 1919, vol. 120, pp. 108–109; Lease from R. S. Livingston to D. G. Price et al., 1 Oct. 1920, vol. 22, p. 288; *Beaumont Journal*, 9 Dec. 1919; Texas, Sec. State, Articles of Dissolution of the Ab-Moor Oil Co., 27 Dec. 1919, Charter No. 023389-0, Div. Inactive Corp.

50. *Angleton Times*, 10 Oct. 1919, 16 Jan. 1920. The date of birth is conjecture; see J. G. Phillips, Jr., to DFS, 11 Apr. 1977. See also interview of J. P. Phillips, Jr., with DFS, 27 Jan. 1978; James F. Weed, Beaumont, to [Seth] Mabry, 6 Apr. 1933, Dr. L. F. Sheffy Memorial Collect., Cornette Lib., WTSU; *Oil Weekly* 16 (10 Jan. 1920): 44; *Oil Trade Journal* 11 (Feb. 1920): 44; 11 (Sept. 1920): 15, 103; *Angleton Times*, 23 July, 30 July 1920; *Houston Chronicle*, 25 July 1920.

51. Texas, Jefferson County, County Clerk, Deed Records, Lease from Gladys City Oil, Gas, and Manufacturing Co. to W. M. D. Lee, 1 Oct. 1920, vol. 205, pp. 284–287; Lease from Rosina and J. O. Davis, T. C. and D. F. Rowe, Joseph H. Tremble to W. M. D. Lee, 6 Nov. 1920, vol. 213, pp. 334–336; *Beaumont Enterprise*, 20 Dec. 1920; Texas, Newton County, County Clerk, Deed Records, Lease from R. S. Livingston to D. G. Price et al., 1 Oct. 1920, vol. 22, p. 288; Lease from R. S. Livingston to D. G. Price et al., 18 Jan. 1921, vol. 22, pp. 546–549.

52. *Houston Chronicle*, 2 Jan. 1921; *Galveston Daily News*, 23 Jan., 3 Apr. 1921; *Oil Trade Journal* 12 (Feb. 1921): 16, 28, 30; *Angleton Times*, 21 Jan. 1921; *Southwestern Oil Trade Journal* 4 (28 Jan. 1921): 13–14.

53. *Oil Trade Journal* 12 (Feb. 1921): 16; *Oil Weekly* 20 (29 Jan. 1921): 51.

54. *Oil Weekly* 20 (5 Feb. 1921): 40; *Galveston Daily News*, 23 Jan. 1921.

Epilogue

1. *Houston Chronicle*, 10 Apr., 24 Apr., 1 May, 15 May, 29 May, 5 June, 16 Oct., 30 Oct. 1921; *Oil Weekly* 21 (9 Apr. 1921): 44; 21 (14 May 1921): 48; 22 (16 July 1921): 48; 23 (29 Oct. 1921): 46; 23 (5 Nov. 1921): 75; *Oil Trade Journal* 12 (May 1921): 15, 26; 12 (Aug. 1921): 16; 12 (Sept. 1921): 17; *Galveston Daily News*, 21 Nov. 1921.

2. *Beaumont Enterprise*, 17 Apr. 1921; *Houston Chronicle*, 8 May 1921; *Oil Weekly* 21 (4 June 1921): 44; 24 (25 Feb. 1922); 55; Texas, Sec. State, Dissolution of the Nineteen Oil Co., 29 Dec. 1921, Charter No. 023920-0, Div. Inactive Corp.; Texas, Brazoria County, County Clerk, Deed Records, Lease from S. E. Bullock, W. M. D. Lee, C. L. Nash, S. W. Pipkin, F. E. Carroll, Monroe Carroll to the Texas Co., 24 May 1922, vol. 176, pp. 183–184; *Houston City Directory*, 1924, p. 973; interview of J. P. Phillips, Jr., with DFS, 27 Jan. 1978.

3. *Angleton Times*, 4 Mar. 1921; *Denver Post*, 21 Mar. 1921; *Houston*

Chronicle, 9 Sept., 8 Nov., 11 Nov. 1923; Texas, Harris County, County Clerk, Marriage Certificate of Captain W. M. D. Lee to Mrs. Leila Schumacher, 7 Nov. 1923, No. 61216, vol. 33, p. 327; *Houston Daily Post,* 22 Sept., 11 Nov. 1923; Texas, City of Houston, Office of the Registrar, Bureau of Vital Statistics, Death Certificate of Mary Leila Lee, 25 Sept. 1967, No. 97595.

4. Texas, City of Houston, Office of the Registrar, Bureau of Vital Statistics, Death Certificate of William M. D. Lee, 6 Jan. 1925, No. 44; interview of J. P. Phillips, Jr., with DFS, 27 Jan. 1978; *Houston Daily Post,* 7 Jan. 1925.

5. *Leavenworth Times,* 9 Jan., 11 Jan. 1925; *Columbus Republican,* 10 Jan. 1925; Burial Certificate of Capt. W. M. D. Lee, 10 Jan. 1925, Mount Muncie Cemetery Assoc. of Leavenworth, No. 13694.

6. Texas, City of Houston, Office of the Registrar, Bureau of Vital Statistics, Death Certificate of William M. D. Lee, 6 Jan. 1925, No. 44.

Bibliography

Manuscripts and Archives

Amarillo, Texas. Amarillo Public Library. John L. McCarty Papers.
Austin, Texas. Texas State Archives and Library. Governor O. M. Roberts Papers.
———. ———. Texas Railroad Commission Annual Reports. Velasco Terminal Railway Papers.
Canyon, Texas. Panhandle-Plains Historical Society Museum. J. N. Browning, "Abstract of Warranty Deed on LS Ranch Holdings."
———. ———. Dick Bussell. "Hunting Buffalo in the Panhandle." Dick Bussell Papers.
———. ———. Cowboy Association Papers.
———. ———. Charles Goodnight. "Recollections." Edited by J. Evetts Haley. Charles Goodnight Papers.
———. ———. L. Gough. "Reminiscenses." L. Gough Papers.
———. ———. Laura V. Hamner Papers.
———. ———. J. J. Long. "My Indian Recollections." J. J. Long Papers.
———. ———. George A. Montgomery Papers.
———. ———. W. B. Munson Papers.
———. ———. L. F. Sheffy Papers.
———. ———. XIT Ranch Papers.
———. West Texas State University, Cornette Library. Dr. L. F. Sheffy Memorial Collection.
———. ———. John Arnot. "Tascosa Recollections." El Reno, Oklahoma. Carnegie Library. Edna May Arnold Papers.
Leavenworth, Kansas. Mount Muncie Cemetery Association of Leavenworth. Burial Certificate of John M. Ferguson, 1906.
———. ———. Burial Certificate of Lina W. Lee, 1900.
———. ———. Burial Certificate of Lucien Lee, 1905.
———. ———. Burial Certificate of Capt. Wm. M. D. Lee, 1925.
Lubbock, Texas. Texas Tech University, Southwest Collection. John Wesley Mooar Papers.
———. ———. Joseph Smith Papers.

Norman, Oklahoma. University of Oklahoma, Western History Collection. W. S. Campbell Papers.

———. ———. Camp Supply Papers.

Oklahoma City, Oklahoma. Oklahoma Historical Society, Division of Archives and Manuscripts. Cheyenne and Arapaho Papers.

———. ———. Kiowa Papers.

Topeka, Kansas. Kansas State Historical Society. Governor T. A. Osborne Papers.

Government Documents

Kansas. Lawrence Public Library. Map of Lawrence, Kansas, 1869.

———. ———. Map of Lawrence, Kansas, 1880.

———. Leavenworth County. Conveyances: 1883, 1901. Vols. 86, 184.

———. ———. Guardianship of Lucien W. Lee. Probate Court, Pre-1935 Papers.

———. ———. Inventory and Settlement of the Estate of Lina W. Lee. Probate Court, 1902.

Louisiana. Jefferson Davis Parish. Conveyances: 1917, 1921. Vols. K–L, U.

New Mexico. San Miguel County. Deed Records: 1884, 1886. Vols. 26, 28, 126.

Texas. Brazoria County. Deed Records: 1888–1889, 1907, 1909, 1915–1917, 1920, 1922. Vols. 1–2, 70, 73, 125, 132, 134, 137, 158, 165, 176.

———. Clay County. Minutes of the Commissioners' Court, 1879. Vol. 1.

———. Court of Civil Appeals. *Houston Transfer Co. vs. Lee*, 1906. *Southwestern Reporter*. Vol. 97.

———. ———. *Lee and Reynolds vs. Henry Flemming*, 1881. *White and Willson*. Vol. 1.

———. Galveston County. Deed Records: 1897. Vol. 159.

———. Harris County. Deed Records: 1905–1906, 1910, 1912, 1915, 1919–1920. Vols. 169, 181, 193, 244, 292, 316, 319, 343, 424, 443.

———. ———. Marriage Certificate of Captain W. M. D. Lee with Mrs. Leila Schumacher, 1923. Vol. 33.

———. ———. Marriage Certificate of James Price Phillips with Selina Harris Lee, 1911. Vol. 4.

———. City of Houston. Office of the Registrar, Bureau of Vital Statistics. Death Certificate of John M. Ferguson, 1906.

———. ———. Death Certificate of Mary Leila Lee, 1967.

———. ———. Death Certificate of Lucien W. Lee, 1905.

———. ———. Death Certificate of Capt. W. M. D. Lee, 1925.

———. Jefferson County. Deed Records: 1911–1912, 1915, 1917, 1919–1920. Vols. 131–132, 134–135, 150, 205, 213.

———. Newton County. Deed Records: 1919–1921. Vols. 20, 22.

———. Oldham County. Brand Records. Vol. 1.

———. ———. Criminal Docket. *Ex Parte Charles Emory*, 1886.

———. ———. Deed Records: 1879–1884, 1886, 1890. Vols. F-1, 1–4, 7, 19, 22, 24–25, 29.

————. ————. Minutes of the Commissioners' Court: 1881–1884, 1886–1887. Vol. 1.

————. Office of the Secretary of State. Division of Inactive Corporations, Austin. Charter of the Ab-Moor Oil Company, 1911.

————. ————. Dissolution of the Charter of the Ab-Moor Oil Company, 1919.

————. ————. Charter of Nineteen Oil Company, 1911.

————. ————. Dissolution of the Charter of Nineteen Oil Company, 1921.

————. ————. Charter of Palacios Oil Company, 1908.

————. ————. Charter of the Velasco Construction Company, 1895.

————. ————. Minutes of Stockholders Meeting of the Velasco Construction Company, 1895.

————. ————. Charter of West Columbia Oil Company, 1906.

————. ————. Charter Amendment of West Columbia Oil Company, 1907.

————. ————. Dissolution of West Columbia Oil Company, 1911.

————. Wheeler County. Civil Docket. *R. E. McAnulty vs. W. M. D. Lee, et al.*, 1882.

————. ————. Civil Docket. L. A. Mosty with Lee-Scott Cattle Co., 1881.

————. ————. Deed Records: 1876, 1878–1880. Vol. 1A.

————. ————. Minutes of the Commissioners' Court, 1881. Vol. 1.

U.S. Congress. House. *Brazos River, Texas.* House Exec. Doc. 109, 50th Cong., 1st sess., 1888.

————. ————. *Brazos River, Texas.* House Exec. Doc. 63, 52d Cong., 1st sess., 1892.

————. Proceedings of 27 July 1888. 50th Cong., 1st sess. *Congressional Record.* Vol. 19, part 7.

————. ————. Proceedings of 7 August 1888. 50th Cong., 1st sess. *Congressional Record.* Vol. 19, part 8.

————. ————. Proceedings of 22 August 1888. 50th Cong., 1st sess. *Congressional Record.* Vol. 19, part 8.

————. ————. Proceedings of 5 April 1892. 52 Cong., 1st sess. *Congressional Record.* Vol. 23, part 3.

————. ————. Proceedings of 16 June 1898. 55th Cong., 2d sess. *Congressional Record.* Vol. 31, part 7.

————. *Deep Harbor, Gulf of Mexico.* House Exec. Doc. 56, 51st Cong., 1st sess., 1890.

————. *Dredge Boat for Use at Sabine Pass.* House Rpt. 212, 55th Cong., 2d sess., 1898.

————. *Improvements at Mouth and Passes of Calcasieu River, Louisiana,* Annual Report of the Chief Engineer, U.S. Army to Secretary of War, H. Doc. 2, 54th Cong., 1st sess., 1895, part 3.

————. *Inquiry into the Postal Star Service.* House Misc. Doc. 31, 46th Cong., 2d sess., 1880.

————. *Letter from the Secretary of the Treasury Transmitting a Report from the Chief of the Bureau of Statistics, in Response to a Resolution of the House Calling for Information in Regard to the Range and Ranch Cattle Traffic in the Western States and Territories.* House Exec. Doc. 267, 48th Cong., 2d sess., 1885.

———. *The Management of the War Department.* House Rpt. 799, 44th Cong., 1st sess., 1876.

———. *Preliminary Examination, Survey and Appropriations [of Rivers and Harbors].* House Doc. 482, 55th Cong., 2d sess., 1898.

———. *Report of the Secretary of the Interior.* House Exec. Doc. 1, 41st Cong., 2d sess., 1869. Vol. 1, part 3.

———. ———. House Exec. Doc. 1, 41st Cong., 3d sess., 1870. Vol. 1, part 4.

———. ———. House Exec. Doc. 1, 42d Cong., 2d sess., 1871. Vol. 1, part 5.

———. ———. House Exec. Doc. 1, 42d Cong., 3d sess., 1872. Vol. 1, part 5.

———. ———. House Exec. Doc. 1, 43d Cong., 1st sess., 1873. Vol. 1, part 5.

———. ———. House Exec. Doc. 1, 43d Cong., 2d sess., 1874. Vol. 1, part 5.

———. ———. House Exec. Doc. 1, 44th Cong., 1st sess., 1875. Vol. 1, part 5.

———. ———. House Exec. Doc. 1, 44th Cong., 2d sess., 1876. Vol. 1, part 5.

———. ———. House Exec. Doc. 1, 45th Cong., 2d sess., 1877. Vol. 1, part 5.

———. ———. House Exec. Doc. 1, 45th Cong., 3d sess., 1878. Vol. 1, part 5.

———. ———. House Exec. Doc. 1, 46th Cong., 2d sess., 1879. Vol. 1, part 5.

———. ———. House Exec. Doc. 1, 46th Cong., 3d sess., 1880. Vol. 1, part 5.

———. *Report of the Secretary of War.* House Exec. Doc. 1, 41st Cong., 2d sess., 1869. Vol. 1, part 2.

———. ———. House Exec. Doc. 1, 41st Cong., 3d sess., 1870. Vol. 1, part 2.

———. ———. House Exec. Doc. 1, 42d Cong., 2d sess., 1871. Vol. 1, part 2.

———. ———. House Exec. Doc. 1, 42d Cong., 3d sess., 1872. Vol. 1, part 2.

———. ———. House Exec. Doc. 1, 43d Cong., 1st sess., 1873. Vol. 1, part 2.

———. ———. House Exec. Doc. 1, 43d Cong., 2d sess., 1874. Vol. 1, part 2.

———. ———. House Exec. Doc. 1, 44th Cong., 1st sess. 1875. Vol. 1, part 2.

———. ———. House Exec. Doc. 1, 44th Cong., 2d sess., 1876. Vol. 1, part 2.

———. ———. House Exec. Doc. 1, 45th Cong., 2d sess., 1877. Vol. 1, part 2.

———. ———. House Exec. Doc. 1, 45th Cong., 3d sess., 1878. Vol. 1, part 2.

———. ———. House Exec. Doc. 1, 46th Cong., 2d sess., 1879. Vol. 1, part 2.

———. ———. House Exec. Doc. 1, 46th Cong., 3d sess., 1880. Vol. 1, part 2.

———. *Survey of Sabine Lake, Texas.* House Doc. 299, 54th Cong., 2d sess., 1897.

———. Senate. Proceedings of 19 April 1876. 44th Cong., 1st sess. *Congressional Record.* Vol. 4, part 3.

———. ———. Proceedings of the Senate Sitting for the Trial of William W. Belknap on the Articles of Impeachment Exhibited by the House of Representatives. 44th Cong., 1st sess., 1876. *Congressional Record.* Vol. 4, part 7.

———. ———. Proceedings of 1 May 1888. 50th Cong., 1st sess. *Congressional Record.* Vol. 19, part 4.

———. ———. Proceedings of 1 August 1888. 50th Cong., 1st sess. *Congressional Record.* Vol. 19, part 8.

———. ———. Proceedings of 7 August 1888. 50th Cong., 1st sess. *Congressional Record.* Vol. 19, part 8.

———. *Improvements at the Mouth of the Brazos River, Texas.* S. Doc. 138, 54th Cong., 2d sess., 1897.

U.S. Court of Claims. *Willis S. Glenn et al. vs. U.S.* Indian Depredation Cases Nos. 1892–1893.

U.S. Department of Commerce. Bureau of the Census. *Seventh Census of the United States, 1850*: Population, Wisconsin, Columbia County, Hampden Township.

Washington, D.C. National Archives. Records of the Bureau of Indian Affairs. Record Group 75. Letters Received by the Office of Indian Affairs, 1824–1881. Letters Received from the Central Superintendency. 1869– 1878.

———. ———. Letters Received from the Cheyenne and Arapaho Agency. 1875–1880.

———. ———. Letters Received from the Kiowa Agency. 1869–1874.

———. ———. Letters Received from the Upper Arkansas Agency. 1869– 1874.

———. Military Records Division, Navy and Old Army Branch. Record Group 92. Records of the Office of the U.S. Quartermaster General, Consolidated Correspondence Files, 1874–1890. Box 555 (1871, 1873, 1877– 1889).

———. ———. Fort Dodge, Kansas. Box 260 (1877).

———. ———. Index 4772 (1872).

———. Record Group 94. Records of the Office of the U.S. Army Adjutant General. Appointments, Commissions, and Personnel. Indexes 2445 (1876), 1475 (1880), 832 (1885), 2974 (1889), 7663 (1890).

———. ———. Medical History of Fort Supply, Indian Territory. Vol. 166 (1868, 1870, 1874).

———. ———. Register of the Appointment of Sutlers Made by the Secretary of War. 4 regs.

———. Record Group 393. Records of the U.S. Army Continental Commands, 1821–1890. Letters Received from Fort Supply, Indian Territory. 1869, 1880–1882.

———. ———. Letters Sent from Camp Supply, Indian Territory. 1869–1877, 1879–1880, 1885–1887, 1889–1890.

———. ———. Letters Sent from Fort Dodge, Kansas. 1872.

———. ———. Letters Sent by the Post Quartermaster, Fort Elliott, Texas. 1876–1877, 1879–1881, 1887.

Wisconsin. Columbia County. Records of the Registrar. Marriage Certificate of W. M. D. Lee to Orlina E. Whitney, 1876. Vol. 6.

Books

Collins, Dennis. *The Indians' Last Fight or the Dull Knife Raid*. Giraud, Kansas: Press of the Appeal to Reason, [ca. 1915].

Cook, John R. *The Border and the Buffalo*. Topeka, Kansas: Crane and Company, 1907. Reprint. New York: Citadel Press, 1967.

Cullis, Lynch, and Edge. *Leavenworth City Directory and Business Mirror*, Leavenworth, Kansas: Daily Commercial Print, 1871–1883.

Directory of the City of Lawrence, for 1871. Lawrence, Kansas: J. T. Atkinson, 1871.

Dubbs, Emanuel, Charles Goodnight, John Hart, et al. *Pioneer Days in the*

Southwest. Guthrie, Oklahoma: State Capital Company, 1909.

An Early History of Columbia County, Wisconsin. Chicago: Culver, Page Hoyne & Company, 1880.

Edwin Green's City Directory. Leavenworth, Kansas: Ketcheson & Hubbell, [ca. 1884].

Gammel, H. P. N. *The Laws of Texas, 1822–1897.* 10 vols. Austin: Gammel Book Company, 1898.

Houston City Directory. Houston: R. L. Polk and Company, 1924.

Morrison and Fourmy's Directory Co., Inc.'s Directory of the City of Beaumont. Houston: W. G. Burchfield and Company, [ca. 1913].

Morrison and Fourmy's General Directory of the City of Houston. Galveston and Houston: Morrison and Fourmy, [ca. 1899, 1901, 1903, 1904, 1909, 1911].

Poe, John W. *Billy the Kid.* Los Angeles: E. A. Brininstool, 1919.

Sanders, Alvin H. *A History of Hereford Cattle.* Chicago: Breeder's Gazette, 1914.

Stenhouse and Sanders' Lawrence City Directory, 1875–1876. Lawrence, Kansas: A. A. Cutler's Excelsior Job Office, 1875.

Stone, Wilbur Fisk. *History of Colorado.* 4 vols. Chicago: S. J. Clarke Publishing Company, 1918.

Sullivan, Dulcie. *The LS Brand.* Austin: University of Texas Press, 1968.

State of Kansas, Census of 1885. Topeka: Kansas State Historical Society, 1969.

Townshend, Samuel Nugent. *Our Indian Summer in the Far West.* London: Charles Whittingham, 1880.

Wright, Robert M. *Dodge City: The Cowboy Capital.* Wichita, Kansas: Wichita Eagle Press, [ca. 1913].

Articles

Fritz, Henry E. "The Making of Grant's 'Peace Policy.'" *Chronicles of Oklahoma* 37 (Winter 1959–1960): 411–432.

Lubers, H. L. "William Bent's Family and the Indians of the Plains." *Colorado Magazine,* January 1936, pp. 19–22.

Mothershead, Harmon, ed. "The Journal of Ado Hunnius, Indian Territory, 1876." *Chronicles of Oklahoma* 51 (Winter 1973–1974): 451–472.

Murphy, John. "Reminiscences of the Washita Campaign and of the Darlington Indian Agency." *Chronicles of Oklahoma* 1 (June 1923): 259–279.

Schofield, Donald F. "W. M. D. Lee, Indian Trader." *Panhandle-Plains Historical Review* 54 (1981): 1–113.

Strickland, Rex, ed. "The Recollections of W. S. Glenn, Buffalo Hunter." *Panhandle-Plains Historical Review* 22 (1949): 21–64.

Wisner, George Y. "The Brazos River Harbor Improvement." *Transactions of the American Society of Civil Engineers* 25 (July–December 1891): 519–567.

Newspapers and Periodicals

American (Lake Charles, Louisiana), 1896.
Angleton (Texas) *Times,* September 1900, 1907–1924.
Austin Daily Statesman, April 1884, February 1888, February 1892.
Badger State (Portage City, Wisconsin), 1854–1856, 1858–1859.
Beaumont Enterprise, 1898, 1911, 1921.
Beaumont Journal, 1911–1921.
Boston Evening Transcript, September–December, 1890.
Breeder's Gazette 1–17 (December 1881–March 1890).
Caldwell (Kansas) *Journal,* June 1886, May 1887.
Caldwell (Kansas) *Post,* January 1880, September 1881, March 1882, March 1883.
Chicago Daily Tribune, November 1886.
Colorado Springs Gazette, August 1890.
Columbus (Wisconsin) *Democrat,* 1874–1897.
Columbus (Wisconsin) *Republican,* 1868–1909.
Cheyenne Transporter (Darlington, Oklahoma), 1880–1885.
Daily Nebraska State Journal (Lincoln), September 1887, September 1888.
Dallas Morning News, 1885–1898.
Democratic Leader (Cheyenne, Wyoming), May 1884.
Denver Post, March 1921.
Denver Republican, November 1891.
Dodge City (Kansas) *Democrat,* January 1886.
Dodge City (Kansas) *Messenger,* February, June 1874.
Dodge City (Kansas) *Times,* 1877–1882.
Evening Standard (Leavenworth, Kansas), 1883–1900.
Evening Star (Washington, D.C.), March–April, 1876.
Field and Farm 1–6 (February 1886–December 1888).
Ford County Globe (Dodge City, Kansas), 1878–1884.
Fort Griffin (Texas) *Echo,* April 1879, August 1880, February 1881.
Fort Worth Gazette, 1886–1896.
Galveston Daily News, July 1879, 1888–1913, 1921–1925.
Globe Live-Stock Journal (Dodge City, Kansas), 1884–1888.
Gulf Coast Oil News [*Oil Weekly*] 9–13 (January 1917–February 1918).
Houston Chronicle, 1905–1925.
Houston Daily Post, 1888–1916, 1919–1925.
Iowa State Register (Des Moines), November 1888.
Kansas City (Missouri) *Star,* September 1886.
Kansas Cowboy (Dodge City, Kansas), 1884–1885.
Las Vegas (New Mexico) *Daily Optic,* January 1888, September 1900.
Leavenworth Times, November 1872, 1874–1875, 1878–1901, January 1925.
Lincoln Daily News, September 1887, September 1888.
New York Times, October–December 1868, 1874–1885.
New York Tribune, February 1872.
Oil and Gas Journal 7–16 (December 1906–December 1917).
Oil Trade Journal 8–16 (March 1917–February 1925).

Oil Weekly [formerly *Gulf Coast Oil News*] 13–21 (May 1918–September 1923).
Picayune Times (New Orleans), April 1896.
Portage City (Wisconsin) *Record*, 1857–1859, 1861.
Republican (Lawrence, Kansas), January 1870.
San Antonio Express, January 1889, October 1891.
Southwestern Oil Journal 4 (28 January 1921).
Stock Grower (Las Vegas, New Mexico), June–September 1887, December 1888.
Stock Grower Journal (Miles City, Montana), 1886–1888.
Tascosa (Texas) *Pioneer*, 1886–1890.
Topeka Daily Capital, September 1887.
Velasco (Texas) *Times* [daily], 1891–1892.
Velasco (Texas) *Times* [weekly], 1891–1893.
Weekly Colorado Chieftain (Pueblo), May 1869, June 1870.
Wichita (Kansas) *Weekly Beacon*, August–December 1880.
Wisconsin State Register (Portage), 1861–1869.
Wyoming County Record (Eaton, Pennsylvania), June 1845.
Yellowstone Journal (Miles City, Montana), 1884–1887.

Interviews

Austen, E. D. G. Interview with J. Evetts Haley, 4 August 1925. J. Evetts Haley Papers. Panhandle-Plains Historical Society Museum, Canyon, Texas.
Baird, R. E. Speech before a history class at West Texas State University as transcribed by A. P. Bralley, 22 August 1933. R. E. Baird Papers. Panhandle-Plains Historical Society Museum, Canyon, Texas.
———. Speech before a history class at West Texas State University as transcribed by J. B. Lewis, 22 August 1933. R. E. Baird Papers. Panhandle-Plains Historical Society Museum, Canyon, Texas.
Bennett, Charles. Interview with Mrs. Larry W. Cook, n.d. Charles Bennett Papers. Panhandle-Plains Historical Society Museum, Canyon, Texas.
Bowers, Newt. Interview with L. F. Sheffy, 13 February 1927. Dr. L. F. Sheffy Memorial Collection. Cornette Library, West Texas State University, Canyon, Texas.
Bussell, R. "Dick." Interview with J. Evetts Haley, 19 July 1926. J. Evetts Haley Papers. Panhandle-Plains Historical Society Museum, Canyon, Texas.
Dobbs, Garrett H. "Kid." Interview with John McCarty and Mel Armstrong, 12 September 1942. John L. McCarty Papers. Amarillo Public Library, Amarillo, Texas.
———. Interview with Mel Armstrong, 13 September 1942. John L. McCarty Papers. Amarillo Public Library, Amarillo, Texas.
———. Interview with John L. McCarty, 20 October 1942. John L. McCarty Papers. Amarillo Public Library, Amarillo, Texas.
East, James. Interview with J. Evetts Haley, 27 September 1927. Dr. L. F.

Sheffy Memorial Collection. Cornette Library, West Texas State University, Canyon, Texas.

Hall, S. A. Interview with J. Evetts Haley, 27 September 1927. J. Evetts Haley Papers. Panhandle-Plains Historical Society Museum, Canyon, Texas.

Henry, J. H. Interview with J. Evetts Haley, 5 May 1925. J. Evetts Haley Papers. Panhandle-Plains Historical Society Museum, Canyon, Texas.

Ingerton, Harry. Interview with J. Evetts Haley, 13 April 1927. J. Evetts Haley Papers. Panhandle-Plains Historical Society Museum, Canyon, Texas.

Jenkins, Jesse. Interview with Laura V. Hamner and Winnie D. Hall, 11 September 1936. Jesse Jenkins Papers. Panhandle-Plains Historical Society Museum, Canyon, Texas.

Jowell, G. N. Interview with J. Evetts Haley, 17 January 1927. J. Evetts Haley Papers. Panhandle-Plains Historical Society Museum, Canyon, Texas.

Lang, John G. Interview with L. F. Sheffy, 13 October 1936. Dr. L. F. Sheffy Memorial Collection. Cornette Library, West Texas State University, Canyon, Texas.

Locke, N. F. Interview with L. F. Sheffy, 23 July 1934. Dr. L. F. Sheffy Memorial Collection. Cornette Library, West Texas State University, Canyon, Texas.

McAllister, J. E. Interview with J. Evetts Haley, 1 July 1926. J. Evetts Haley Papers, Interview File. Panhandle-Plains Historical Society Museum, Canyon, Texas.

Merry, S. P. Interview with J. Evetts Haley, 21 August 1926. J. Evetts Haley Papers. Panhandle-Plains Historical Society Museum, Canyon, Texas.

Mooar, J. Wright. Interview with J. Evetts Haley, 25 November 1927. J. Evetts Haley Papers. Panhandle-Plains Historical Society Museum, Canyon, Texas.

———. Interview with J. Evetts Haley, 12 April 1936. W. S. Campbell Papers. Western History Collection, University of Oklahoma, Norman, Oklahoma.

———. Interview with Frank P. Hill, J. B. Slaughter, Jr., and Jim Weatherford, 15 May 1936. J. Wright Mooar Papers. Panhandle-Plains Historical Society Museum, Canyon, Texas.

———. Interviewer unidentified, 29 May 1938. J. Wright Mooar Papers. Southwest Collection, Texas Tech University, Lubbock, Texas.

Nelson, O. H. Interview with J. Evetts Haley, 13 July 1926. Dr. L. F. Sheffy Memorial Collection. Panhandle-Plains Historical Society Museum, Canyon, Texas.

———. Interview with J. Evetts Haley, 26 February 1927. J. Evetts Haley Papers. Panhandle-Plains Historical Society Museum, Canyon, Texas.

O'Loughlin, Ellen. Interview with J. Evetts Haley, 17 July 1926. J. Evetts Haley Papers. Panhandle-Plains Historical Society Museum, Canyon, Texas.

Phillips, J. P., Jr. Interview with Donald F. Schofield, Amarillo, Texas, 27 January 1978.

Simpson, George A. Interview with L. F. Sheffy, 30 November 1929. L. F. Sheffy Papers. Panhandle-Plains Historical Society Museum, Canyon, Texas.

Stickley, Vas. Interview with J. Evetts Haley, undated. J. Evetts Haley Papers. Panhandle-Plains Historical Society Museum, Canyon, Texas.
Webster, A. H. Interview with J. Evetts Haley, 9 April 1927. J. Evetts Haley Papers. Panhandle-Plains Historical Society Museum, Canyon, Texas.
Wynne, Jesse. Interview with L. F. Sheffy, June 1934. Dr. L. F. Sheffy Memorial Collection. Cornette Library, West Texas State University, Canyon, Texas.

Letters

Arps, Louisa Ward. Letter to Donald F. Schofield, 7 May, 12 June, 8 and 10 November, 22 December 1976, 1 January 1977.
Phillips, J. G., Jr. Letter to Donald F. Schofield, 11 April, 18 October 1977.
Quinlan, Patricia, Alumnae Director, St. Agnes Academy, Houston, Texas. Letter to Donald F. Schofield, 26 April 1977.
Smith, Joseph H. Letter to Donald F. Schofield, 13 January, 4 March 1977.
Sprader, Richard L., Assistant Director of Public Relations, American Angus Association, St. Joseph, Missouri. Letter to Donald F. Schofield, 24 January 1977.
Sutton-Doland, Ruth. Letter to Donald F. Schofield, 27 March, 20 April 1977.

Index